The Theology of Abraham Bibago

The Theology of Abraham Bibago

A Defense of the Divine Will, Knowledge, and Providence in Fifteenth-Century Spanish-Jewish Philosophy

Allan Lazaroff

The University of Alabama Press
University, Alabama

Library of Congress Cataloging in Publication Data

Lazaroff, Allan.
The theology of Abraham Bibago.

(Judaic studies ; 9)
Bibliography: p.
1. Bibago, Abraham ben Shem-Tob, 15th cent.
Derekh emunah. 2. Jewish theology. 3. Philosophy,
Jewish. I. Title. II. Series.
BM550.B53D44 1980 181'.3 77-10611
ISBN 0-8173-6906-6

TO
ELONA
whose patience, devotion
and self-sacrifice
made this study possible

Contents

Acknowledgments

I wish, inadequate as it may be, to express my profound indebtedness to Professor Alexander Altmann of Brandeis University, at whose suggestion this study was undertaken and under whose guidance it progressed. His vast erudition and scholarly discipline and his concern and encouragement have been a model and inspiration for me. I also wish to thank Professor Shlomo Pines of the Hebrew University for graciously sharing with me some of his penetrating and enlightening insights during my stay in Jerusalem. The responsibility for the study that follows is of course my own.

I am most grateful to Dr. Philip Lown, whose generosity and devotion to Jewish scholarship enabled me to spend a year as a Lown Research Fellow and so to complete a good part of the research for this study. I also wish to express my appreciation to the National Foundation for Jewish Research and to the Memorial Foundation for Jewish Research, from whom I received grants that were of great aid to me in completing this study.

Finally, I wish to acknowledge with gratitude the kind assistance of Professor Leon J. Weinberger, the general editor of this Judaic Studies Series. His support of the publication of this volume has gone well beyond the usual editorial functions.

Preface

The expulsion of the Jews from Spain in 1492 was a cataclysmic tragedy in Jewish history similar to the destruction of the first and second temples at an earlier period and to the European Holocaust in the present century. In the difficult decades of the fifteenth century before the expulsion, rationalist philosophers were a leading faction in the Jewish community. The philosophers consequently bore responsibility in the eyes of their contemporaries for the increasing oppression. The pious attributed Jewish suffering to divine wrath at the assimilationism of the philosophers. For their part, the philosophers did not just attempt to synthesize Judaism and philosophy. They were also more and more concerned with defending Judaism against the force behind the oppression and later the expulsion--namely, Christianity. There was a growing orthodoxy and supernaturalism among philosophers and a trend toward eclecticism.

One of the foremost Jewish philosophers and communal leaders of this period was Abraham Bibago. His theology exhibits many of the characteristics of the age. He was somewhat more of a consistent Averroist than were other contemporary Jewish philosophers, but he used his Averroism to offer an orthodox defense of the philosophy of Maimonides against the criticisms of Gersonides, Crescas, and the radical Averroists. Further, Bibago used his philosophy to comfort and exalt the Spanish Jews by arguing that divine providence accompanied them because of the intellectual superiority they had acquired through the Torah. His blend of rationalism, supernaturalism, and practical faith soon aroused the praise and criticism of both philosophers and traditionalists.

In spite of their importance, Bibago's ideas and philosophy have not yet been analyzed and published. The purpose of this study is to outline the major trends of Bibago's thought as they present themselves in the theology of his chief work, _Derekh 'Emunah_ (=_DE_), (_The Path of Faith_). The investigation undertaken in the following pages reveals the vigor and rigor of philosophy and theology in the last decades of Spanish Jewry.

A Note on Transliteration

The Hebrew in this book is transliterated according to the following system, which, with some modifications, is the one recommended by the Journal of Jewish Studies.

א	'	כּ	k	◌ָ	a
בּ	b	ך, כ	kh	◌ַ	a
ב	v	ל	l	◌ֲ	a
גּ	g	ם, מ	m	◌ֶ	e
ג	g	ן, נ	n	◌ֵ	e
דּ	d	ס	s	◌ֱ	e
ד	d	ע	^{c}	◌ְ	e
ה	h	פּ	p	(only shewa' na^{c} is transliterated)	
ו	w	ף, פ	f		
ז	z	ץ, צ	ṣ	◌ִ	i
ח	ḥ	ק	q	◌ֹ	o
ט	ṭ	ר	r	וֹ	o
י	y	שׁ	sh	◌ֻ	u
(after a, at end of word)	i	שׂ	s	וּ	u
		תּ	t		
		ת	th		

1. Dagesh Ḥazaq (forte) is indicated by doubling the English letter, except for the Hebrew letter shin. The prefix "ha" in titles is followed by a dash instead of a doubling of the next letter.

2. Proper names and some words that have a usual English form are rendered in that form.

The Theology of Abraham Bibago

1. Bibago's Life, Works, and Influence

Very little is known about the life of Abraham ben Shem Ṭov Bibago. There is even some doubt about the correct form of his name. His father is sometimes called Yom Ṭov instead of Shem Ṭov.[1] Further, there is wide disagreement among the earliest sources in regard to the correct form of his family name.[2] He has been identified with a certain Abram Bivagch who presided over the circumcision of a wealthy converso at Huesca in 1465,[3] and this form of the family name has been widely accepted recently in Israel.[4] Since the form "Bibago" is not among the forms that occur most frequently in the earliest sources,[5] it could well be that "Bivagch" or "Bivach" is indeed the correct form of our author's name. Since, however, he has been known as Bibago over the past few centuries, I have continued to use this traditional form.

The earliest date that we have for Bibago is 1446, which is when he completed a commentary on Aristotle's Posterior Analytics at Huesca in Aragon.[6] The postscript of a copy of Narboni's commentary on al-Ghazālī's "Intentions of the Philosophers" says that it was concluded in 1471 at Saragossa at the academy of the philosopher R. Abraham ben Bibag'.[7] Bibago himself gives a report of a discussion he had in his youth at the court of King John of Aragon,[8] the reference evidently being to John II, who ruled from 1458 to 1479.[9] It seems then that Bibago lived at first at Huesca and later moved to Saragossa perhaps between 1466 and 1470. Bibago also mentions that he used to deliver sermons in the synagogue on Sabbaths and festivals.[10] It seems likely that he died around 1489.[11]

The period in which Bibago lived could be described as the calm between the storms. After the widespread destruction of the Jewish communities in Castile and Aragon between 1391 and 1412, the Jewish population of Aragon remained small, unlike that of Castile. There were no large Jewish centers, not even in the bigger cities, and Jews were not so prominent in public life as they had been earlier. Alphonso V and John II, however, were relatively tolerant monarchs, and Jewish life in Aragon at this time was calmer than it was in Castile, which was again upset by widespread disturbances around the middle of the century.[12] There was a creative revival of Aristotelian and Averroist philosophy, and the philosophers became a leading faction in the Jewish community.[13] The conversos, however, were a more serious problem than they had ever been because of the unprecedented persecutions that marked the beginning of the fifteenth century.[14] Finally, in 1484 the Inquisition of Ferdinand and Isabella came to Saragossa,[15] presaging the expulsion of all Jews from Spain in 1492.

Bibago was characteristic of the philosophical community leaders of the period. His chief work, Derekh 'Emunah (The Path of Faith), was in many ways a response to the circumstances of the times in which he lived. In response to the challenges of Christianity and philosophy, Bibago argued that Judaism was the one true and rational faith that brought salvation to the believers among the Jewish people. In response to the dire straits in which his people found themselves, Bibago argued that God knows and cares for them. The first of the three major parts of his book is devoted to this latter goal. The four chapters of this first part deal with the divine will, knowledge, providence, and purpose in this world.[16] The second of the three major parts of the book deals with man and faith. The first chapter of this second part discusses the nature of man,[17] and the second chapter deals with the cosmic role of intellect and its importance for man's salvation.[18] The third chapter describes the hindrances preventing man's salvation,[19] and the fourth treats of the ways in which faith overcomes these hindrances.[20] The fifth chapter discusses the acquisition of faith through tradition,[21] and the sixth chapter argues from five presuppositions that Moses, the first transmitter of this tradition, never sinned.[22] The seventh and last chapter in this second part develops the definition of faith.[23] The third and last part of the book concerns various doctrines that compose the content of faith. The first chapter in this part discusses the basic principles of faith, the second discusses miracles, and the third the arguments for creation.[24] The fourth chapter deals with theoretical and practical commandments and the future world.[25] The book concludes with a discussion in the fifth chapter of Maimonides' thirteen principles of faith.[26]

The book was published for the first and only time in the autumn of 1521 in Constantinople. It was most likely written in Saragossa toward the end of Bibago's life, perhaps around the year 1480.[27] The four manuscripts available seem to date from the sixteenth century, and three of them are defective. Cambridge-Trinity College 121, which may be the oldest of the manuscripts,[28] begins on page 2b and ends in III-3, page 86d.[29] Munich 43.17 only goes through the first chapter of the second part, to page 37, is also missing the introduction, and is erroneously entitled as well.[30] Paris 995.2 is also defective at the beginning, lacking the first chapter and part of the second.[31] Thus the only complete manuscript is Paris 747.[32]

Among the authors and sources mentioned by Bibago in this work, the one most frequently cited is Maimonides, who is usually called simply "the Master" (ha-Rav).[33] He is referred to on nearly every other page of the book and is sometimes cited several times on the same page.[34] While Bibago generally does not specify the particular work of Maimonides to which he is referring, the reference most of the time is to the Guide of the Perplexed.[35] Occasionally Bibago mentions the particular part and chapter of the Guide to which he is referring.[36] He also refers to Maimonides' Mishneh Torah[37] and to his "Mishnah Commentary" on the talmudic tractate 'Avoth[38] and on chapter eleven of the tractate Sanhedrin.[39] Bibago also draws frequently from Maimonides without bothering to mention him by name.[40]

Conversely, Bibago may also attribute an idea to Maimonides and then interpret it according to, say, ibn Rushd.[41]

Bibago is lavish in his praise of Maimonides on both intellectual and religious grounds,[42] and he declares his devotion to him.[43] In one of the rare passages in the book that are frequently quoted,[44] Bibago is sharply critical of those who attack Maimonides in order to appear pious in the eyes of the multitude.[45] He himself often defends Maimonides by trying to reinterpret Maimonides' more radical positions in a more traditional manner.[46] The future world, Bibago says, can be interpreted according to both Maimonides and the rabbis,[47] but in a case of conflict one should follow rabbinic tradition.[48]

Bibago, however, also exhibits a degree of independence in regard to both Maimonides and the rabbis. He argues that diversity of opinion is a requirement for the discovery of truth[49] and that Maimonides himself has said that profound matters can have many interpretations.[50] He therefore openly disagrees with Maimonides on several issues.[51] As for his independence in regard to rabbinic tradition, he says that if there is no precedent in it for his view that Moses never sinned, this does not constitute an objection to this view, for a child on a giant's shoulder can see farther.[52]

The other Jewish philosophers to whom Bibago refers by name are Saadia,[53] Isaac Israeli,[54] Abraham ibn Ezra,[55] Joseph ibn Kaspi,[56] Moses Narboni,[57] Samuel ibn Tibbon,[58] Gersonides,[59] and Moses Naḥmanides.[60] Bibago also mentions 'Onqelos,[61] Rabbenu Ḥanan'el,[62] Rashi,[63] Tosfos,[64] Rabad,[65] Targum Yonathan,[66] and the 'Arukh.[67] The works of Jewish mysticism that he cites are the Hekhaloth,[68] Shiᶜur Qomah,[69] Sefer Bahir,[70] the Zohar,[71] and the Maᶜarekheth ha-'Elohuth.[72] He also mentions a well-known phrase from the Sefer Yeṣirah.[73]

Of the Islamic philosophers, Bibago mentions ibn Rushd[74] and ibn Sīnā[75] most frequently. He calls ibn Rushd a great philosopher[76] and refers specifically to the following of his works: The Treatise on the Possibility of Conjunction (Sefer 'Efsharuth ha-Devequth),[77] The Destruction of the Destruction (Happalath ha-Happalah),[78] Treatises on Nature (Ma'amarav ha-Ṭivᶜiyyim),[79] Epitome of Metaphysics (Qiṣṣuro lemah She-aḥar),[80] Commentary on the Metaphysics, chapters 6 and 11,[81] Commentary on the Book of Demonstration (Sefer ha-Mofeth, i.e., the Posterior Analytics),[82] and The Book of Celestial Phenomena (Sefer ha-'Othoth ha-ᶜElyonoth).[83] Bibago also calls ibn Rushd "the inquirer" (ḥoqer)[84] and the "wise one" (ḥakham).[85] He does not apply any such praiseworthy appellations to ibn Sīnā, although he does call ibn Sīnā the teacher and beloved of Maimonides.[86] Of ibn Sīnā's works the only one mentioned by name is his "Oriental Philosophy."[87] Still, in the six cases in which Bibago notes the divergent views of ibn Rushd and ibn Sīnā, Bibago himself does not state a preference for one or the other,[88] and he refers to each of them the same number of times, twenty-one. It should nevertheless become more apparent during the course of this study that the dominant influence was that of ibn Rushd.[89]

Other Arabic authors and works cited are the following: al-Fārābī and his denial of the possibility of conjunction,[90] al-Ghazālī[91] and his works The Destruction of Philosophy (Happalath ha-Pilosofim, in Arabic, Tahāfut al-Falāsifah)[92] and On Nature (ha-Ṭivᶜiyoth),[93] ibn Bājja and his Letter of Farewell ('Iggereth ha-Peṭirah),[94] the astronomer Isaac al-Zarkil,[95] the fable book Kelilah we-Dimnah,[96] and pseudo-Empedocles.[97]

Of the Greek authors and works, Bibago refers by name to Aristotle[98] and the following of his works: the Prior Analytics (Sefer ha-Heqesh),[99] the Posterior Analytics (Sefer ha-Mofeth),[100] the Topics (Sefer ha-Nissuah),[101] the Physics (Sefer ha-Shema^c),[102] On the Heavens (Sefer ha-Shamayim weha-^{c}Olam),[103] On the Celestial Phenomena (Sefer ha-'Othoth ha-^{c}Elyonoth),[104] On the Soul (Sefer ha-Nefesh),[105] On Animals (Sefer Ba^{c}ale Ḥayyim),[106] the Metaphysics (Mah she'aḥar),[107] and the Ethics (Sefer ha-Middoth).[108]

The other Greek authors mentioned by Bibago are Heraclitus,[109] Democritus,[110] Pythagoras,[111] Socrates,[112] Plato,[113] Epicurus,[114] Clearchus,[115] Alexander of Aphrodisias,[116] Themistius[117] and his book On the Soul,[118] Galen,[119] Euclid,[120] Lucretius,[121] and Ptolemy[122] and his Almagest[123] and Quadripartium.[124]

Bibago makes a few references to "some Christian scholars" in the Derekh 'Emunah[125] and says that he had studied a little of their theology in his youth.[126] In this book, however, the only Christian author to whom Bibago refers by name is Eusebius. He recounts Eusebius's version of Clearchus's account of the meeting between Aristotle and a Jewish sage.[127] As is well known,[128] in Bibago's version the account of the meeting turns into an assertion that Aristotle himself was Jewish.[129] It has been suggested recently that this change in the story is due to a misprint in the Latin translation of Eusebius published in 1470.[130]

In addition to the Derekh 'Emunah, the only other work by Bibago to have been published was a small homiletic one on the topic of creation. It is called Zeh Yenaḥamenu (This One will Comfort Us), in reference to Gen. 5:29, and was printed in Salonica in 1522.[131] It is also extant in two manuscripts[132] and is mentioned by Bibago in the Derekh 'Emunah.[133]

In addition to these two printed works, there are six other works by Bibago extant in various manuscripts. Of these the most significant is a lengthy "Supercommentary to ibn Rushd's 'Middle Commentary on Aristotle's Metaphysics'," extant in Munich 357.6 and 57.2.[134] The original Arabic of ibn Rushd's "Middle Commentary on Aristotle's Metaphysics" is evidently no longer extant and no Latin translation is known. It is extant in two Hebrew translations, the most common one being that made by Kalonymus ben Kalonymus in 1317.[135] Bibago, however, evidently had some good Arabic texts before him and used them to correct the Kalonymus translation, which he considered especially deficient in the sixth chapter.[136] This work would therefore seem to indicate that Bibago knew Arabic. In it Bibago also compares ibn Rushd's "Middle Commentary" to his "Long Commentary" and to his "Epitome."[137]

In his introduction Bibago says that long years of exile and oppression have led to a decline of the sciences among his people and that he is writing this supercommentary to restore philosophy to its prominence among his people and to teach them how to respond to the questions of the heretic.[138] The philosophic sources that he mentions are generally those to which he refers later in the Derekh 'Emunah.[139] In addition, he mentions the following Christian philosophers by name: Boethius, Duns Scotus, Ockham, and Nicolas Bonet.[140] Bibago also summarizes a treatise by Yeda^{c}yah Bedershi on individual forms[141] and refers to three other philosophical and scientific treatises written by himself.[142]

A second work extant in a manuscript, Paris 995.1,[143] is called "Sefer ᶜEṣ Ḥayyim (The Tree of Life)," and, like Zeh Yenaḥamenu, deals with the topic of the creation of the world.[144] It is mentioned three or four times in the Derekh 'Emunah[145] and attempts to disprove the contention of the philosophers that the eternity of the world can be proven.[146] A third work, a "Commentary on Aristotle's Posterior Analytics (Sefer ha-Mofeth),"[147] is extant in two manuscripts, Paris 959.2 and Vatican 350, the latter possibly an autograph.[148] As we have seen, this was written in 1446 in Huesca[149] and is thus one of Bibago's earliest works, as well as one of the only two to have a definite date.[150] Bibago says that he followed the commentary of ibn Rushd and defended him against the criticism of Gersonides. Bibago had before him only a poor Latin translation of the Posterior Analytics,[151] which indicates that he knew Latin as well as Arabic. Bibago mentions this "Commentary on Aristotle's Posterior Analytics" in his "Supercommentary on the Metaphysics."[152]

A fourth work extant in a manuscript, Paris 1004.3, is a small collection of short philosophic essays written in response to various questions put to the author.[153] The anonymous "Ma'amar be-Ribuy ha-Ṣuroth (Treatise on the Plurality of Forms)," Paris 1004.1, is most likely the essay on this topic that Bibago says he wrote.[154] There are finally two letters to Moses Arondi, Parma 457.4, written in 1470.[155]

In addition to these two printed works and these six works extant in manuscripts, there are several other works that are mentioned by Bibago in the Derekh 'Emunah and in the "Supercommentary on the Metaphysics." These works are evidently no longer extant. In the Derekh 'Emunah, Bibago summarizes a treatise that he wrote on the significance of sacrifices as a means of bringing us close to God by helping us to conquer our material parts.[156] He also mentions a treatise that he wrote in order to defend Maimonides against the objections that Naḥmanides raises in his Perush ha-Torah.[157] Finally, on the last page of the Derekh 'Emunah Bibago mentions a work, "Maḥazeh Shaddai (The Vision of the Almighty),"[158] in which he refutes those ancient philosophers and astronomers who interpret resurrection naturally and say that it occurs every day.[159] The two compositions that Bibago says he wrote on the question of creation are most likely the "Sefer ᶜEṣ Ḥayyim" and Zeh Yenaḥamenu.[160]

In his "Supercommentary on the Metaphysics" Bibago also refers to a couple of his works that are no longer extant. He twice mentions his "Commentary on Aristotle's Physics"[161] and twice his "Commentary on the Kullīyāt," ibn Rushd's medical work.[162]

Finally, Saul ha-Kohen Ashkenazi, in a letter to Isaac Abravanel, mentions a short essay by Bibago on corporeal forms. Saul Ashkenazi understands this essay to be a defense of ibn Rushd in response to a question by Eli Habillio.[163]

We should also mention here two works extant in manuscripts that have either been attributed to Bibago or may possibly have been written by him. One is a fifteenth-century Spanish manuscript in the Sassoon Library, no. 702, which contains a collection of homilies on the Torah and, according to a note by a previous owner, was written by Rabbi Abraham ben Shem Ṭov Bibago. There is, however, no evidence beyond this note to indicate Bibago's authorship.[164] A second is a brief medical manual that in Paris 1181.1 and 1182.1 is said to have been written by Rabbi Abraham the son of Shem Ṭov.[165] It seems to be the Paris manuscript on medicine that Wolf attributed to Bibago.[166] Neubauer, however, said that the author was Abraham of Tortosa, who lived in the thirteenth century and was the son of Shem Ṭov ben Isaac.[167]

Bibago's influence and popularity in his own generation and in the sixteenth century seem to be almost as extensive as his writings. It has been well known since 1839 that Isaac Abravanel (1437-1508) borrowed extensively from Bibago's discussion of Maimonides' thirteen principles at the end of the Derekh 'Emunah when Abravanel was writing his own work, the Rosh 'Amanah, on the thirteen Maimonidean principles.[168] Abravanel, however, does not mention Bibago in this work. Abravanel also neglects to mention Bibago in his response to Saul ha-Kohen Ashkenazi, although he notes in passing all the other philosophers that Saul Ashkenazi had mentioned in his letter.[169] Ashkenazi had referred to Bibago as a "perfect sage" (ḥakham shalem).[170]

Isaac Arama (1420-1494) also does not mention Bibago by name, but Joseph Delmedigo reports that Arama followed Bibago constantly.[171] Arama says that he had heard that Moses did not sin at all from "one of the wise and important philosophers of our people."[172] Arama's statement that he had "heard" this has suggested to some that Arama knew this not from having read the Derekh 'Emunah but rather from his personal acquaintance with Bibago.[173] Ibn Verga, in Sefer Sheveṭ Yehudah (The Rod of Judah, first published in 1550), also does not mention Bibago by name, but he does briefly describe the response of "one of our great sages" before King John of Aragon to the question of why Jews believe in creation and not in Jesus.[174] The reference is clearly to the discussion that Bibago recalls at the end of Derekh 'Emunah.[175]

Azariah de Rossi (1513-1578) gives Bibago as well as Maimonides as a source for the view that the other nations derived their knowledge from the Jews,[176] and he also reports Bibago's story about Aristotle being Jewish.[177] Gedalya ibn Yaḥya (1515-1587) also recounts Bibago's story about Aristotle's being Jewish, and he adds another report found in Bibago about a meeting between a Jew and a Greek.[178] The Italian rabbi, Judah Moscato (1530-1593), mentions these and other passages from the Derekh 'Emunah in his commentary to Judah Halevi's Sefer ha-Kuzari.[179]

Joseph Delmedigo (1591-1655), who as we saw associated Arama with Bibago, also favorably describes Bibago's division of natural science and theology into two sections each, one of which in each case is available to non-Jews.[180] On the other hand, the Kabbalist Meir ibn Gabbai (1480-1540) complains of Bibago's partiality to Greek philosophy.[181] Similarly Jacob ibn Ḥabib (1460-1516), while admitting that a few of Bibago's homilies may have a certain charm, explains that he excluded them from his ᶜEn Yaᶜaqov because as philosophical allegories they were rhetorical distortions of the texts.[182]

The sixteenth-century Kabbalist in Safed, Solomon ha-Levi Alkabeṣ, refers to Bibago frequently and not in an unfavorable light.[183] A section of the Derekh 'Emunah can be found in an anthology of Kabbalist selections in a sixteenth-century manuscript in a Maghrebi hand in the Sassoon Library.[184] The Sefer ha-Miqnah by Josel of Rosheim (1478-1554), a leader of German Jewry, has recently been shown to be based on the first third of Bibago's Derekh

'Emunah, although Bibago's name is not mentioned in the work.[185] Finally, Montefiore 289 is a summary of the last two parts of the Derekh 'Emunah in a German hand.[186]

Despite Bibago's prolific work and his broad influence during the fifteenth and sixteenth centuries, however, the only extensive monograph about him that has been published is the bibliographical essay written by Steinschneider almost a century ago.[187] Yiṣḥaq Baer has therefore called for a study of Bibago's theological system.[188]

In the following chapters I shall discuss Bibago's references in the Derekh 'Emunah to the proofs for God's existence and his general observations on the divine attributes, as well as his defense of the divine will, knowledge, and providence in particular. The study will conclude with a summary of the basic characteristics of Bibago's theology, characteristics that may well hold for his entire philosophical system.

2. The Existence of God

Scholasticism in the fourteenth and fifteenth centuries did not pay much attention to traditional metaphysical topics such as the proofs for the existence of God.[1] Similarly Bibago, like Judah Halevi but unlike Maimonides, does not have a formal discussion of these proofs in his Derekh 'Emunah. His references, however, to the ways in which we can know God's existence indicate elements characteristic of his thought.

We can know that God exists, says Bibago, either by faith or by rational proofs.[2] Faith in this regard is not inferior to a rational proof. Believing that God exists and that the contrary is impossible constitutes knowledge whether or not the belief is arrived at by syllogisms. It is the conclusion of an argument that constitutes knowledge, not the postulates and proofs.[3] Thus the existence of God is taught in the first few words of the First Commandment, "I am the Lord your God."[4]

Knowledge of God is the subject of faith,[5] but since faith is a science,[6] Bibago raises the question of whether the subject of science can be proven in that science. It would seem that it cannot be proven because the subject in a science comes before a demonstration in that science, not after it. Bibago, however, says that the truth lies with those who say that it is only an a priori demonstration that cannot be applied to the subject of a science, not an a posteriori one.[7] Both of these kinds of demonstration, Bibago explains later, are proofs of existence through the principle of causality. An a priori demonstration (mofeth sibbah) reasons from cause to effect, as when we deduce the motion of the sphere from its mover or smoke from fire. It is the primary and true demonstration and gives absolute knowledge. An a posteriori demonstration (mofeth re'ayah) reasons from effect to cause, as from the moved to the mover or from smoke to fire.[8]

The a posteriori or cosmological[9] proof that is taught by faith is the proof from creation. As found in the Muslim Kalām and in early Jewish philosophy, the proof from creation has two parts, a demonstration that the world came into existence and an application of the principle of causality that nothing can change or come into existence without a cause.[10] Maimonides, however, had established that the creation of the world could be neither proved nor disproved and so should be accepted from prophecy.[11] So Bibago explains that the creation of the world, that is, the "Account of the Beginning" (ma^caseh bere'shith), as he calls it, can be known neither through an a priori demonstration nor through an a posteriori demonstration and so is taught by true faith.[12]

Bibago therefore says that the proof from creation is a mean (memuṣṣa^c) between faith and philosophy[13] because creation is accepted on faith, but from there the demonstration proceeds philosophically by the principle of causality.[14] The proof is an easy, quick, and certain path to knowledge of God's existence,[15] for according to Bibago, as we have seen, a doctrine of creation based on faith is not inferior to one based on rational proof. Maimonides had also said that the doctrine of creation quickly and easily shows the existence of God,[16] evidently because it is a first or axiomatic intelligible that what comes into existence must have a creator outside itself.[17] For Maimonides, however, a conclusion drawn from principles accepted on authority, while permissible,[18] would hardly be certain.

Another advantage of the proof from creation, says Bibago, is that it leads not just to a first mover or cause but to a God Who performs miracles at will, Whose providence extends to this lowest of worlds and Who knows us as individuals.[19] It should finally be noted that Bibago mentions a proof of God's existence from miracles as another a posteriori proof, in addition to the one from creation, that is taught by faith.[20] In another comment on the same biblical verse, however,[21] Bibago says that these miracles indicate the divine providence.[22]

The rational or philosophical proofs for God's existence to which Bibago refers are also a posteriori or cosmological ones. He usually says in this regard that we can know God's existence from the motions of the heavens[23] and especially from the motion of the first sphere.[24] On one occasion he specifies the perpetuity of the celestial motions as the source of the proof.[25] On another occasion, however, Bibago says that even a blind person could know God's existence from feeling the motion of water in earth as it makes mud. This motion would be impossible without the circular motion that comes from the heavens, and the heavens cannot be moved by another material mover if one is to avoid an infinite regress. They must, therefore, be moved by an immaterial, unmoved mover who is the First Being.[26]

This proof and the references to the celestial motions recall Maimonides' first proof for the existence of God. Maimonides traced all motion and change in this world back to the motion of the sphere, which in turn was shown to be moved by an immaterial, immovable mover. It is especially the Aristotelian thesis of the perpetuity of the celestial motion, which Maimonides mentioned at the end of the proof, that demonstrates that the first cause is separate from the sphere.[27] This proof from motion is based on Aristotle's analysis of motion in the eighth book of his Physics. Ibn Rushd used it to prove God's existence because he identified God with the Unmoved Mover and said that God Himself was the First Intelligence Who moved the first sphere.[28]

As Bibago frequently mentions this proof from motion, which ibn Rushd used, so Bibago frequently notes, also in agreement with ibn Rushd, that God Himself is the Mover of the first sphere.[29] It is after all only fitting, Bibago says on one occasion, that this simple and universal motion be attributed to a simple, universal being.[30] Usually, however, Bibago derives his opinion from Ps. 68:5, "Extol the Rider of the <u>ᶜAravoth</u>," <u>ᶜaravoth</u> here being interpreted as in B. T. Ḥagigah 12b as "heavens" because of Deut. 33:26, "The Rider of the heavens is helping you." Were the mover of the heavens not God, it would hardly be proper to extol him.[31] In fact this is an example, says Bibago, of an important issue on which philosophers are divided but concerning which faith and the Torah give us the information we need for our felicity.[32]

In regard to his opinion that God moves the first sphere directly and that His existence can be proven from motion, ibn Rushd was in opposition to ibn Sīnā, who held that God emanates a first intelligence which then moves the first sphere.[33] Since the mover whose existence is established by the proof from motion is not God according to ibn Sīnā, he used a slightly different cosmological proof that employed the categories of possibility and necessity and concluded with a Being that exists necessarily (<u>meḥuyyav</u> <u>ha-meṣi'uth</u>).[34] Maimonides, who according to Bibago agrees with ibn Sīnā that God is not the mover of the first sphere,[35] also uses ibn Sīnā's version of the cosmological proof as his third proof for God's existence.[36] Ḥasdai Crescas used a slightly modified version of this proof,[37] and his student Joseph Albo said that, unlike the proof from motion, Maimonides' third proof was "strong and indisputable."[38]

Bibago, however, does not clearly refer to ibn Sīnā's version of the proof at all. In fact, in only one passage in the <u>Derekh 'Emunah</u> does Bibago speak of God as the Necessary Existent, and that is in the context of a proof for the divine unity.[39] Further, ibn Rushd says that his own proof is not only a posteriori but also physical in character, that any metaphysical proof for the existence of a First Principle of separate beings must similarly have a basis in physics,[40] and that ibn Sīnā's method is like that of the Kalām.[41] Bibago similarly, in his one rehearsal of the proof from motion, emphasizes that this proof is based on premises that agree with existence, as Maimonides says,[42] and that are drawn from corporeal and sensible objects.[43] This is in opposition to those who, as Maimonides says of the Mutakallimūn, do not use premises in the divine science that agree with existence.[44]

Bibago does occasionally speak of knowing God's existence in terms of sufficiency and insufficiency of existence. He considers it rationally necessary that the derivative beings of this world require a self-sufficient source of their existence.[45] He also notes that the beings of this lower world prove the existence of God better than the higher beings because the natural deficiency of the lower beings makes their dependence upon God for their existence more obvious.[46] In no case, however, does he use the categories of the possibility and necessity of existence. Bibago also refers to what has been called the proof from the conservation of the world in existence when he argues that the world needs a maintainer as well as a creator[47] and that the sole Maintainer of the world in existence is God and not any other cause.[48] This proof, which is consistent with the eternity of the world, can also be called a proof from divine providence[49] and indeed was mentioned by Bibago first in his discussion of providence.[50]

On one occasion Bibago says that we know God's existence through the perfection of His actions.[51] Since both artificial and natural actions are purposive,[52] Bibago seems to refer here to a teleological proof from design.[53] He also finds evidence for the existence of a maker in the relationship of the parts of the body and cites as proof Job 19:26, "From my flesh I know God,"[54] a verse frequently used in the teleological proof.[55] In a reference to a "microcosm" proof for God, Bibago says that man can come to know the existence of God through knowing his own rational faculty.[56] Finally, Bibago says that one can know God's existence through knowing "the ways of existence"[57] and through knowing "all the parts of existence."[58] Since he does not specify how this latter knowledge leads to the knowledge of God's existence, presumably it would be through one of the previously mentioned proofs.

Thus Bibago's references to proofs for God's existence through faith and reason indicate a posteriori and physical proofs in the tradition of ibn Rushd, not ibn Sīnā.

3. The Divine Attributes

The ways of proving God's existence are also often the ways of speaking about God.[1] Philo's causal proofs for the existence of God led him to speak about God through His causal relations to the world, that is, through His actions.[2] The divine actions were one of the two categories of divine attributes knowable to man in later Christian, Muslim, and Jewish philosophy.[3] Negative attributes are the other category of divine attributes in the church fathers and in Arabic philosophy.[4] Maimonides allowed only actions and negations of privations as descriptions of God and specifically excluded essential attributes,[5] but later Jewish and Christian philosophers did use positive attributes.[6] Toward the end of the fifteenth century, however, some of the Spanish-Jewish philosophers returned to the theory of negative attributes.[7]

Citing Maimonides, Bibago also initially divides the divine attributes into two classes, negative attributes and attributes of action.[8] God must be described by negative attributes instead of positive ones because in the first place the latter would imply a plurality in the divine nature. For the described and the description must differ and must be two.[9] Further, God must be described negatively because of His hiddenness from us and because of the absolute difference between His attributes and ours.[10] When we say "strong," therefore, in reference to God, we intend thereby "not weak," and when we say "wise," we mean "not ignorant."[11]

In his explanation of Maimonides' thirteen principles of belief at the end of the Derekh 'Emunah, Bibago interprets the first four principles in terms of negative attributes.[12] The first principle, the concept of God's existence, Bibago interprets as a negation of His absence[13] in both senses of the word "existence" (meṣi'uth). If the word refers to hammeṣi'uth haṣṣodeq, that is, the affirmation of the correspondence of reality to our ideas of it, then the proposition that God exists is true as long as He is not absent, even if our ideas of Him do not correspond exactly to what He really is. If the word "existence" refers to the unity of essence and existence in the First of all existences, then in this case also in asserting God's existence we negate the denial of this unity of essence and existence.[14]

This twofold meaning of "existence" to which Bibago refers can be found in the works of ibn Rushd. One sense of "existence," according to ibn Rushd, is synonymous with the "true"[15] and is a logical concept in the mind affirming the correspondence of reality to our idea of it. The other, more primary sense of "existence" is that of the most universal genus of real entities outside the mind. In this ontological sense it is the opposite of nonexistence and is related to the ten categories.[16] It is not the case, as ibn Sīnā thought it was, that existence can be separated as an accident from the quiddity of a thing. This is so not just in God but in all things. It is only existence in its logical sense that can be separated from the quiddity of a thing.[17]

Moses Narboni accuses Maimonides of not distinguishing these two meanings of "existence" and says that he instead follows ibn Sīnā in this question of essence and existence.[18] Unlike Narboni's criticism of Maimonides on this point, Bibago, as we have seen, tries to make Maimonides' negative interpretation of the divine attributes consistent with ibn Rushd's twofold interpretation of existence.

Bibago says that the second, third, and fourth articles of belief in Maimonides' creed--the divine unity, incorporeality, and eternity--deny three ways in which God might be limited or classified.[19] The divine unity is interpreted as a negative attribute because it denies of God numerical plurality[20] and indeed negates of Him number as such.[21] Further, by unity Bibago may mean only uniqueness and not simplicity. In his discussion of faith, Bibago specifies simplicity along with unity, incorporeality, and eternity as accidental characteristics of the subject of faith.[22]

Bibago also describes four proofs that there is one God and not two.[23] The first proof is based on the impossibility of the necessary existent being other than it is[24] and on the difference required between any two necessary existents.[25] A second necessary existent must differ in some manner from the first necessary existent, for otherwise there would be only one necessary existent and not two. The first necessary existent, however, must be necessarily existent in its own peculiar manner.[26] The second necessary existent, therefore, must be necessarily existent in a way different from that of the first necessary existent, but this counters our definition of necessary existence as a unique characteristic.[27] This, Bibago says, is the best proof for the divine unity and is the meaning of the Shema[c],[28] the confession of divine unity using the Tetragrammaton, for Maimonides explained that the Tetragrammaton refers to God as the Necessary Existent.[29]

The second proof is based on the universe being one organic whole like a human individual.[30] This unitary whole must then have one mover,[31] not two. Some say that because the upper and lower worlds differ,[32] there are two movers, but Bibago maintains that the two worlds differ only as do the parts of one body. The third proof uses in its first half what Maimonides calls the method of "reciprocal hindering," a method he attributes to the Mutakallimūn.[33] If, Bibago says, there were two equal gods, they could never do anything. If, however, they were not equal, the greater then is God.[34] The fourth proof is that two or more gods would participate in the genus "god," and this genus would then be naturally prior to the gods themselves, an obviously absurd conclusion.[35]

Maimonides' third article of belief, the divine incorporeality, is interpreted negatively by Bibago as a denial that God is limited by place[36] and as a denial that He is either composed of matter and form or divisible into parts.[37] The latter denial is similar to

Maimonides' contention that the composition of body out of matter and form and its divisibility into dimensions are both proofs for the incorporeality of God, to Whom no composition or divisibility can pertain.[38] Maimonides held that all bodies, even the heavenly ones, are composed of matter and form at least equivocally.[39] Bibago, however, notes that Maimonides' second proof, the divisibility of body into dimensions, is valid for those who, like ibn Rushd, believe that heavenly bodies are divisible into dimensions but are not composed of matter and form.[40]

Maimonides' fourth article of belief, the divine eternity, is interpreted negatively by Bibago as a denial of generation, creation, and corruption in regard to God, for what is generated or created must have a generator or creator, and so God cannot have been generated or created.[41] Bibago further says that God's rule over the stars is shown in His changing the astrological future that the wicked Haman prepared for the Jews, and that this proves that He alone is eternal.[42] Later Bibago says that eternity is a negation of limitation by time.[43]

Bibago associates the last nine articles of Maimonides' creed with the divine actions.[44] He here further subdivides the divine actions into two classes. The first subdivision of the divine actions corresponds to the fifth article of the creed, the worship of God.[45] The remaining eight articles correspond to divine actions that are enduring to the living (providence) and dead (retribution), partial deeds in the past (prophecy and the revelation to Moses), a general deed in the past (the Torah and its eternity), or are future deeds to the living (the coming of the Messiah) and the dead (the resurrection).[46] In an earlier section Bibago offers a somewhat different subdivision of the divine actions into attributes of "perception" (hassagah), such as seeing and hearing, and actions proper, such as mercy and grace.[47]

In spite of his assertions that the divine attributes are either negations or actions, Bibago does on one occasion refer to the "essential" attributes.[48] These are, he immediately notes, nothing additional to the divine essence, as Maimonides has said,[49] for Bibago had agreed that the problem with positive attributes is that they add something to the deity.[50] These essential attributes are identified with the ways (derakhim) of God, which are also identical with the divine essence. These "ways" are the sources of the divine actions and are the object of Moses' request for knowledge in Exod. 33:13. As we learn from Ps. 103:7, the rest of the people of Israel knew only the divine actions, not the "ways" or sources of the actions.[51] Bibago's interpretation of Exod. 33:13 differs from that of Maimonides, who said that the "ways" are the divine actions, not the sources of the actions.[52] Bibago compares them to properties in a human soul, although God of course is not a soul.[53] On the other hand, these "ways" are also the parts of existence derived from God, and knowledge of them is not the same as absolute, essential knowledge of the divine.[54]

Ḥasdai Crescas asserted of God essential attributes, in spite of Maimonides' sharp criticism of essential attributes and his advocacy of negative attributes.[55] Joseph Albo exhibits the influence of his teacher Crescas as well as the influence of Maimonides in asserting of God both negative and positive attributes.[56] Bibago, therefore, in this reference to essential attributes, may also have been influenced by Crescas, although Bibago's basic position was, as we have seen, like Maimonides in asserting of God only negations and actions. It should be noted, however, that Bibago's term here for essential attributes, te'arim ᶜasmuthiyyim, differs slightly from the term used by Crescas, te'arim ᶜaṣmiyyim.[57] Further, Crescas, like Maimonides, said that the "ways" of Exod. 33:13 referred to the divine actions.[58] He differed from Maimonides in referring Moses' second question in Exod. 33:18 to these essential attributes instead of to the divine essence.[59] Bibago, however, says that the "ways" refer to the essential attributes.[60] Like Crescas, he distinguishes these essential attributes from the divine essence[61] and, like Maimonides, he refers Moses' second question in Exod. 33:18 to the divine essence.[62]

In his references to the divine goodness, Bibago also seems to combine the interpretations of Maimonides and Crescas. On the one hand, Bibago, like Maimonides, says that being is good and that the good is being.[63] On the other hand, Bibago's references to the divine goodness also seem to reflect the influence of Crescas, part of whose originality lay in making the divine goodness the primary and unifying content of our idea of God.[64] Like Crescas, Bibago refers to the absolute goodness of God,[65] identifies His goodness with His essence,[66] and says that this goodness is the purpose of His actions.[67] Somewhat like Crescas's student Albo, Bibago says that the divine goodness is absolute because it expects no reward.[68] The doctrine that the divine mercy and grace are the divine essence was cited later in Bibago's name by Solomon Alkabeṣ.[69]

In addition to his references to the divine goodness, Bibago's references to the divine infinity may also reflect the influence of Crescas, for Crescas emphasized the infinite nature of God as well.[70] For Crescas, one of the major differences between the divine attributes and the attributes of all other existents is the infinity of the former and the finitude of the latter.[71] Similarly Bibago, after noting the Maimonidean distinction between divine attributes as identical with the divine essence and the attributes of creatures as accidental to their essence,[72] adds that the former are infinite and the latter finite.[73] Crescas speaks of infinity in two senses, infinity of intensity (beḥozeq) and infinity of time.[74] Bibago similarly says that God is infinite in both senses of infinity, that is, that He is infinite in power and infinite in duration,[75] and he attributes this distinction to the "philosopher."[76]

In this chapter we have discussed Bibago's general classification of the divine attributes and his treatment of those specific attributes that we shall not deal with in separate chapters. We have seen that in several instances Bibago sought to synthesize Maimonides' theory of negative attributes with the theories of ibn Rushd (whom Bibago mentions frequently) and Ḥasdai Crescas (whom Bibago mentions not at all). We turn now to the three divine attributes to which Bibago devotes the first three chapters of his book, namely, the divine will, knowledge, and providence.

4. The Divine Will

The dissolution of the harmony between faith and reason that had prevailed in thirteenth-century Christian scholasticism led not only to the scepticism of nominalism but also to a theological reaction on the side of faith. The more conservative authors of the fourteenth century emphasized the divine will and knowledge and, given the breach now felt in the continuity of existence, tried to reconcile these with man's free will.[1] Characteristic of this group is Thomas Bradwardine (1290-1349), whose chief work is not a comprehensive commentary but a treatise divided into three parts that deal respectively with God's existence and attributes, man's free will, and the meeting of the two.[2]

In Jewish philosophy in Christian Spain and France in the fourteenth century, the problem of free will also became a major topic and in the fifteenth century there arose a conservative tendency to emphasize the supernatural activities of God.[3] The divine providence seems to have been an important theme in the work of several Spanish-Jewish thinkers in the fifteenth century, among them Ḥasdai Crescas.[4] It is in this spirit that Bibago, writing in the last half of the fifteenth century, divides his treatise into three parts that deal respectively with the divine will and providence, the human soul and faith, and theological topics such as creation and miracles.[5]

Maimonides' discussion of providence in the third book of his _Guide of the Perplexed_ deals more specifically with the topics of the divine purpose, knowledge, and providence.[6] So Bibago's first three chapters in the first part of his _Derekh 'Emunah_ deal with these same three subjects in the same order.[7] When Bibago in fact begins his book by asking whether the divine actions have a final end or purpose, he says that this same question was raised by Maimonides in the thirteenth chapter of the third part of the _Guide_.[8]

The problem, says Bibago, according to those who deny any purpose in the divine acts, is that a final end implies a deficiency both in the act and in the agent himself. For the end completes and limits acts, which must therefore not be perfect in themselves. The end or purpose similarly perfects the agent who intends to achieve it and so implies a deficiency in the agent himself. Neither God nor His acts can be deficient, of course, and so the divine acts cannot be committed for a final end or purpose.[9]

This problem of the deficiency of divine actions that are performed toward a final end is not mentioned by Maimonides in the chapter of the Guide referred to by Bibago.[10] In that chapter Maimonides argues, in opposition to those who say that man is the final end of the universe,[11] that there is no ultimate end for the universe as a whole, although there are of course final ends in nature. The problem raised by Bibago, that the divine will implies a deficiency in the deity and that the divine actions cannot be done for a final end, was mentioned, however, by the Neoplatonic and Arabic philosophers who derived the world from God by necessity. Thus Plotinus, according to whom the world is eternal and produced by necessity,[12] says that there is no desire or willingness to produce intellect that intervenes between the One and intellect, for this would imply that in the One there is the imperfection of not yet having what it wishes to have.[13] There is no previous design or craftsmanlike reflection in the production of the world.[14] The Arabic philosophers al-Fārābī and ibn Sīnā similarly deny that the divine actions have a final end,[15] and ibn Sīnā also denies any deficiency in God because of a desire for what He lacks.[16] The philosopher in Judah Halevi's Sefer ha-Kuzari begins his speech by arguing, in words very similar to those of Bibago, that the Creator has no will or final end because the completion of the end is the perfection of the agent, who before this must therefore have been deficient.[17] Finally, ibn Rushd also says that will occurs in man and animals to perfect a deficiency in their essence and that this obviously cannot be the case with God.[18]

Thus, although Maimonides does not refer to this argument that Bibago reproduces, namely, that divine actions for a final end are deficient, Maimonides' denial in this chapter that the world as a whole has an ultimate final end may have seemed to many to place Maimonides in the camp of those philosophers who did use this argument, who denied a final end to the divine actions and who derived the world from God by necessity. Bibago's purpose in this first chapter of the Derekh 'Emunah is to deny that this opinion of the philosophers is Maimonides' opinion.[19]

This is not to say that the philosophers who derived the world from God by necessity, who denied a final end in the divine actions, and who felt volition implied a deficiency in the agent also in fact denied a divine will. They rather asserted of God a will independent of final ends, implying no deficiency in God and consonant with the production of the world by necessity. This consistency between necessity and volition may be based on the conception of a voluntary act in Greek philosophy as one that not only involves knowledge but also is free from external compulsion.[20] Since "necessity" is used by Aristotle to apply to what is compelled by something external to itself as well as to what could not be otherwise,[21] it might be possible for an action to be voluntary insofar as it was free of external compulsion and yet also be necessary insofar as it was determined by the agent's own simple nature and so could not be otherwise.[22]

Perhaps it was in this sense that Plotinus, who as we saw denied that the world was produced by design and said that desire would imply a deficiency in God, also explained at length that the One possesses will insofar as it is self-caused and self-determined and does not just happen to be.[23] Later philosophers associated the divine will with a satisfaction or delight in God at the emanation of the universe.

Thus al-Ghazālī reports that according to the philosophers God's will is His satisfaction in knowing that His perfection is attained in the emanation of the universe.[24] Maimonides similarly attributes to Aristotle the opinion that the First Cause wills what is necessarily derived from it and rejoices and takes pleasure in it.[25] Isaac Albalag also says that the divine will is the delight God takes in what emanates from Him.[26] As ibn Rushd had said, the philosophers do not deny that God wills, but they do deny that His will implies a deficiency in Him as the empirical will does in human beings.[27]

The philosophers, however, were not the only ones to assert that God wills and yet to deny that His actions also have a final end. According to al-Shahrastānī, the orthodox Islamic position is that no final cause prompted God to create the universe because He cannot profit or suffer harm.[28] Maimonides ascribes to the Ashᶜariyya, an Islamic sect, the view that everything comes about through the divine will but that the divine actions have no final end.[29]

Maimonides himself, however, clearly associated will, purpose, and final ends. Thus, in citing Aristotle's opinion that the First Cause wills what is necessarily derived from Him, Maimonides immediately adds that this willing is not called purpose and that the notion of purpose is not included in it.[30] Of those who derived the divine actions from the divine will alone and not from the divine wisdom, that is, the Ashᶜariyya, Maimonides says that according to them God intends or purposes what He does, but this intention is still not toward any final end.[31] Maimonides' own opinion seems closer to that of the Muᶜtazila, the Islamic sect that derived the divine actions from the divine wisdom[32] and upheld a final end for these divine actions.[33] Thus Maimonides not only frequently emphasizes the notion of purpose along with will,[34] he also affirms the importance of an ultimate end to existence and to the divine actions in I-69[35] and III-25,[36] in spite of his apparent denial of such an ultimate end in III-13.[37] Even at the beginning of III-13 Maimonides insists that every agent who acts with a purpose must necessarily have an end in view.[38]

For Bibago as well the divine actions have a final end[39] and are the result of the divine wisdom as well as will.[40] The divine will for him also includes both the notions of purpose and a final end.[41] On the other hand, the problem of avoiding a deficiency in the deity, the problem with which Bibago began his book, leads to a denial not only of final ends but also of the divine will, for one who wills an action does so for the perfection of its final end.[42] Bibago therefore turns in the first chapter to an analysis and defense of the divine will to solve this problem and to support his explanation of Maimonides.

Bibago first divides all agents truly deserving the name "agent" into two kinds, natural and voluntary.[43] There are two characteristics that distinguish these two kinds of agents from each other. First, a natural agent such as fire acts unconsciously without knowledge of its action or its result, whereas a voluntary agent such as man is conscious of his action and acts with knowledge. Second, a natural agent can perform only one of two opposite actions essentially, the other being performed, if at all, only accidentally. Fire, for example, only heats essentially and cools, if at all, only accidentally. A voluntary agent, on the other hand, can perform either of two opposite actions essentially, both being possible for him.[44]

According to some, Bibago continues, there is a third intermediate type of agent, an agent by necessity, that is similar in the first respect to a voluntary agent and is similar in the second respect to a natural agent. Like a voluntary agent, the necessary agent is conscious of its action but, unlike a voluntary agent, the necessary agent acts without intention or change. Like the natural agent, the necessary agent performs only one of two opposite actions without change, but unlike the natural agent, the necessary agent is conscious and knows its action.[45]

Some philosophers further say, according to Bibago, that God is such an agent by necessity because He would be deficient if He were a natural or a voluntary agent. He would be deficient if He were a natural agent because a natural agent lacks knowledge. He would be deficient if He were a voluntary agent because a voluntary agent acts by intention, presumably thus lacking the goal he intends to achieve. God's actions therefore, according to this opinion, proceed from Him necessarily as light proceeds from the sun, except that God knows His actions and this knowledge is in fact the cause of these actions.[46]

Bibago agrees that God cannot be a natural agent because a natural agent is deficient.[47] For Bibago, however, the deficiency of the natural agent is not just its lack of knowledge, but its inability to perform either of two opposite actions.[48] An agent who can perform essentially only one of two opposite actions is a deficient agent, says Bibago, even if his one action comes about through knowledge. This deficiency then applies equally well to an agent by necessity, who in this respect is no better off than a natural agent, for of what use is his knowledge to him if he does not have the power to do the opposite? If, on the other hand, he has the ability to do either of two opposite actions, he is then a voluntary agent, for the definition of will is the ability to do an action and its opposite.[49]

One of Bibago's major arguments against God's being an agent by necessity, then, is that such an agent is as deficient as a natural agent in its inability to perform either of two opposite actions. This performance of two opposites does not imply any plurality in the deity, Bibago adds, any more than the duality of the "now" (<u>ᶜattah</u>) as the end of the past and the beginning of the future detracts from its simple basic unity.[50] It was the failure to understand that one God could perform opposite actions that led to the ancient heresies of dualism and polytheism, for some evidently believed that opposite effects must be produced by different powers or deities.[51] It was for such a heretical view that a man called Mani was executed by King Shabur. So, says Bibago, heretics who deny the unity of God are called, because of Mani, <u>minim</u>,[52] just as one who believes that man's ultimate felicity is in this world is called an <u>'epiqurus</u> because such was the belief of the man Epicurus.[53]

A second argument used by Bibago to show that God is not an agent by necessity is related to the first argument about opposite actions. An agent by necessity, Bibago says, performs only one action constantly without change and in accordance with the necessity of its essence. The divine actions, however, change from time to time.[54] Change such as this is of the essence of will and without it there would be no will. God is therefore a voluntary and not a necessary agent. In spite of such change in the divine actions and will, Bibago adds, there is no change in the deity, although Bibago admits that we are ignorant of how this is possible.[55] God can do whatever He wants whenever He wants without any change occurring in Him, but because the divine will is not like the human will, we don't know how this is possible.[56]

This problem of the change implied in willing as against the divine immutability is the primary issue raised by Joseph Albo in his discussion of the divine will,[57] a discussion that includes many of the elements found in Bibago's treatment of the subject. Albo's solution of the problem, somewhat like that of Bibago, is to restate our ignorance of the divine will.[58] Bibago, however, unlike Albo, says that the divine will does indeed change, although, because the term "will" is used of the divine and human wills only equivocally, this does not result in any change in God.[59] Albo does not speak of change in the divine will, which is identical with the divine essence. Also Maimonides, to whom Bibago refers for support in this matter,[60] says that the divine will does not change.[61]

The problem of change and the divine will in relation to the issue of creation was dealt with by Joseph ibn Ṣaddiq.[62] Al-Ghazālī also speaks at length about change and the divine will when he discusses creation.[63] The apparent shift in the focus of the discussion from the problem of change and the divine will to the related concept of will as the ability to perform opposite actions, as in Bibago, may be connected with a shift from the issue of creation to the issue of the divine providence and miracles.[64]

The third argument used by Bibago against God's being an agent by necessity is based on the dissimilarity between God and the world and is in fact the argument that Bibago discusses first, although we have listed it here third. The argument is that something generated by necessity from another thing must be similar to and related to that other thing somehow, and everyone agrees that nothing is similar and related to God.[65] In the earlier Neoplatonic and Arabic philosophy, a basic dissimilarity between God and the world was the unity of God and the multiplicity of the world. The fundamental problem was to derive a composite world from one God and still be consistent with the corollary of the above principle that only one simple being can proceed from a simple being.[66] When Bibago sets out to demonstrate rationally the lack of similarity and relation between the Creator and His universe, the distinction he uses is not unity and multiplicity but the infinity of God and the finite dimensions of the world. If God is infinite, then by the above principle of the similarity of necessarily related beings, the world generated from God by necessity would also have to be infinite. If the dimensions of the world are finite, it is because the world derives from God not by necessity but by will.[67]

In regard to the finite dimensions of the universe, Bibago refers in a general way to the measures and motions of the heavens. The only particular fact specified by him is the revolution of the outermost sphere once in twenty-four hours.[68] Maimonides, in arguing for the production of the world by will and purpose, referred to many specific facts about the heavens that could not be explained on the assumption of a necessary order in both the sublunar and celestial worlds.[69] Judah Halevi, though arguing primarily against the theory of chance instead of necessity, also sought to establish the generation of the world by the divine will through referring to specific facts about the heavens and earth,[70] among them the revolution of the outermost sphere once every twenty-four hours.[71] Neither Halevi nor Maimonides, however, argued for the divine will from the lack of relation and similarity between God and the world because of the infinity of God and the finite dimensions of the world. Thus, although Bibago's arguments for the divine will from the measures of the heavens are reminiscent of similar arguments in Halevi and Maimonides, one clearly distinguishing element in Bibago's argument is the concept of the divine infinity, which, as we have already seen, the fifteenth-century Jewish philosophers[72] had inherited from, among others, Duns Scotus and Ḥasdai Crescas.

Bibago takes up an objection to this argument based on ibn Rushd's contention that the revolution of the outermost sphere once in twenty-four hours is indeed necessary for maintaining the existence of the world. Bibago answers that the limitation of the speed of the sphere for the end of maintaining the world in existence is indicative of generation not by necessity but by purpose and will.[73] He in fact agrees later that the revolution of the outermost sphere at the speed necessary to maintain the world is a sign of divine wisdom,[74] and he also agrees later with ibn Rushd that the dimensions of the sun being exactly right for maintaining the world is a sign of the divine providence.[75] Bibago consequently seems to be arguing here for the divine will not on the basis of irregularities in nature but rather on the basis of a regular natural order that cannot come from God by necessity because of the divine infinity.[76] The element of the divine infinity in Bibago thus seems to have altered the structure of the arguments about divine will and necessity from what they had been in al-Ghazālī, Halevi, and Maimonides.

In addition to this rational distinction between the infinity of God and the finite dimensions of the world as a ground for the absence of a relation of necessity between God and the world, Bibago also derives the lack of such a relation or similarity between them from the prophetic books. From Ps. 89:7 we see that even the spheres that are eternal a parte post and the immaterial intellects that seem most similar to the deity are not similar. From Isa. 40:18, 25 we see that God and His creatures cannot even be compared because they are not in the same genus.[77] Bibago concludes that the divine activity in the world in spite of this rationally and traditionally proven separation between God and the world is like a miracle unless we assume that God is a voluntary agent.[78]

Although the separation between God and the world in Bibago is distinguished from that found in Maimonides by the element of infinity, the concept of a gulf between God and the world is common to both Bibago and Maimonides.[79] It is also characteristic of the fourteenth-century Christian scholastics who in this regard opposed the Arabic necessitarian philosophies with their gradations and analogies of being between God and the world.[80] Whereas the more Neoplatonic philosophies of necessity derived the world from God only indirectly through intermediaries, many Jewish and Christian thinkers insisted that the gulf between God and the world could be bridged directly as well by the divine will.[81]

Thus Bibago's fourth and last argument against God's being an agent by necessity is related to his third argument based on the dissimilarity between God and the world, much as his second argument is closely related to his first.[82] This fourth argument is that an agent by necessity operates only through intermediaries and only upon properly prepared objects, whereas God, Bibago insists, operates either with or without intermediaries and upon whomever He so desires, whether they are prepared or not,[83] although most of the time He does in fact act through intermediaries.[84] The sin of the twelve spies in the biblical story, Bibago says, was in thinking that God is restricted by these two limitations of agents that operate by necessity.[85] One might add that the requirement of intermediaries between God and the world was, according to Bibago, a basis for idolatry.[86]

In addition to these four rational arguments against God's being an agent by necessity, Bibago also argues that this doctrine would conflict with such basic articles of faith as creation, miracles, the divine providence, and retribution.[87] Some of the details of this conflict between these beliefs and the doctrine of necessity are mentioned in various sections of the book. In regard to creation, Bibago says in his discussion of creation that the opposite of the theory of creation, namely, the theory of the eternity of the world, is based on the world's having emanated by necessity from the deity.[88] The argument is that if the deity that emanates the world by necessity is eternal, then the world that is emanated by necessity is also eternal.[89] Further, like the doctrine of necessity, the doctrine of the eternity of the world also negates the beliefs concerning miracles, the divine providence, retribution, and divine revelation as well.[90]

In addition to the eternity of the world being implied by God's being a necessary agent, the doctrine of the creation of the world is clearly associated by Bibago with God's being a voluntary agent.[91] It is not just that in this case the doctrine of creation is possible and unobjectionable.[92] God's being a voluntary agent implies that He is a creator,[93] and indeed creation cannot even be conceived without this corollary.[94]

Maimonides, in his discussion of the creation or eternity of the world, had based this question upon the issue of the production of the world by will or by necessity.[95] As Bibago says that the doctrine of necessity destroys basic Jewish beliefs, so Maimonides had said that the doctrine of the eternity of the world destroys the Law in its principle and gives the lie to every miracle.[96] Maimonides explicitly denies that one can believe in both the eternity of the world and its production by will and purpose.[97] Isaac Abravanel similarly says that the issue of the creation or the eternity of the world is really the issue of its production by necessity or by will.[98]

As for miracles, Bibago later says that they are also inconsistent with the doctrine of the eternity of the world,[99] which we have just seen is based on the doctrine of the production of the world by necessity.[100] Bibago notes that both al-Ghazālī and ibn Sīnā believe that miracles are consistent with the doctrine of the eternity of the world.[101] For Bibago, however, miracles clearly indicate that God is a voluntary agent because such changes are the result of the divine will.[102] Miracles are therefore associated with the will of God[103] and are in fact used by Bibago to shed light on the problem of how to avoid change in the deity because of change in the divine will.[104] For Judah Halevi, miracles are the chief argument for free will in God.[105] Divine providence as well, which extends below the sphere of the moon to man because of man's reason, does so in virtue of the divine will and miracles.[106]

Retribution, or reward and punishment for one's deeds, also comes not according to necessity or nature but by the divine will and providence.[107] This indeed is one of Bibago's principal explanations for the problem of theodicy, that is, for the suffering of the righteous and the prosperity of the wicked in this world.[108] Since the reward of the righteous and the punishment of the wicked occur not naturally but miraculously by the divine will and providence,[109] the righteous suffer when, for reasons known only to God, He wills not to miraculously reward the righteous[110] and instead leaves them to the effects of nature, chance, and the stars. While they are under the miraculous care of the divine will, the righteous do not suffer nor do the wicked prosper.[111]

Prophecy is not one of the concepts listed by Bibago in this first chapter as being negated by the doctrine of necessity.[112] In later chapters Bibago says that he follows Maimonides in basing prophecy also on the divine will.[113] The one exception is Moses, who, because he had reached the level of the angels, prophesied not by the divine will but by necessity.[114]

Finally, from the references in the discussion of divine retribution to the divine providence and will and to miracles,[115] and from the references in the discussion of miracles to the divine providence and will,[116] and from the association of the doctrine of creation with the divine providence and will and miracles,[117] we can see that these concepts all mutually imply each other for Bibago and that the doctrine of the necessary generation of the world must indeed negate the whole complex.

Since, therefore, the belief in the generation of the world by necessity negates doctrines basic to the faith of Judaism, and since it has also been shown by four arguments to be philosophically and rationally untenable, Bibago rejects the notion that God is an agent who acts by necessity.[118] Since Bibago also rejects the possibility of God's being a natural agent as obviously wrong,[119] he concludes that God is an agent by will.[120] This divine will, Bibago immediately adds, is of course absolutely different from ours, and the term is used of God and man only equivocally,[121] as we have seen,[122] for we have no concept of the divine will.[123]

Bibago's classification of agents into natural and voluntary ones has ample precedent.[124] This twofold classification, however, may be a distillation of more complete lists of causes that often include chance as well.[125] Although it did not suit Bibago's purpose and schemework in this first chapter to mention chance at the beginning of it, he somewhat later in the chapter notes four types of actions in this world, those by nature, by choice, by chance, and through the stars.[126] This classification, as Bibago himself says,[127] is based on Maimonides' threefold division of the proximate or intermediate worldly causes into natural, voluntary, and accidental ones.[128] In good Aristotelian fashion,[129] however, Maimonides says that chance is only an excess of what is natural and that most causes are either natural or voluntary,[130] thus reducing the list to the basic twofold classification of natural and voluntary causes. Bibago also eliminates chance by saying that it occurs on a minority of occasions[131] and that it is really our name for our ignorance of the true cause.[132]

Of the two characteristics by which Bibago distinguishes the voluntary from the natural agent, namely knowledge and the ability to perform opposite actions,[133] knowledge had long been agreed upon as a basic requirement for a voluntary agent. Both Plato and Aristotle had said that a voluntary action could not be done from ignorance.[134] Al-Ghazālī also said that will necessarily implies knowledge and ibn Rushd agreed that knowledge is included in the definition of will.[135] Although Maimonides calls both the celestial intellects and spheres and the corporeal forces angels, he differentiates the corporeal forces as things of nature because they do not apprehend their acts, whereas the celestial intellects and spheres apprehend their acts and have will and free choice.[136] Isaac Albalag says that a voluntary agent is distinguished from a natural one by not being separated from knowledge,[137] a phrase almost exactly duplicated by Bibago,[138] and Menaḥem ben Abraham Bonafos[139] defines a natural agent as one that acts without knowledge and a voluntary one as the opposite.[140] Shem Ṭov ben Joseph ibn Shem Ṭov, in his "Commentary" on the Guide, even speaks not of natural agents and voluntary agents but of natural agents and conscious agents, or agents by knowledge.[141] Bonafos and Shem Ṭov, like Bibago, use fire and man as examples of the opposing types of agents.

That it is through knowledge alone, however, that the First Cause necessarily generates the universe seems to go back at least to ibn Sīnā.[142] Al-Ghazālī says that the philosophers' opinion is that the world proceeds necessarily from the divine essence as light does from the sun or as heat does from fire, except that in regard to God this emanation is caused by God's knowledge of the universe, which is identical with His knowledge of His essence.[143] Judah Halevi similarly attributes to the philosophers the opinion that the divine knowledge alone is sufficient to determine any particular time or one of a pair of opposites without the addition of will or power.[144] Maimonides also seems to be referring to ibn Sīnā when he describes Aristotle's derivation of the universe from the First Cause by necessity as being not like the procession of a shadow from a body, heat from fire, or light from the sun, but rather like the derivation of an intellectum from an intellect.[145]

Like al-Ghazālī and Maimonides in the passages referred to, Bibago, as we have seen, also uses the simile of the sun to describe the agent by necessity, adding of course that the deity differs in operating through knowledge.[146] The simile of the sun goes back at least to Plotinus,[147] in whose thought, however, the distinction of the One from the sun is not knowledge, for the One is above knowledge and intellect.[148] Thus ibn Sīnā's system, in which the world emanates necessarily from God because of His knowledge, seems to combine the Neoplatonic emanation by necessity with the Aristotelian God of intellect.[149] Al-Ghazālī in fact chides ibn Sīnā for contradicting his fellow philosopher who says that the universe follows necessarily from the divine essence but not through knowledge.[150] Ibn Sīnā does not deny a divine will but rather identifies it with this divine knowledge.[151] He does deny, however, that the divine actions have a final end.[152]

Bibago's description of the view that God is an agent operating necessarily through knowledge seems to fit ibn Sīnā's opinion on the subject very well. Since the two characteristics distinguishing natural and voluntary agents for Bibago are knowledge and the ability to perform either of two opposite actions, the intermediate necessary agent would preserve the symmetry of Bibago's scheme if it were not only like the voluntary agent in acting through knowledge but also differed from it in performing only one of two opposite actions. Bibago says, however, that the necessary agent differs from the voluntary one in acting without purpose or change,[153] characteristics that ibn Sīnā ascribed to the agency of the First Cause.[154]

One of Bibago's main arguments, however, against God's being an agent by necessity, as ibn Sīnā contended, was that such an agent lacked the other characteristic of a voluntary agent in addition to knowledge, namely, the ability to do either of two opposite actions essentially. This characteristic of the will seems to go back to Philo's interpretation of the biblical tradition.[155] For Philo, a voluntary action was not, as it was for Plato and Aristotle, an action done with knowledge and without external compulsion.[156] This has been called a relative concept of freedom.[157] Philo's concept of the absolute freedom of the will meant in God the power to intervene miraculously in nature, and it meant in man the similarly miraculous and divinely derived power to choose freely between alternatives.[158]

According to Judah Halevi, the Kalām view of the divine will is that God can do the opposite of everything that He does. His omnipotence inclines equally to either of two opposites and must be directed to one or the other by the will.[159] This is very similar to al-Ghazālī's statement that God could have willed the opposite of every work that exists through His will and that, since His power encompasses the opposites, there must be a will that directs the power to one or the other.[160] Maimonides also said that the true reality and quiddity of will is to will and not to will,[161] and that every agent acting by purpose and will and not by nature accomplishes many different acts.[162] Earlier he had pointed out that precisely this was the issue of dispute between the adherents of the Law and the philosophers, namely, that what exists is made by will and is not a necessary consequence and that it could have been made differently from what it is.[163]

Among the Christian scholastics it was especially Duns Scotus, and William of Ockham after him, who said that will in its primary act is free with regard to opposite acts.[164] It has been contended, in fact, that the reputed "voluntarism" of Duns Scotus, instead of being some sort of irrationalism, consists precisely in his insistence that the free will is capable of choosing other than it does.[165] Abner of Burgos, who had converted from Judaism to Christianity, said that the distinction between a voluntary and a natural agent was that the latter could perform only one of two opposing actions in accordance with its nature, whereas a voluntary agent could perform either one according to its nature.[166] Joseph Albo also distinguished natural agents, which could do only one thing essentially, from voluntary agents, who can perform opposite actions at will.[167]

Al-Ghazālī, in arguing against the philosophers' view of God as an agent acting necessarily through knowledge, had insisted upon only a twofold classification of agents into natural and voluntary ones. He concluded that the philosophers who derived the world from God by necessity were in effect reducing God to a natural agent.[168] If it is objected that the world is derived necessarily from God through His knowledge, which is not the case with natural agents such as the sun,[169] al-Ghazālī answers that as long as the divine will is denied, the additional factor of knowledge seems to make little difference.[170]

In response to al-Ghazālī's criticism of the philosophers, ibn Rushd used an Aristotelian analysis to show that God operates by both knowledge and will. In Aristotle's philosophy, it was because of a rational formula that a potency associated with that rational formula could be capable of contrary effects, whereas a nonrational potency produces only one effect.[171] Thus the ability to produce contrary effects that in the biblical-Philonic framework was a function of the free will is in Aristotle's thought a function of reason. It is appetency or will that then decides which of the opposites is to be done. Without this decision of will, both opposites would be done at the same time, which is impossible.[172]

Ibn Rushd similarly says that if God operated only by knowledge, in knowing two opposites He would necessarily perform them both at the same time, which is impossible. He therefore has an additional attribute of will or choice through which He performs one of the two opposite acts that He knows.[173] Thus ibn Rushd, who said that al-Fārābī and ibn Sīnā introduced into philosophy some of the theological notions of the Kalām,[174] seems himself here to be utilizing an Aristotelian concept to effect somewhat of a compromise between ibn Sīnā and the Kalām on the issue of the divine will. In this response to al-Ghazālī's criticism of the philosophers, ibn Rushd, unlike ibn Sīnā, implies that the divine will is not identical with the divine knowledge and that the world is not generated by the divine knowledge alone.

This agency through the divine will, ibn Rushd adds, of course does not have the deficiencies of agency through the human will, such as the need to better oneself through the desired object.[175] The divine agency is even further from natural agency, for a natural agent acts without knowledge and final ends.[176] Therefore the division of agents into natural and voluntary ones is not exhaustive, for God is neither one nor the other and possesses instead an agency superior to both. He can thus be said to will only equivocally, for only He can understand how His will is not subject to the deficiencies of human wills.[177] Further, ibn Rushd insists that, although each of the opposites is possible for the deity, He always performs the better of the two.[178]

Isaac Albalag repeats ibn Rushd's position that God's agency is superior to that of the voluntary or natural agent and that He always chooses the better alternative.[179] However, Albalag refers specifically to this divine agency as being intermediate between the natural and voluntary agency.[180] He describes this intermediate divine agent according to ibn Sīnā's formulations as an agent acting necessarily through knowledge and possessing will insofar as He takes delight in what emanates from Him.[181]

It is therefore possible that Bibago was influenced by Albalag in his description of the agent who acts necessarily through knowledge as a third type of agent intermediate between the natural and voluntary agents. Albalag was evidently well known in the fifteenth century, for Shem Ṭov ibn Shem Ṭov, Isaac ben Shem Ṭov ibn Shem Ṭov, Abraham Shalom, and Isaac Abravanel are all critical of his doctrines and mention him by name.[182] Further, Bibago's response to Albalag's position was similar to that of al-Ghazālī to ibn Sīnā. Like al-Ghazālī, Bibago tries to eliminate this third type of agency and to reduce it to a natural agency by saying that it is deficient as a natural agency even if it does operate through knowledge.[183]

It should be noted that the Aristotelian analysis of choice that ibn Rushd used to modify ibn Sīnā's theory of necessary emanation differs also from the biblical-Philonic free will in the following manner. In Aristotle's philosophy, both man and animals can act voluntarily.[184] Both are moved by the same motive force, appetency (orexis),[185] so that human will and animal impulse are not really different in kind.[186] What distinguishes man from animals, according to Aristotle, is not his free will but his reason, so that choice is characteristic of man's volitions because choice involves a rational principle.[187] In the biblical-Philonic tradition, man is distinguished by the divine gift of free will.[188] In spite of this distinction, however, ibn Rushd may have been playing upon the similarity between the two concepts in his use of the Aristotelian concept of choice in his answer to al-Ghazālī. Duns Scotus, also playing upon this shift in the concept of choice between opposites from the realm of reason to that of the will and playing as well upon the different concepts of reason involved, tries paradoxically to prove that according to Aristotle's division of rational and nonrational powers, the intellect is "nonrational" (in the Aristotelian sense of rational choice) in that it acts automatically in the presence of evident truth, whereas the will (biblical-Philonic) is "rational" in that it can freely choose or not choose an object known through reason.[189]

Whereas ibn Rushd used the Aristotelian analysis of rational choice from the Metaphysics to describe the divine agency, Bibago, following Maimonides,[190] uses Aristotle's analysis of volition and choice from the Nicomachean Ethics to describe man's freedom. All animals act voluntarily (beraṣon), but only man, insofar as he is rational, has choice. If one denies that man has choice, he also denies that man is rational,[191] which, however, would be like denying that man is man.[192] Later Bibago refers to man's rational choice (beḥirah sikhlith).[193] Bibago, however, says that man has choice not only because he is rational, but also because he has a material part that conflicts with his rational part and so forces him to choose between them. Therefore it is not just nonrational animals that lack choice. Beings that do not have a material part, such as angels and God, also do not have choice and will.[194] This denial of will and choice to God seems to conflict with Bibago's earlier, lengthy defense of God as an agent by will Who can perform either of two opposing actions. Further, in the same section Bibago says that this power of choice was given man by God so that man could worship God.[195] This denial of choice to God may reflect a more philosophic strain in Bibago's thought.

In his first chapter, however, Bibago interprets Maimonides' concept of the divine will in terms of the biblical-Philonic tradition found also in the Kalām and in scholastics like Duns Scotus, namely, as the ability to perform either of two opposite acts. This interpretation of the concept of the divine will in Maimonides may partially explain the latter's criticism of ibn Sīnā.[196] In view of the religious and almost mystical aspect of ibn Sīnā's philosophy and considering his apparent attempt to work out a compromise between the philosophers and the Kalām, one might have expected Maimonides to be more sympathetic to ibn Sīnā.[197] One factor in Maimonides' reservations concerning ibn Sīnā may be the differences between them regarding the freedom of the divine will, which Maimonides himself says is one of the basic issues between the philosophers and the adherents of the Law.[198] In view then of ibn Sīnā's somewhat unsatisfactory synthesis, Maimonides may have been attempting a new synthesis incorporating the biblical-Philonic notion of the free divine will.

In this first chapter Bibago may have been interpreting ibn Rushd in this way as well on the basis of ibn Rushd's application to the divine will of Aristotle's doctrine of rational choice.[199] Thus, when Bibago says that action by knowledge is no added advantage unless the opposite action is also possible,[200] he may not be eliminating the middle type of action by necessity as al-Ghazālī had done.[201] He may be saying instead that, given ibn Rushd's application of the Aristotelian doctrine of rational choice to the divine actions, action by knowledge implies choice between opposites.

Further, although the principal object of Bibago's arguments concerning the divine will are the philosophers like ibn Sīnā who derive the world by necessity from the divine knowledge, Bibago would also disagree over this issue of the will with those more voluntaristic philosophers such as Crescas who derive the world from God by both will and necessity. Maimonides had explicitly denied the possibility of a combination of will and necessity in a theory of the eternal emanation of the world from the divine will,[202] and Isaac Abravanel said that Crescas's opinion was identical with this theory here described as unsatisfactory by Maimonides.[203] Crescas had said that the will is nothing but the necessary procession of existences from the rational forms because of a superabundance of goodness.[204] This possibility of a union of free will and necessity is based, as we saw, on the Greek conception of relative free will[205] and goes back most notably to Augustine who, it is interesting to note, describes the will as a delight much as the later philosophers of necessity did.[206]

In addition to insisting that God is a voluntary agent Who can perform either of two opposite actions, Bibago says that either action can also be performed essentially (<u>be^c^eṣem</u>), whereas a natural agent can perform only one of two opposite actions essentially and the other, if at all, only accidentally (<u>bemiqreh</u>).[207] Opposite actions, in other words, can come from the one God whether the actions are in the category of essence or whether they are in the category of accidents.[208] Like Maimonides,[209] Bibago says that an essential action is the opposite of an action by chance since an essential action completes its goal and so relates its end to its beginning. It has, that is, a certain constancy for the duration required to achieve its end.[210]

Bibago discusses two other characteristics that distinguish an essential agent from an agent that acts accidentally. First, an agent that acts essentially knows its action. Second, an essential agent remains in existence as long as its product does, and its product goes out of existence when the agent does, as is the case with essential causes and effects. Thus, according to these two criteria, a human father is not the essential agent of his son's existence. First, he does not know the exact moment of his son's conception and so is not aware of his action. Second, his son may endure after him. God, on the other hand, is our true Father, for as a voluntary and essential agent He is aware of His action as He performs it and He endures for the duration of His effect.[211]

Bibago thus says that a voluntary agent also can (and in the case of God must) be an essential agent. Bibago's contemporary

Shem Ṭov ben Joseph ibn Shem Ṭov, on the other hand, restricted essential agency to what Bibago calls the necessary agent and so denies that a voluntary agent can act essentially. Essential agency for Shem Ṭov is the distinguishing characteristic of an agent that operates through knowledge like a voluntary agent and yet is not a voluntary agent.[212] Initially, an agent acting essentially was one of the meanings of a natural agent. That is, a natural agent was one that moved according to its nature or essence. Maimonides evidently used "naturally" and "essentially" interchangeably in his discussion of intermediate causes.[213] Aristotle had said that the primary sense of "nature" is the essence of things that have in themselves, as such, a source of movement.[214] Similarly Judah Halevi defined "nature," according to the philosopher, as the principle and cause in a thing by which it moves and rests essentially, not accidentally, adding that this is how we distinguish natural agents from accidental ones.[215]

It was in this sense of "nature" that the church father Athanasius had said that a man begets a son by nature because the son is the proper offspring of the father's substance.[216] Although in Athanasius "nature" as well as "necessity" were terms used in opposition to "will," the terms "naturally" and "essentially" came eventually to be used also not in opposition to "will," since "naturally produced" meant produced from the essence of God but not by necessity.[217] Isaac Albalag notes that the problem of whether one or more actions can come from an agent essentially is the result of a confusion between essential and accidental agents. It is in accidental agents that the number of actions equals the number of accidents, but the agent who operates essentially through reason can perform many different actions equally.[218] Essential actions thus came to be attributed to voluntary agents as well, as in Bibago, although the original association of essence and nature may explain the opposition of essential and voluntary agency in Shem Ṭov ben Joseph ibn Shem Ṭov.

Having thus established that God is a voluntary agent Who can perform either of two opposite actions essentially, Bibago turns to a second major theme of his first chapter, and insists and reiterates in various ways that God not only created the world by the divine will but also constantly maintains the world in existence by means of the divine will.[219] God is not like the architect of a house who builds the house at first and then leaves it to endure solely by its own nature and essence, so that the house would not go out of existence if its architect went out of existence. According to both the philosophers and the theologians, the opposite is the case in regard to God and the world. The world, unlike the house, would disappear were it not for its maintenance by the divine will, whereas God endures forever, even after the destruction of His creatures.[220]

For the divine will is the direct coefficient in all events in nature, and thus these events become vehicles and instruments for the divine will.[221] According to the philosopher as well, nature is unintelligent, but the philosopher says that the active intellect guides nature toward its final end, whereas we, says Bibago, attribute this guidance to the divine will.[222] This divine coefficiency, for example, is why man cannot live on bread alone,[223] for the essence of bread cannot nourish without the divine will. This also is the lesson of the manna.[224] Consequently from this point of view there is no longer a distinction between natural and artificial deeds, since natural events are artificial insofar as they are the result of the divine will.[225]

The proof for the divine will as a coefficient cause comes from miracles. Because miracles are obviously from the divine will, they indicate to us the less obvious element of divine will in natural events.[226] As an example, Bibago supposes a man born suddenly with fully developed faculties. This man would, says Bibago, think that the colors he saw were their own cause until, failing to see them after sunset, he would realize that they require sunlight as well to be seen. In a similar way, miracles show us that natural causes by themselves are insufficient.[227]

On the other hand, since Bibago believes that God generally acts through intermediaries,[228] he carefully insists that this coefficiency of the divine will does not negate the existence of natural and voluntary intermediate causes in this world.[229] As to how man's free will can be maintained along with this divine coefficiency, Bibago simply draws an analogy, saying that, as the divine knowledge does not compromise the realm of possibility, so the divine will does not compromise man's free choice, although in both cases we are ignorant of how this comes about.[230]

This emphasis upon the direct agency of the divine will, which evidently goes back at least to Philo and the Muslim Kalām, did not in all systems of thought allow for natural and voluntary intermediate causes as well.[231] Maimonides says that the Muslim Ash^{c}ariyya ascribed each atom in this world directly to the divine will and so denied natural and voluntary intermediate causes.[232] The neo-Augustinian Christian scholastics of the fourteenth century usually emphasized the divine coefficiency in all worldly events at the cost of man's absolute free will.[233] Judah Halevi, however, as Bibago was to do later, insists upon the direct agency of the divine will in this world as well as upon natural and voluntary intermediate causes. Although he emphasizes God's continuing maintenance of the universe through His will, he also says that God implanted in things the power of self-preservation and that this divine maintenance does not impair man's free choice.[234] Bibago followed Halevi in this respect.

The issue of the divine will seems to have been associated usually with the problem of the creation or eternity of the world.[235] Al-Ghazālī, for example, devoted so much of his defense of the doctrine of creation to a discussion of the divine will that ibn Rushd accused him of changing the subject.[236] Maimonides also, as we have seen, felt that the question of the eternity or creation of the world hinged upon its generation by necessity or by will.[237] Judah Moscato, the sixteenth-century commentator on Sefer ha-Kuzari, quotes a passage from Bibago's discussion of the divine will and adds that it comes from Bibago's discussion of creation.[238] Bibago certainly considered the doctrine of creation to be an axiom of the Torah,[239] but his emphasis is also clearly upon the maintenance of the universe by the divine will, not upon its creation. This indicates that his basic theme in this discussion of the divine will and in the first third of his book is the divine providence, not creation.[240]

Toward the end of the first chapter, Bibago raises the question of how to account for evil in the world if the divine will is at least the coefficient cause of everything in the world. Bibago offers three possible answers. First, evil partakes somewhat of the good insofar as it is the sword of God and serves thus as an instrument of the divine will, evidently to punish the wicked.[241] Second, evil may come from the necessity of matter (hekhraḥ haḥomer) in the process of generation in this world, since new forms arise because of the privation inherent in matter.[242] Third, evil helps the righteous remain steadfast, for such steadfastness is the result of seeing the suffering of the wicked in their punishment.[243]

Bibago finally returns to the question that he had raised at the beginning of this first chapter, namely, the final end of the divine actions. Final ends, says Bibago, are either the end served by the action or the end that the agent has in mind,[244] for the two are not necessarily the same. For example, the garments made by a tailor will serve to clothe someone, but the end that the tailor has in mind is to make a profit. Since all natural works, not to speak of artificial ones, have a final end, the divine actions certainly serve a final end insofar as the actions themselves are concerned.[245] That all natural as well as artificial works have a final end was the view of Aristotle.[246] Aristotle himself did not associate this purely natural teleology with the conscious purpose of a higher being,[247] but it is usually assumed that later religious thought did associate this teleology with the conscious purpose of God.[248] Bibago's clear distinction between the final ends of natural works or the divine actions on the one hand and the final ends of the divine agent on the other seems to indicate that such an association between natural teleology and the divine purpose was not automatically and necessarily made even in the Middle Ages.

Having decided that the divine actions are for a final end, Bibago turns to the question of whether or not the divine agent acts for a final end. Either assumption would seem to imply a deficiency in God. If He does act for a final end, He would seem to lack that end, as we saw at the beginning of this chapter. If He does not act for a final end, His actions would be like those of an unintelligent being, which is absurd. The resolution of the problem depends upon the distinction between external and internal ends. If an agent acts for an end external to himself, one can then imply that the agent lacks that end. If, however, God acts for the sake of His own essence, an internal end, this does not imply any deficiency in Him.[249]

This, Bibago concludes, solves our initial problem about the thirteenth chapter in the third part of the Moreh Nevukhim.[250] Maimonides' intention there was to deny that the universe as a whole has a final end external to the essence of God. This denial is correct, for God's final end is His essence. Maimonides himself says in that chapter that the only final end of existence as a whole is the divine will or wisdom, which is identical with the divine essence.[251] Thomas Aquinas and Ḥasdai Crescas had also said that God's final end for this existence is His essence.[252]

In summary, we have seen that Bibago, in his first chapter, interprets Maimonides' concept of the divine will in an orthodox and conservative way in terms of the biblical-Philonic concept of a free divine will. Bibago's particular formulation of this freedom of the will, that the will can perform either of two opposite actions, can be found in the Muslim Kalām and was emphasized among the scholastics by Duns Scotus. On the basis of four rational proofs and on the basis of tradition as well, Bibago specifically denies that God acts necessarily through knowledge alone, as ibn Sīnā contended. Averroists such as Isaac Albalag had interpreted ibn Rushd in this manner and had said that the divine agency acting necessarily through knowledge was intermediate between a natural and a voluntary agency.

In addition, Bibago may have been arguing against those more voluntarist philosophers such as Crescas who, utilizing the Greek concept of a relatively free will, had followed Augustine in combining both will and necessity. Bibago further emphasized that the divine will had a purpose and final end, and we have seen that this interpretation of Maimonides opposes not only the philosophers but also the Muslim Ash^{c}ariyya, according to whom the divine will has no final end. Finally, although Maimonides' primary discussion of will and necessity is in relation to the problem of the creation or eternity of the world, Bibago's long discussion of the coefficiency of the divine will in all worldly events, even man's free choice, indicates that Bibago's primary concern is with the divine providence. The chapter of the Moreh Nevukhim with which Bibago began his discussion of the divine will is from Maimonides' discussion of providence. So, having completed his treatment of the divine will, Bibago turns in his second chapter to the next major issue in the topic of providence, the divine knowledge.

5. The Divine Knowledge

When Bibago raised the problem of divine actions for final ends implying a deficiency in God, he noted that this led to a denial of divine knowledge as well as to a denial of the divine will. Divine knowledge of individual or newly created things implied that the divine intellect was perfected by this knowledge and had before been deficient.[1] Having established in the remainder of the first chapter that God acts by will without such action involving a deficiency in His nature, Bibago turns now in the second chapter to a defense of the principle that God's knowledge encompasses all things, even individual and newly created things. This principle, Bibago says, is in fact the basic axiom of his whole thesis.[2]

Bibago first mentions some of those who have denied this principle of divine knowledge. Among them are the followers of Epicurus, Democritus, and Lucretius, who assert that chance is the only cause operative in the world.[3] In the second book of his Physics, Bibago says, Aristotle refuted this theory of chance by showing that chance events occur only on a minority of occasions when there is a deviation from the essential purpose of the event. Since what happens by chance is posterior to and incidental to what occurs as a result of essential causes, it is impossible that all things happen by chance. Thus, those advocates of chance who would deny essential causes are forced by this definition of chance to admit essential causes.[4] We however, Bibago says, believe that all events, both essential and by chance, are caused at least partially by the divine will and differ only in duration, the essential divine acts exhibiting a greater consistency and completeness in fulfilling their purpose.[5] According to those who say that all events are by chance, no knowledge either divine or human of these events could ever be completed or perfected.[6]

A second group of those who deny the divine knowledge assert that God is too exalted to be cognizant of our mundane affairs and that His knowledge does not extend below the sphere of the moon.[7] As the first group that Bibago said denied the divine knowledge, the Epicureans, corresponded to the first of the five theories of divine providence listed by Maimonides, so this second group that Bibago says denies the divine knowledge corresponds to Maimonides' second theory of providence, the one he attributes to Aristotle.[8] In Maimonides' second theory of providence, the individual events of the sublunar world are left to chance. Bibago combines this second theory of providence with Maimonides' description of idolatry in the Mishneh Torah and says that this lower world is governed by the stars, which are worshiped as divine intermediaries.[9] He thus expresses his agreement with Maimonides' view that the idolators originally believed in God but denied His direct knowledge of and providence over this sublunar world.[10]

The second group of those who deny the divine knowledge are thus the idolators, and of them Bibago mentions three kinds. The first are the astrologers who believe that the propitious times for human actions are determined by the stars and who prognosticate according to the stars. The second kind consists of those who produce and use talismans at the propitious times and with the proper incantations in order to influence and harm others.[11] The third kind of idolator that Bibago mentions is one who worships imaginary forms of animals or plants or imaginary beings such as ᶜaza'el and shedim. The references to shedim in rabbinic literature can be explained, Bibago says, although he specifies that one ought not to be called a heretic for either believing or disbelieving in them.[12] These imaginary beings of course have no relationship to knowledge, for knowledge pertains only to rational forms, not imaginary ones.[13]

In addition to the Epicureans and idolators, the two groups that he describes as denying divine knowledge, Bibago also mentions the opinion of Themistius in this regard, but he does not elaborate.[14]

In contrast to these denials of divine knowledge, Bibago asserts the view of the Torah that God knows everything, both the universals and the particulars and the things that come into existence both in the future and in the past.[15] Although God Himself is immaterial, He miraculously knows the matter that is the basis of individuality, so how much more obviously does He know man according to man's rationality, which is his essence.[16] Bibago emphasizes that God knows not only men's deeds but also their thoughts and that, unlike human judges and kings, God judges men both according to their deeds and according to their properties or habits from which their deeds follow.[17] God also judges men according to the ultimate effects of their actions, which are not always apparent to other men and may indeed be the opposite of what they seem to be. Yet this divine foreknowledge does not in any way compromise the realm of the possible and human free will.[18]

Bibago marshals four arguments in support of the divine knowledge. First, lack of knowledge of particulars would ordinarily be an imperfection, but God is free of all deficiencies because He is free of the source of all deficiencies, matter.[19] As for the argument of the philosopher that some things, such as the disordered particulars of this lower world, are better not known, Bibago answers that this applies only to men who can be affected and harmed by knowledge. For God all knowledge contributes to His perfection.[20] Further, the knowledge of particulars is, if anything, superior to that of universals, for the particulars have an independent existence and have been called the primary substance (ᶜeṣem ri'shon), whereas universals exist only in the particulars. Thus if any knowledge were a deficiency, it would be the knowledge of universals, for the existence of universals is a deficient type of existence.[21] It therefore pertains to God's perfection to know the particular things of this world.

In response to opinions such as that of ibn Sīnā that God knows particulars only through their universal causes,[22] Thomas Aquinas said that it would be an imperfection in God if His knowledge extended only to universals[23] and that God's perfection dictated that He know particulars, even though they are individuated by matter.[24] In Jewish philosophy Maimonides had already said that the philosophers, in order to avoid imputing negligence to God because of the disordered state of human individuals in this world, fell into the worse imputation of ignorance.[25] Gersonides' later extension of the divine knowledge to only the general order of forms was said by him to be part of the divine perfection and to involve no ignorance,[26] but Ḥasdai Crescas returned to asserting God's knowledge of particulars as particulars in order to avoid imputing to God the deficiency of ignorance.[27]

A second argument used by Bibago to prove the divine knowledge of particulars is really the fourth and last in Bibago's list, but like his first argument it also is based on the divine perfection. If God did not know the individual beings of this world, then a man because of his knowledge would be closer to perfection than God, which is absurd. The argument is also based on our ranking individuals according to their knowledge.[28] A third argument, really the second mentioned by Bibago, is that God must know all things in order to be their essential agent, for knowledge is one of the two requirements for essential agency, and without it the agency would be only accidental.[29]

The fourth and last argument, really the third in Bibago's list, is his other major argument for divine knowledge of particulars. Since God knows His essence as it truly is, He knows Himself as the principle of all beings because He made them. He therefore knows those beings of which He is the principle, since otherwise He would not know His essence as their principle.[30] Bibago refers in this regard to Maimonides' statement that God is the principle and efficient cause of all things other than Himself.[31] Maimonides had also said that God, in knowing the true reality of His immutable essence, knows the totality of what necessarily derives from all His acts.[32]

Further, Bibago says that God, in knowing all things through His knowledge of His essence, knows them in their most excellent form and that all things exist in God in a most perfect and exalted existence.[33] Ibn Rushd had said that God knows all existents in their noblest mode of existence because of His knowledge of His essence,[34] and this opinion was quoted by Narboni[35] and repeated by Efodi.[36] Bibago explains that God possesses knowledge in this highest degree because He is the cause of all knowledge, and the cause of anything possesses it in the highest degree.[37] In asserting that the divine knowledge is the cause of all other knowledge, Bibago was in the footsteps of Maimonides and Crescas, who also asserted the causative nature of the divine knowledge.[38] Simon ben Ṣemaḥ Duran, on the other hand, said that the divine knowledge is not the cause that Saadia and Judah Halevi said it was.[39] Bibago also says, as Maimonides does, that God's knowledge is His essence.[40]

After these four arguments for the divine knowledge of particulars,[41] Bibago repeats Maimonides' basic criticism of the philosophers' denial of divine knowledge, namely, that they compare the divine attributes to the attributes of His creatures. The two sets of attributes, however, are different in kind, for the divine attributes are identical with the divine essence, whereas the attributes of the creatures are added to their essence. Further, the divine essence and its attributes are infinite, whereas the created existences are finite.[42] Therefore, Bibago says, Maimonides' view is that God knows things even before and after they are in existence without any change in His knowledge and that He knows many things with one simple knowledge. We are ignorant of how this is possible, however, for knowledge is predicated of God and others only equivocally.[43]

Bibago further cites Maimonides' list of five differences between the divine and human knowledge.[44] The first is that God's one, simple knowledge can encompass many things that differ even in genus and species. Man's knowledge, on the other hand, achieves some unity only when a relationship or common element is involved, but human knowledge of discrete individuals such as a horse and man is plural.[45] Maimonides had simply said that God's knowledge, while being one, corresponds to many different known things belonging to various species.[46] Gersonides had objected that this unity in the divine knowledge did not constitute a distinction between it and human knowledge. Human knowledge also achieves some unity insofar as we have a conception of the intelligible order and entelechy of the forms of things. Since the unity of the divine knowledge is of the same kind, although incomparably greater, the unity itself is not the distinguishing characteristic.[47] Bibago's formulation of Maimonides' first distinction thus incorporates Gersonides' objection and attempts to answer it. Since the divine knowledge, according to Bibago, maintains its simple unity even though it knows individuals, the divine knowledge is still distinct from human knowledge even though the latter achieves a certain unity in its conception of the general order of things.[48]

Bibago's formulation of Maimonides' second distinction between the divine knowledge and human knowledge also reflects Gersonides' criticism of Maimonides. Maimonides again simply says that the divine knowledge may have as its object something that does not exist.[49] Earlier he had specified that this pertains to things that at some time come into existence, in which case He knows about their coming into existence beforehand. On the other hand, things that never come into existence and so are absolutely nonexistent are not objects of the divine knowledge just as things nonexistent for us are not objects of our knowledge.[50] Gersonides had argued that God knows the particulars only as part of the intelligible order from which they derive their existence; His knowledge does not come from the particulars themselves. Since this intelligible order is always in existence, it <u>is not necessary</u> for God to know nonexistent things.[51] Bibago, as if in response to Gersonides, says that it <u>is necessary</u> for the divine knowledge to encompass nonexistent things both before and after they come into existence. Mindful of Gersonides' comment about the divine knowledge in this regard, Bibago says that human knowledge could not encompass nonexistent objects because it consists of the abstraction of forms from existent objects. Forms of nonexistent objects would thus have no means of entering into human knowledge.[52]

The third distinction listed by Maimonides is that the divine knowledge can have as its object something that is infinite.[53] The philosophers, Maimonides had said, who deny divine knowledge of nonexistents and the infinite, say that God knows only the permanent immutable species, but the speculative opinion of those who adhere to a Law is that the divine knowledge extends in a certain sense to all the individuals of the species.[54] Gersonides objects, as he had objected in the case of divine knowledge of nonexistents, that the divine knowledge of the infinite is not necessary according to his theory because he says that God knows all things in respect of their unity, not in that respect in which they are individual, multiple, and infinite.[55] Bibago answers, as he had done in the case of Gersonides' objection to Maimonides' first distinction, that men can know an infinite number of things only insofar as they possess unity through their universals, but this is not knowledge of the infinite as such. God, on the other hand, can know an infinite number of individual things as individual, something impossible for men because knowledge for them necessarily implies limitation.[56]

Gersonides lists in fourth place Maimonides' fifth distinction between divine and human knowledge, namely, that God's knowledge that one of two possibilities will come about does not actualize that possibility.[57] That the divine knowledge does not compromise the nature of the possible is, according to Maimonides, a fundamental principle of the Law.[58] As in the previous cases, Gersonides says that God's knowledge of the general order of things does not compromise the possibility of things nor eliminate man's free choice in regard to them as particulars. Also as in previous cases, Gersonides implies that this does not constitute a distinction between divine and human knowledge, for the knowledge of particular future events that human beings receive in dreams and prophecies does not compromise the possible nature of these events nor eliminate human free choice in regard to them because these prophecies and dreams come as advice and warning.[59]

Bibago, evidently following Gersonides, also places as fourth in his list Maimonides' fifth distinction concerning the divine knowledge of possible events. He agrees with Maimonides that God's knowledge of future particular events does not determine these events. If God knows that a certain man will commit idolatry, this does not eliminate the possibility of his not committing idolatry. If this were not the case, the man could not be punished for the idolatrous act, for one cannot be punished for a transgression committed under compulsion.[60]

Bibago also draws from Gersonides the classifications of human knowledge that make it impossible to say that men could know the future without compromising the possible, as God does. If, for example, one knew that one of two opposites was going to occur, but also knew that it was possible for the second opposite to occur, this is not called "knowledge" (yediyᶜah) but "thought" (maḥashavah). If one knew that either one of two opposite events would occur, but did not know which one of the two it was going to be, this also is not called "knowledge" but "perplexity" (mevukhah). If one thought that one of two opposites was going to occur and the other opposite in fact occurred, this is certainly not "knowledge" but simply "error" (ṭaᶜuth). These three ways of knowing are all opposed to knowledge proper. If, however, one did certainly know that one of two opposites was going to occur and that the other could not occur, this is indeed knowledge, but it compromises the possible nature of the opposite.[61]

Bibago rejects as "thought" an explanation of the divine foreknowledge that he attributes to some Christian sages. According to this view, God knows the mixtures and compositions from which our inclinations and actions come so that He can predict what we are going to do without depriving us of the free choice of doing the opposite. For example, if a scholar and a warrior entered a room in which a book and a sword were lying on a table, one knows that the scholar will most likely pick up the book and the warrior the sword, but this does not eliminate the possibility of the opposite occurring.[62] Abraham Shalom offers a similar explanation of the divine foreknowledge, using as an example the physician's ability to make predictions on the basis of his medical knowledge.[63] Bibago, however, rejects this solution because the knowledge involved is only probable and so deficient and distinctly inferior to the perfect knowledge that pertains to God.[64]

Like Gersonides, Bibago lists as fifth and last Maimonides' fourth distinction of divine knowledge, that it remains unchanged in spite of its knowledge of the changing particulars in this world. Maimonides had asserted the immutability of the divine knowledge in apprehending things that come into existence in time, even though knowing the actualization of the potential in our knowledge of existent things is additional knowledge above and beyond what we know in knowing that a thing will exist.[65] Gersonides notes that the divine knowledge cannot change because it is identical with the divine essence, which certainly cannot change.[66] In line, however, with his thesis of comparing instead of distinguishing the divine and human knowledge, Gersonides says that human knowledge also does not change insofar as it considers things as part of a general order.[67] Like Gersonides, Bibago says that God's knowledge cannot change because it is identical with His essence.[68] Since Bibago, however, wants to reestablish Maimonides' distinctions between the divine and human knowledge, Bibago insists that human knowledge of things that have come into existence does change. Like Maimonides, Bibago also says that a thing has in its existence something additional to what it had before it came into existence. Since human knowledge is derived from the objects, as we noted in discussing the second distinction, our knowledge of things that come into existence must undergo change similar to the change in the objects themselves.[69]

Thus in each of the five distinctions that Maimonides had drawn between the divine and the human knowledge, Gersonides sought to establish continuity and Bibago responded by reestablishing the distinctions. Gersonides had also described eight philosophical objections to the divine knowledge of particulars.[70] Bibago recounts these eight objections, although he does not mention that they are found in Gersonides, and he briefly notes that Maimonides' five distinctions can be used to solve the problems raised by these objections.[71]

Bibago finally takes up four criticisms by Gersonides of Maimonides' theory of divine attributes in general and of his theory of the divine knowledge in particular. The first criticism is that, since our knowledge is derived from the divine knowledge, the relationship between the two is one of priority and posteriority (qedimah we'iḥur), and the terms are ambiguous or amphibolous (mesuppaqim), not equivocal (beshituf gamur).[72] Gersonides himself had not called the terms in a relationship of priority and posteriority "ambiguous," but had simply said that they were comparable (meshuttefeth).[73] The Arabic philosophers al-Fārābī, ibn Sīnā, al-Ghazālī, and ibn Rushd, as well as most Christian and Jewish philosophers after Maimonides, were in common with Gersonides in asserting that the divine and human knowledge were related by priority and posteriority, not as equivocal terms, as Maimonides had maintained.[74] Bibago's answer to Gersonides' criticism is that human knowledge is not derived from God's knowledge as human existence is derived from God's existence. This would be the case if the divine knowledge were an attribute added to the divine existence. Since, however, God's knowledge is identical with His essence, it is in this respect that His knowledge is the cause of our knowledge, that is, in the same way that His essence is the cause of all things in existence. Divine knowledge is no more the cause of our knowledge than is a divine whiteness the cause of white things in this world.[75]

Gersonides' second criticism of Maimonides' distinction between the divine and human knowledge is that we ascribe the attribute of knowledge to God because of the attribute of knowledge in us. Whenever an attribute is ascribed to one subject because of the presence of the attribute in another subject, the attributes cannot be related only equivocally so that they have only their name in common.[76] If the term "knowledge," in other words, is not the same in the premise and in the conclusion, the syllogism by which we attribute knowledge to God is an equivocation, which is not a valid form.[77] Duns Scotus had also argued that unless there was a common middle term with a univocal meaning, there could be no argument from creatures to God.[78]

Bibago's answer is that equivocal terms need differ only in their final distinction, but not in every way. Thus the divine and human knowledge do have in common "perception" (hassagah).[79] This "perception" is, according to Crescas, what constitutes the positive content of the divine knowledge in addition to its being the contrary of ignorance.[80]

On the other hand, the community of "perception" is a community of name alone as well, for the unity of knowledge, knower, and known in the divine knowledge is different from the unity in the knowledge of both humans and angels. In the latter two cases, the knowledge is externally caused, in humans by the objects perceived and in angels by the Deity from Whom the knowledge is derived. The unity of knowledge, knower, and known in God, however, is a perfect simplicity, for His knowledge is not derived from anything but is itself the cause of other things.[81] Bibago in this seems to be following Moses Narboni, who criticized Maimonides for comparing the unity of the divine knowledge to that of human knowledge.[82]

In spite of his assertion that attributes can be ascribed to both God and man only equivocally,[83] Maimonides evidently compared the unity of the divine knowledge with that of human knowledge.[84] Bibago, in his answer to Gersonides' second criticism of Maimonides, seems to say that the degree of superiority of the divine knowledge is sufficient to warrant calling the use of the term in this case equivocal. Although Isaac Albalag had spoken of the degrees of the unity of knowledge leading up to the ultimate simplicity of God, he also ended up with a negative theology like that of Maimonides.[85] It is interesting to note in this regard that Bibago on one occasion offers a threefold division of the divine attributes, listing, in addition to negative attributes and attributes of action, attributes of perception.[86]

Gersonides' third criticism of Maimonides is that attributes which we wish to deny of God, such as corporeality and motion, cannot be ascribed to God and man in an equivocal sense. If they were so ascribed, they could just as easily be affirmed of God as denied of Him, for the terms in a set of contraries must have a common meaning in order to be contraries. In a similar way, those positive attributes that we wish to affirm of God, such as knowledge, cannot be ascribed to God and man in an equivocal sense, for if this were so we could just as easily deny them of God as affirm them of Him. As for the contention that we deny corporeality of God because it is a deficiency and affirm knowledge of Him because it is a perfection,[87] Gersonides notes that the terms "knowledge" and "corporeality" are not perfections or deficiencies; rather their significations are. If these significations were reversed, then "corporeality" would be affirmed of God because it is a perfection and "knowledge" would be denied of Him because it is a deficiency.[88]

Thomas Aquinas and Duns Scotus had raised a similar objection against the complete equivocality of attributes ascribed to God.[89] Bibago, in his paraphrase of Gersonides' criticism, says that the word "man," used equivocally of a real man and a picture, can be both affirmed and denied of the picture.[90] In his response, Bibago also cites the example of "eye" (<u>ᶜayin</u>) used to refer to the seeing eye and to the "eye of day." If we say that the "eye of day" is not an eye, this would be true if "eye" refers to the seeing eye. If, however, it refers to the eye of day, then we are contradicting ourselves. Similarly, if "knowledge" is used equivocally of divine and human knowledge, it can be both affirmed and denied of God. It can be affirmed of God insofar as it refers to divine knowledge, but it must be denied of God insofar as it refers to human knowledge. Bibago therefore admits Gersonides' contention concerning positive attributes applied equivocally to God and man, namely that they can be both affirmed and denied of God. In regard, however, to attributes such as motion that are denied of God, Bibago says that in cases such as this Gersonides' objection is not valid, for the denial is meant to exclude all possible meanings of the term.[91]

Gersonides' fourth objection, according to Bibago,[92] is that even if knowledge is ascribed to God through a complete equivocation, the divine knowledge would still comprise contradictory characteristics such as mutability and immutability. Gersonides adds that Maimonides' objective in asserting that God knows particulars seems to have been to avoid attributing ignorance to God in the popular sense of "ignorance."[93] Bibago, in his paraphrase of this fourth objection, interprets this to mean that if God's knowledge did not change along with the objects of His knowledge, He would be ignorant of the new objects.[94] Bibago's answer is that human knowledge changes along with its objects, but that these objects, though transitory in themselves, do not change insofar as they are known by God.[95]

Bibago thus reasserts what he feels to be Maimonides' contention that God knows individual and transitory things without such knowledge implying any deficiency in the divine nature. This is possible because the divine knowledge differs from human knowledge in five ways. On the basis of these differences Bibago responds to four criticisms of Gersonides based on his view of the divine knowledge as analogous to human knowledge and so extending to particulars only insofar as they participate in the general order. In his response Bibago also seems to have utilized the views of Averroists such as Narboni. Bibago concludes his discussion of the divine knowledge by reiterating the moral significance of God's knowledge of individuals.[96]

6. The Divine Providence

Bibago's discussion of divine providence, like his discussion of the divine knowledge, is in many ways a response to Gersonides. Bibago begins his discussion of divine providence in the third chapter of the Derekh 'Emunah by pointing out that the denial of both providence and knowledge to God is often a result of the problem of the suffering of the righteous and the prosperity of the wicked.[1] Maimonides had also said that the lack of order in the circumstances of human individuals had led many philosophers to deny the divine knowledge,[2] but in Gersonides' discussion of divine providence the suffering of the righteous is a dominant theme to which he returns again and again.[3]

Further, Gersonides frequently specifies that the problem for divine providence that is posed by the suffering of the righteous is a result of our experience.[4] As if in response, Bibago on the one hand says that our experience is not always reliable[5] and on the other hand says that divine providence is substantiated by our experience of miracles.[6] He in fact defines a miracle (nes) as the good received through providence.[7]

Bibago, however, follows both Gersonides and Maimonides in extending divine providence to men because of their rationality and according to the degree of their development of their reason. According to Maimonides, divine providence extends to the individuals of the human species because they are endowed with intellect.[8] This providence varies in measure from individual to individual in proportion to their intellectual perfection.[9] Further, this providence is said in one chapter to mean that God watches over these human individuals and rewards and punishes them according to their just desserts.[10] Later, Maimonides says that evils come to men only in the absence of providence.[11] Gersonides said that divine providence extends only to some human individuals because of their acquired intellect[12] and because of their closeness to the active intellect.[13] Both agreed that providence extends only to the species in the case of other animals.[14]

Bibago relates providence to the specific difference in each class, which in the case of man is intellect.[15] In the case of animals other than man, the individuals participate only in the general providence of species, namely, the preservation of the species. They act naturally according to the characteristics of the species, so that their actions are performed without choice and are not even completely voluntary.[16]

In regard to the human species, however, providence extends to its individual members so that their individual souls are preserved along with the species as a whole.[17]

Divine providence thus manifests itself in the human species in the form of the intellect, and this is why man's intellect is the reason that he is said to be in the divine image.[18] Divine providence further extends to the individuals of the human species to the degree of their perfection of their intellects,[19] so that an individual human being devoid of intellect would also be devoid of providence.[20]

Because the human actualized intellect is like the celestial intellect, the extension of divine providence to individual human beings according to their intellect does not imply any diminution in the divine any more than does the extension of providence to the individual spheres and intellects in the heavens.[21] Also because of this similarity between the human and celestial intellects, saying that human beings are the purpose of creation implies no diminution in the status of the angels or celestial intellects, for it is equivalent to saying that the rational part of the universe is the purpose of creation.[22] Divine providence also extends to the material bodies of human beings in a secondary sense, that is, insofar as they are ruled by that reason in which divine providence primarily manifests itself.[23]

In agreeing with Maimonides and Gersonides that divine providence extends to human beings according to their intellect, Bibago disagrees with Crescas, who bases divine providence on the divine will and love instead of intellect. For example, Crescas had also raised the problem of the divine providence for individual human beings in this lowly world implying a diminution in the divine. Unlike Bibago, Crescas had answered that a divine providence based on love is not affected by the lowliness of the creature loved. Instead of varying according to the degree of intellect, divine providence for Crescas varies in proportion to the divine love.[24] According to Crescas, the interpretation of divine providence in terms of union with the active intellect is a result of the desire to avoid attributing to God knowledge of particulars. Crescas, however, has no such desire, for he also interprets divine providence in terms of retribution, and the divine knowledge of particulars is a necessary prerequisite for retribution.[25]

Bibago also follows the common practice of associating his doctrine of divine providence with his theory of the divine knowledge.[26] Maimonides, for example, had said that the discussions of divine providence and knowledge are connected.[27] Bibago, at the end of the Derekh 'Emunah, says that the divine knowledge and providence are indeed one and the same principle of faith.[28] The various views concerning the divine providence and the proofs supporting them are parallel to those concerning divine knowledge.[29] As he had done in his discussion of the divine knowledge,[30] Bibago notes in his discussion of providence that divine ignorance of any of the details of this world would mean a deficiency in the divine knowledge.[31]

As those opposed to the divine knowledge of individual human beings were the philosophers of chance and the astrologers,[32] so those who are not governed by divine providence are said by Bibago to be left to the rule of chance and the stars.[33] Maimonides had said that one abandoned by providence is left to the sea of chance.[34] Maimonides in fact presents this as his solution to the problem of the suffering of the righteous. One who apprehends God correctly by participating in the divine intellectual overflow is watched over by divine providence and can never suffer any kind of evil during the time of this apprehension. It is only when he is distracted from this apprehension that the evils of this world may befall him.[35] As we saw earlier, Bibago had similarly explained the suffering of the righteous as the result of being left to the effects of chance and the stars.[36] Gersonides, admitting that evils caused by the stars are still attributable to God, had answered that the true rewards of the righteous are of a distinctly human and spiritual nature and that the physical suffering in this world is often only an apparent evil.[37] Crescas, in his response to the problem of theodicy, agreed that our true rewards are spiritual and that the evils of this world are often only apparently so.[38] Bibago did not dwell on these two points but, like Maimonides, he attributed the suffering of the righteous to the effects of chance and the stars in the absence of providence.[39]

Further, as the opposite of a happening by chance was, according to Bibago and Maimonides, something effected by essential agency,[40] and as essential agency was associated by Bibago with the divine knowledge,[41] Bibago also associates essential agency with divine providence.[42] Those who believe that the fortunes of human individuals are governed by celestial causes instead of by the divine will are said by Bibago to substitute chance for essential agency.[43] The motions of the heavens do influence this lower world but only accidentally and as intermediaries, the essential cause being the divine will.[44] Bibago thus asserts that the causality of the heavens is by chance.

That the motions of the heavens are the cause of the qualitative differences in this lower world is attested to by our sense experience.[45] The means by which the celestial spheres influence this world is the "conjectural" or "natural heat" (_ḥom meshuᶜar_, _ḥom ṭivᶜi_) that is part of the process by which things in this world acquire both essential and accidental forms.[46] Aristotle in his _Meteorologica_ had said that the influence from the heavens comes only from their motions.[47] Thus Bibago says that one who denies that the heavens influence this world along with the divine will is contradicting both reason and our senses.[48] That this world is influenced by the spheres as well as by the celestial intellects was also the view of Maimonides, who added that this was the basis of astrology.[49] This does not mean, Bibago says, that Maimonides believed in astrology, as many have contended. Maimonides was simply stating the empirically and rationally verified fact that the proximity and remoteness of the spheres causes qualitative differences in this world such as heat and cold and wetness and dryness.[50] This influence of the stars is thus a physical influence upon the material things of this world.[51]

Theoretically, if one knew all of these celestial causes, such as the motions of the spheres and the measures of this conjectured heat, one could predict what would happen in this world. Such knowledge, however, is in fact impossible. Since these causes are infinite, they could never be known by the human mind, which can only grasp what is limited. Further, Isaac al-Zarkil wrote a book proving mathematically that the heavens cannot assume the same position twice. One could not, therefore, predict what will happen in the future through knowing what followed in the past upon a certain configuration of stars, for this same configuration of stars could never be repeated.

Astrologers therefore cannot predict the future through knowledge of the celestial movements, for these movements are only accidental causes of what happens in this world. Only the prophet can make such predictions, but this is not because of his knowledge of these celestial causes. It is because he is in connection with the essential cause of what happens in this world, namely, the divine will.[52]

Bibago inserts a lengthy refutation of astrology into his discussion of providence because, he says, belief in the claims of astrology was so widespread in his day.[53] There were complaints that Averroist philosophers explained the miraculous events of Jewish history through the conjunction of heavenly constellations and said that all depends not on divine providence but on fate.[54] This association of philosophy with astrological doctrines that denied divine providence is what, according to Bibago, led some to forbid the study of philosophy until after one had acquired faith.[55] Those Christian theologians of the preceding century whose defense of the divine will opposed philosophic necessitarianism also opposed astrology and the doctrine that events are determined by the stars.[56]

Although Maimonides was also opposed to astrology,[57] Bibago notes many passages in rabbinic literature that seem to indicate that our fate is controlled by the stars.[58] While Bibago believed, like Maimonides, that the spheres exert a physical influence upon this world, he felt that the further assertion that the stars control the events of our lives contradicted our human freedom of choice, which is the basic axiom upon which the entire Torah is built.[59] Bibago therefore contends that none of the rabbis espoused astrology to the extent of believing that human actions are necessarily determined by the heavenly constellations.[60] Some may have believed that the stars give us an inclination to certain actions without impinging on our free choice, but most of the rabbis rejected even this interpretation of astrology.[61] In order to explain some rabbinic passages, however, Bibago did have to say that the Hebrew word _mazal_, which ordinarily designates a constellation of stars, may also be used equivocally to designate a cause in general that determines us, whether it be divine or astrological.[62]

It is in regard to the belief of some rabbis that the stars influence our material state in this world that Bibago notes that our true rewards are after all spiritual and concern our distinctly human part, the soul.[63] These spiritual rewards are evidently the same as the true goods that come to us in a proper manner, as opposed to those goods and evils whose disorderly distribution constitutes the problem of theodicy.[64] It is the belief in divine providence, Bibago says, that gives us the confidence to expect such rewards for our obedience to the commandments.[65]

Thus Bibago, like Maimonides, speaks of the divine providence both as functioning in terms of reward and punishment and as varying according to intellect.[66] These two interpretations of divine providence need not be mutually exclusive. Divine providence according to intellect may not mean that one is rewarded for intellect but rather that one is watched over by providence according to the degree of his intellectual perfection and that the result of being so watched over is that one is rewarded for his good deeds and punished for his bad deeds. Animals, who have no intellect and so no individual providence, are not punished or rewarded but are subject to good and evil only by chance. There are thus, as Bibago says, two kinds of evils according to their causes, those that result from chance and so may result in the suffering of the righteous, and those that come as a just punishment to those who, because of their intellect, are under the government of providence.[67] It must be a theory like this that Crescas intended to criticize when he said that, according to its premises, only the righteous and those who found divine favor are punished by providence for their transgressions, the fate of everyone else being left to the stars.[68]

This relationship between reason and a providence of reward and punishment could be based on the Aristotelian theory of rational choice. Since the Aristotelian theory is that only rational beings can exercise free choice,[69] only they can act out of a choice between right and wrong, and so only they can be rewarded or punished for their actions. This combined theory of providence according to both intellect and reward and punishment, however, is not supported by one of the last chapters in Maimonides' Guide. Maimonides seems to say there that one who is under divine providence can suffer no evil at all.[70] Bibago also says, as part of his interpretation of the biblical story of Cain's punishment, that the inferior type of providence that accompanies our human practical intellect affords some protection from harm.[71]

The topic of the divine providence is tied up with the question of the divine immanence and transcendence. Bibago concludes his chapter on providence by asserting that God is both transcendent and immanent, that He is exalted beyond the world and yet maintains it and is beneficent to it.[72] At the beginning of the chapter Bibago had noted that some think that God is too exalted to be concerned with this lower world.[73] Bibago answers that in this regard even the heavens, insofar as they are material, are too lowly to be compared to God and so are not worthy of His concern.[74] As we see from Isa. 3:6, God is indeed absolutely separate from all three parts of the existent universe[75] and yet miraculously His presence fills the world and He is active in it.[76]

Bibago spells out this divine transcendence and immanence further by specifying that God is separate from the world in that there is no "mixture" (ᶜeruv) or "union" (hit'aḥduth) between Him and any part of the world, yet He is in the world by a "connection of existence" (heqsher meṣi'uth).[77] Bibago had just previously said that the human intellect (sekhel) is bound up with its material body by such a connection of existence, not by a "connection of mixture" (heqsher ᶜeruv), since things that differ in genus cannot intermix in their parts.[78] The separate intellects are also said to be related to their celestial spheres by a connection of existence.[79]

Because Bibago uses this connection of existence to explain the divine transcendence and immanence, he says that he has no need, as Maimonides does, to explain that it is the limitation of the human intellect that prevents us from understanding how God is both separate from the world and yet provident with respect to even the most contemptible part of it.[80] Maimonides' view in this regard, however, is not surprising, Bibago continues, since Maimonides' teacher ibn Sīnā also failed to make this distinction. In his oriental philosophy, Bibago reports, ibn Sīnā said that Aristotle agreed with the Sabeans that God is not separate from the world.[81] Aristotle's true opinion, according to Bibago, is that God is indeed separate from the world and is bound up with the world by a connection of existence, not a connection of mixture.[82] It is interesting to note that some modern Western interpreters agree that ibn Sīnā upheld the biblical view of a transcendent God, whereas ibn Rushd conceived of God as being more immanent.[83]

As God is both immanent and transcendent because He is related to the world by a connection of existence just as the human intellect is related to the body, so God is exalted above the world and yet provident with regard to it just as the human soul is exalted and yet is provident in regard to the human body. For God is the soul of the world, says Bibago, and all existence can indeed be compared to one human individual. In a human being, the soul is borne upon the vital spirit, which is borne in turn by the heart, which in turn is the most important member of the body. In the universe, this lower world is like the body, the celestial spheres can be compared to the heart and the angels or separate intellects can be compared to the vital spirit.[84] Then as the soul is the form of the vital spirit, so God is the form and soul of the realm of the angels.[85] As the soul governs all parts of the body, so God governs all the parts of existence. The human soul, however, governs the body naturally and not by will and knowledge, whereas the divine providence is a function of the divine will and wisdom.[86]

Bibago also says that the divine presence, the shekhinah, as well as the divine providence, is related to the people of Israel by a connection of existence, as the intelligible is to the intellect.[87] Providence, Bibago had said, is one of the two meanings of the word shekhinah according to Maimonides. In this sense it means the presence of the divine in a person or a people according to their intellect. The word, however, has two distinct meanings because it is used equivocally. The other meaning is the created light, and this refers to the sensible manifestations of the divine.[88] Naḥmanides had criticized Maimonides for saying that the term shekhinah referred to something created instead of saying that it referred to God Himself.[89] Bibago's answer is that Naḥmanides had failed to note that shekhinah, according to Maimonides, can refer to the divine providence as well as to the created light.[90] Bibago, on another occasion, says that shekhinah refers to the Active Intellect, which is apprehended by a connection of existence.[91]

Whereas Maimonides spoke of a general and individual providence,[92] Bibago, like Crescas, speaks of the divine providence that attaches to the people of Israel as well.[93] A special providence also attaches to the Levites, the priests, and the king and distinguishes them from the rest of the people of Israel.[94] Unlike Crescas, however,[95] Bibago says that this providence attaches to Israel, as it does to all human beings, because of their intellect. Because the intellect of Israel has been perfected through the Torah, providence is found among them more than among other peoples.[96] Israel indeed was so perfected by the Torah at Mount Sinai that their souls and bodies were united into one essence.[97]

The perfection of the intellect is aided by moderate circumstances. Therefore, Bibago says, providence attaches to Israel also because they are a moderate people living in a moderate place, the land of Israel, and worshiping God at moderate seasons of the year, the fall and the spring.[98] One living outside the land of Israel can be said to be like an atheist because he lacks one of the conditions that bring Israel closer to God.[99] One of the reasons that providence was greatest at the Temple in Jerusalem is that this is the most moderate place in the land of Israel, so the intellect of the people of Israel is most developed here.[100] In the same vein, the reason for the destitute material condition of the people of Israel and its seeming lack of providence is the lack of moderation in its deeds.[101]

The present long exile of the people of Israel, however, is not due only to their past misdeeds but is also a preparation for the eternal redemption. The first or Egyptian exile was also not one of punishment but was rather to purify Israel to receive the Torah. The second or Babylonian exile was indeed one of punishment alone, but this third and longest exile in which Israel presently finds itself is both a punishment for past sins and a purification for future redemption.[102]

The exile of Israel among the nations of the world is like the exile of the rational faculty among the other powers of the soul.[103] Egypt can be compared to the sensual faculties, Babylonia to the material imagination, and Edom[104] to the more intellectual and spiritual part of the imagination. The people of Israel, however, can be compared to the pure intellect[105] and so are called "Man" (_'adam_), for the distinguishing characteristic of mankind is its intellect.[106]

Since, as we have seen, providence is found in proportion to intellect,[107] providence attaches more to the people of Israel than to any other nation.[108] Further, since faith is defined as a rational property of the soul that is conceived from traditional premises[109] and that actualizes and perfects the intellect,[110] the people of Israel through their true faith can achieve ultimate felicity.[111] This constitutes Bibago's "path of faith" (_derekh 'emunah_).

Bibago's theory of divine providence thus asserts that providence is according to intellect, as was maintained by philosophers such as Maimonides and Gersonides. Bibago also emphasizes, however, not only individual providence but also the special providence that attaches to the people of Israel.

7. Conclusion

This study of the theology in the Derekh 'Emunah indicates the presence of three general factors that may well characterize Bibago's thought as a whole. They are a certain rationalism and empiricism resulting from the influence of Maimonides and ibn Rushd, a traditional and somewhat antimetaphysical supernaturalism that reasserted itself in late scholastic Augustinianism and nominalism, and a particularism and nationalism characteristic of Halevi.

The combination of the first two factors means that Bibago offers an orthodox interpretation of Maimonides' often ambiguous philosophy. Like his contemporary Abraham Shalom, he vigorously defends Maimonides, in his case especially against Gersonides. He classifies the divine attributes into negations and actions and interprets the thirteen principles of faith in terms of this classification. Like Maimonides, he argues against the philosophers' derivation of the world by necessity and in favor of a divine will that is free to perform different actions and that is associated with purpose and final ends. Also in Maimonides' footsteps, he asserts that God knows individual and transient things and that His providence extends to men according to their intellect.

The influence of ibn Rushd, however, seems to be at least as pervasive as that of Maimonides. Bibago often interprets Maimonides in terms of ibn Rushd and tries to make their doctrines consistent, although he acknowledges that Maimonides was a student of ibn Sīnā. Whereas Maimonides uses both ibn Rushd's physical proof for God's existence and ibn Sīnā's more metaphysical one, Bibago refers only to ibn Rushd's physical proof from motion, and he mentions the Necessarily Existent only in regard to the divine unity. He similarly reiterates ibn Rushd's view that God moves the first sphere directly and says that Maimonides followed ibn Sīnā in this regard. We have also seen that Bibago could find support from ibn Rushd for his view that the divine will was a factor in addition to the divine knowledge in the derivation of the world, in opposition to ibn Sīnā's view that the world proceeds necessarily from the divine knowledge alone.

On two basic issues that separated Maimonides and the Aristotelians from Crescas, Bibago clearly sided with Maimonides. Like Maimonides and the philosophers, Bibago conceived of the basic relationship between God and man in intellectual terms. He also asserted free will of both God and man. Bibago shared with Crescas, however, certain similarities to the more orthodox theologies of late scholasticism. He emphasizes, for example, the divine infinity and goodness. He does not have a special discussion of the metaphysical proofs for God's existence, but he does speak of the divine will as a coefficient cause in worldly events. He also speaks more of faith than of prophecy and refers to the proof from creation as a valid proof because it is based on faith.

Finally, somewhat like Judah Halevi and Crescas, he speaks of a special salvation available to the Jewish people because of the Torah. In Bibago's case, it is the faith of the Jewish people that makes rational truth available to them all with a certainty that does not differ from knowledge. It was this message of rational faith and special divine providence that Bibago's _Derekh 'Emunah_ brought to the Spanish Jews before the expulsion and that made it a major theological work of the sixteenth century.

Notes

List of Abbreviations

Arabic	Moses Maimonides. Dalālat al-hā'irīn. Ed. S. Munk and I. Joel. Jerusalem, 1930.
DE	Abraham Bibago. Derekh 'Emunah. Constantinople, 1521.
JAOS	Journal of the American Oriental Society.
JQR	The Jewish Quarterly Review.
HTR	The Harvard Theological Review.
HUCA	The Hebrew Union College Annual.
MGWJ	Monatschrift für Geschichte und Wissenschaft des Judenthums.
MH	Levi Gersonides. Sefer Milḥamoth ha-Shem. Riva di Trento, 1560.
MN	Moses Maimonides. Sefer Moreh Nevukhim. Trans. Samuel ibn Tibbon. Commentaries by I. Abravanel, A. Crescas, Efodi, and Shem Ṭov ben Joseph. Jerusalem, 1959-60.
MT	Moses Maimonides. Mishneh Torah.
OH	Ḥasdai Crescas. 'Or ha-Shem. Vienna, 1859.
PAAJR	Proceedings of the American Academy for Jewish Research.
Pines, "Scholasticism"	Shlomo Pines. "Scholasticism after Thomas Aquinas and the Teachings of Ḥasdai Crescas and his Predecessors." Proceedings of the Israel Academy of Sciences and Humanities, vol. 1, no. 10 (Jerusalem, 1967), pp. 1-101.
ST	Thomas Aquinas. Summa Theologica.
SteAbr	Moritz Steinschneider, "Abraham Bibago's Schriften," MGWJ 32 (1883): 79-96, 125-44, 239-40.
SteHU	Moritz Steinschneider. Die Hebräischen Übersetzungen des Mittelalters and die Juden als Dolmetscher. Berlin, 1893.
TAT	Ibn Rushd (Averroes). Tahāfut al-Tahāfut. Ed. M. Bouyges. Beirut, 1930.

TAF — Abū Ḥāmid al-Ghazālī. Tahāfut al-Falāsifah. Ed. M. Bouyges. Beirut, 1927.

ZotCatP — Hermann Zotenberg. Catalogues des Manuscrits Hébreux et Samaritains de la Bibliothèque Impériale. Paris, 1866.

Chapter One
Bibago's Life, Works, and Influence

1. All the Paris manuscripts of Bibago's works (nos. 747, 959.2, 995.1-3, and 1004.3) refer to him as the son of Yom Ṭov. See ZotCatP, pp. 121, 169, 178, and 180. His father's name is also Yom Ṭov in the manuscripts of his "Supercommentary to ibn Rushd's 'Middle Commentary on Aristotle's Metaphysics.'" See Moritz Steinschneider, Die Hebräischen Handschriften der K. Hof- und Staatsbibliothek in München (Munich, 1875), p. 167; also SteAbr, pp. 129 and 138. Yom Ṭov also occurs in the manuscript of Bibago's two letters to Moses Arondi, Parma 457.4. See Giovanni Bernardo de Rossi, MSS. Codices Hebraici Biblioth. I.B. de-Rossi (Parma, 1803), 2:49-50.

Shem Ṭov, however, occurs in DE, p. 2a, and in other early sources, and Steinschneider has no doubt that the reference is to the same person. SteAbr, p. 79, no. 1. See also Steinschneider, Catalogus Liborum Hebraeorum in Bibliotheca Bodleiana . . . (Berlin, 1852-60), p. 670.

2. Our printed text, DE, 2a, has "Bivagi," and so does Joseph Delmedigo in his Maṣref le-Ḥokhmah, published 1629, p. 8b. Jacob ibn Ḥabib, in his cEn Yacaqov, published 1546, p. 51b, has "Bivag," and so does Azariah de Rossi in his Me'or cEnayim, published 1574, p. 91b. Abraham Zacuto, in his Sefer Yuḥasin, published 1566, has "Biva'gi," and Meir ibn Gabbai, in his cAvodath ha-Qodesh, published 1567, has "Biva'gi'" (pt. 3, ch. 16). Solomon ha-Levi Alkabeṣ, in his Manoth ha-Levi, published 1585, has "Biva'sh," p. 180a, and so does Bartolocci in his Bibliotheca Magna Rabbinica, published 1675, p. 17. Gedalya ibn Yaḥya, in his Shalsheleth ha-Kabbalah, published in 1586, has "Bivaṣ," and so does Shabbethai Bass in his Sifte Yeshenim, published 1680. Bass also once has the form "Biwa'"sh." Saul ha-Kohen Ashkenazi, in a letter published in 1574, has the form "Bivig'," p. 10b. Paris 908 has "Biva'ġ" at the end. See ZotCatP, p. 158. For other and even stranger forms, see G. B. de Rossi, MSS. Codices, 2:49-50.

3. Yiṣḥaq Fritz Baer, Die Juden im Christlichen Spanien, vol. 2 (Berlin, 1936), no. 410, pp. 486-94, especially n. 4 on p. 486; idem, A History of the Jews in Christian Spain (Philadelphia, 1966), 2:295-98, 384-87.

4. For example, Chaim Wirszubski, ed., Flavius Mithridates Sermo de Passione Domini (Jerusalem, 1963), pp. 72-75: Azriel Shoḥet's notes to Yiṣḥaq Baer's edition of Solomon ibn Verga's Sefer Sheveṭ Yehudah (Jerusalem, 1947), pp. 175, 179, 194.

5. Shabbethai Bass, in his Sifte Yeshenim (Amsterdam, 1680), has "Bi Ba'go" on pp. 17b and 93b along with other forms. Johann Christoph Wolf seems to have been the first to use "Bibago" in Latin characters. See his Bibliotheca Hebraea, vol. 1 (Hamburg, 1715), no. 60, p. 35; vol. 3 (Hamburg, 1727), no. 60, p. 23. G. B. de Rossi, MSS. Codices, 2:49-50, seems to agree with Wolf, as does Steinschneider in SteAbr, and so "Bibago" became the commonly used form. If Baer is correct, it could be that the different forms of the name in the early

literature are attempts to transliterate into Hebrew characters the last consonantal sound in "Bivagch." One of these ways of transliterating this sound, g̱̀, eventually became go by an erroneous transformation that is easy in the Hebrew script, and so we have "Bibago." Professor Frank Talmage of the University of Toronto, however, has suggested to me orally that "Bibago" could well be the Castilian form of "Bivagch."

6. Salomon Munk, Mélanges de philosophie juive et arabe (Paris, 1859), p. 507; ZotCatP, MS. no. 959.2, p. 169.

7. Munk, Mélanges de philosophie, p. 507; ZotCatP, MS. no. 908, p. 158, listing Ancien fonds 347, however, not 348, as in Munk. The scribe Isaac ben Ḥabib says that he completed the copy on 7 Teveth 5232, which Munk says is equivalent to 17 December 1471. ZotCatP, however, has 1472.

Eliakim Carmoly said that he possessed a manuscript in which Isaac ben Ḥabib testifies that he was a student in the academy of R. Abraham b. Bivag in Saragossa in 1470 and that Bivag was then an old man working on his last literary effort, the Derekh 'Emunah. Israelitische Annalen, 29 March 1839, p. 101. Steinschneider, however, could find no such manuscript in the catalogue of Carmoly's library and so he doubted the references to the Derekh 'Emunah. SteAbr, p. 80, n. 3. It should be noted that Carmoly's other information and references in that passage are not very accurate. Abraham Zacuto also says that Bibago is from Saragossa. See the Sefer Yuḥasin ha-Shalem (London, 1857), p. 226b.

8. DE III-5, 99a-b. In the references to DE, the Roman numerals indicate the part number, the first set of Arabic numerals the chapter number, and the following Arabic numerals the page numbers. Each page has four columns, and these are indicated by the letters a, b, c, or d after the page number.

9. Heinrich Graetz, Geschichte der Juden (Leipzig, 1890), vol. 8, pp. 219-20; Ḥayyim Michal, 'Or ha-Ḥayyim (Frankfurt a. M., 1891), no. 255, p. 122; Azriel Shoḥeṭ's notes to Baer's edition of ibn Verga's Sefer Sheveṭ Yehudah, p. 194. Graetz in one place (p. 219) suggests that Bibago may have been a physician at the court. Graetz gives no source for this conjecture, but it is probably based, first, on Bibago's references to one medical work that he wrote (no longer extant), and second, on the possibility that another medical work extant in manuscripts may have been written by him. See the description of his works later in this chapter. On page 227, however, Graetz says that King John of Aragon had at his court a Jewish physician, Abiator ibn Crescas, and the semiphilosophical author Abraham Bibago. Here Bibago is named, but someone else is the court physician.

On King John II of Aragon and his reign, see Henry John Chaytor, A History of Aragon and Catalonia (London, 1933), ch. 16, pp. 234-44; Jaime Vicens Vives, Juan II de Aragon (Barcelona, 1953).

This discussion, which Bibago says took place in his youth, could therefore not have been before 1458, which is when John II began to reign. Thus Bibago must have been a very young man indeed, perhaps in his late teens, when in 1446 he wrote his "Commentary on Aristotle's Posterior Analytics."

10. See the beginning of the small collection of homilies by Bibago called Zeh Yenaḥamenu (This One Will Comfort Us), [Salonica] 1522.

11. Baer says that R. Abraham Bivach was already dead when in 1489 the Inquisition brought to trial at Huesca those who had conducted the circumcision of the converso there twenty-five years earlier. Baer adds that Bivach may indeed have died several years before the trial in 1489, although his brother Isaac, who had conducted the circumcision with him, was still alive then. Jews in Christian Spain, 2:385 and 489.

Abraham Zacuto, whose Sefer Yuḥasin was written in 1504 and first published in 1566, says that Bibago lived at the same time as Rabbi Isaac ben Jacob Canpanton of Castile, who died in 1463. See the London 1857 edition, p. 226b. David Gans, on the other hand, mentions Rabbi Abraham, the author of the Derekh 'Emunah, twice, once in association with Rabbi Shem Ṭov, who wrote homilies on the Torah and flourished in 5249 (1488-89), and Rabbi Abraham, the author of Neweh Shalom, who died in 5252 (1491-92). In the next column Rabbi Abraham, the author of the Derekh 'Emunah, is mentioned again, but this time it is after the expulsion from Spain and in association with Isaac Arama and Jacob ibn Ḥabib. Gans's Ṣemaḥ David was first published in Prague in 1591. See the Warsaw 1859 edition, pp. 15 and 73. Quite likely it is because of Gans's work that the index to Shabbethai Bass's Sifte Yeshenim, first published in 1680, says that Bibago flourished in 5249 (1488-89).

Zacuto's association of Bibago with the rabbi who died in 1463 cannot be taken too literally since we have already seen that Bibago seems to have still been alive by at least 1471. Bibago may have begun to write and become prominent during the days of Rabbi Canpanton, but he evidently outlived him. A way to utilize the information of Baer and the first reference in Gans would be to place Bibago's death in the first couple months of 1489. He would thus have still been around in 5249 (1488-89) and yet have died before the trial of 1489 began. Gans's second reference to Bibago after the expulsion can be explained by the fact that, as we shall see, both Isaac Arama and Jacob ibn Ḥabib were indeed associated with Bibago, although both also outlived Bibago.

12. Baer, Jews in Christian Spain, 2:244-47, 277-82.

13. Ibid., pp. 252-58; Harry A. Wolfson, Crescas' Critique of Aristotle (Cambridge, Mass., 1929), p. 31; Ḥaim H. Ben-Sasson, "The Middle Ages," in his History of the Jewish People (Cambridge, Mass., 1976), pp. 612, 613.

14. Baer, Jews in Christian Spain, 2:270-77; Ben Zion Netanyahu, The Marranos of Spain from the Late XIVth to the Early XVIth Century According to Contemporary Hebrew Sources (New York, 1966).

15. Baer, Jews in Christian Spain, 2:358-67.

16. DE I-1, 2c-8a; I-2, 8a-16b; I-3, 16b-27c; I-4, 27c-34a.

17. DE II-1, 34a-37d.

18. DE II-2, 37d-43a.

19. DE II-3, 43a-48b.

20. DE II-4, 48b-53b.

21. DE II-5, 53b-60b.

22. DE II-6, 60b-67c.

23. DE II-7, 67c-72d.

24. DE III-1, 72d-79a; III-2, 79a-86b; III-3, 86b-89c.

25. DE III-4, 89c-95c.

26. DE III-5, 95d-102d.

27. There are three considerations that make this year, or the two or three following it, a likely date for the composition of the work. First, it seems that Bibago's quotation from Eusebius in DE II-3, 46c, is from a Latin translation of the Praeparatio Evangelica that appeared in 1470, so that the Derekh 'Emunah would seem to have been written at least after 1470. Wirszubski, Flavius Mithridates, p. 75; Baer, Jews in Christian Spain, 2:489.

Second, we have seen that Bibago mentions a discussion that he had in his youth at the court of King John of Aragon, the reference being evidently to John II, who reigned from 1458 to 1479. In the book Bibago thus looks back to an event of his youth that could not have occurred before 1458. This makes it likely that the book was written about fifteen or twenty years after 1458, perhaps even after the reign of John II had ended.

Third, the Derekh 'Emunah is undoubtedly Bibago's last work and so written late in his life, since in it he either directly or indirectly refers to all his other known works with the exception of the small collection of philosophical articles in Paris 1004.3 and the two letters to Moses Arondi in Parma 457.4. Bibago's "Commentary on Aristotle's Physics" is not mentioned in the Derekh 'Emunah, but it is referred to in Bibago's "Commentary on the Metaphysics" (see SteAbr, pp. 127 and 135), and this latter in turn is mentioned in the Derekh 'Emunah.

All of these considerations indicate that the Derekh 'Emunah was written around 1480 or shortly thereafter. It has been conjectured that one of the manuscripts of the Derekh 'Emunah, Cambridge-Trinity College 121, may have been written in 1458. This conjecture is unlikely in view of the preceding evidence that the work was probably composed a couple decades later and in light of the possibility that the manuscript is from the sixteenth century. See Ḥava Fraenkel-Goldschmidt, ed., Sefer ha-Miqnah, by Josel of Rosheim (Jerusalem, 1970), p. 42, n. 21.

On the title, see DE, Introd., 2c and Ps. 119:30. The Constantinople edition of 1521 (5282) was reproduced in 1969 in Farnborough, England by Gregg and in 1970 in Jerusalem by Meqoroth. The latter reprint is minus pages 98-101. An abridged edition with introduction and notes by Ḥava Fraenkel-Goldschmidt was published in Jerusalem in 1978 by Mosad Bialik. The book is called Derekh 'Emunah ha-Gadol by Bass (Sifte Yeshenim, p. 17b, no. 32) and Wolf (Bibliotheca, 1:35 and 3:23) evidently, according to Steinschneider (SteAbr, p. 80, no. 3), in order to distinguish it from the smaller book of the same name that was published in 1539 by the Kabbalist Meir ibn Gabbai (see Bass, no. 31). Meir ibn Gabbai, it should be noted, criticizes Bibago in another of his works. See n. 181.

28. For a discussion of these manuscripts, see Ḥava Fraenkel-Goldschmidt's Introduction to her edition of Josel of Rosheim's Sefer ha-Miqnah p. 42, and her abridged edition of DE, pp. 40 and 301.

29. Herbert Loewe, Catalogue of the Manuscripts in the Hebrew Character Collected and Bequeathed to the Trinity College Library by the Late William Aldis Wright (Cambridge, 1926), pp. 115-16. Microfilm copies of almost all the manuscripts mentioned here are in the Institute of Microfilmed Hebrew Manuscripts at the National and Hebrew University Library in Jerusalem. There this Cambridge-Trinity College manuscript is no. 12215.

30. It is called "Ya'ir Netiv" ("A Path Lights," from Job 41:24). See Moritz Steinschneider, Hebräische Bibliographie, 20 (1880): 134; idem, Die Hebräischen Handschriften, 2nd ed. (Munich, 1895), p. 29. This is Hebrew University microfilm no. 1150.

31. ZotCatP, p. 178; Fraenkel-Goldschmidt, ed., Sefer ha-Miqnah, p. 42, n. 22; Hebrew University microfilm no. 14680.

32. ZotCatP, p. 121; Hebrew University microfilm no. 12053. Montefiore 289 is a summary. See n. 186.

33. He is also sometimes called Ha-Rav ha-Moreh, "The Master, the Guide," in reference to his chief philosophic work, the Moreh Nevukhim (The Guide of the Perplexed). See, e.g., DE I-2, 14c; I-3, 17a, 21d, 23d. He is also occasionally called Ha-RaMBaM, the acrostic from Rabbi Moshe ben Maimon. See, e.g., DE I-1, 2c, 3b; I-2, 8b, 10b; II-3, 46c, 47d; II-5, 58d.

34. He is occasionally mentioned several times in the same column. See, e.g., DE I-3, 24d; II-2, 38a-b; II-4, 49c; II-6, 64a. It is interesting to note that Maimonides is hardly mentioned at all in Bibago's discussion of miracles in DE III-2, 79d-86b.

35. For example, in DE I-2, 9d, the reference is to Moreh Nevukhim (hereafter called MN) I-16; in I-2, 12b, it is to MN I-10, etc. In the references to MN the Roman numerals indicate the part number, the first Arabic numerals the chapter number, and the remaining Arabic numerals followed by a or b the page numbers.

36. For example, in DE I-2, 14c, Bibago specifies MN I-45 and III-24.

37. For example, in DE II-7, 68d, he mentions "Hilkhoth Teshuvah," III-14, in III-1, "Hilkhoth Yesode Torah" VIII, etc.

38. In DE I-2, 13a.

39. In DE II-5, 59a.

40. For example, in DE I-4, 31d, from MN I-18.

41. See the discussion of Maimonides' first principle of divine existence at the beginning of chapter three.

42. DE II-3, 46c; III-1, 75d.

43. DE III-5, 99c.

44. SteAbr, p. 90, n. 15; The Jewish Encyclopedia, 3:139a, Encyclopedia ᶜIvrith, 8:258, s.v. "Bibago, Abraham."

45. DE II-3, 43b.

46. Bibago tries, for example, to bring Maimonides' view of sacrifices as an anti-idolatry measure (MN III-32) into line with his own view of their cosmic significance (DE I-3, 24d). His own view, it should be noted, is similar to the view of Judah Halevi (Sefer ha-Kuzari, II-25, 26).

Bibago also wrote an essay, no longer extant, in which he defends Maimonides against the criticisms of Moses Naḥmanides in his Perush ha-Torah. See the end of the description of Bibago's works in this chapter.

47. DE III-4, 93b.

48. Ibid., 93d.

49. DE III-3, 84d. This is Bibago's explanation of the necessity for the dispersion of the human race as recounted in the story of the Tower of Babel.

50. DE III-5, 97b. Bibago cites this as support for his practice of giving more than one philosophic interpretation of the same biblical verse. For example, Gen. 2:2 is interpreted differently in DE I-2, 10b

and in II-6, 61b; 1 Kings 19:11-12 is interpreted differently in I-2, 10d and II-3, 45b; Ps. 82 is interpreted differently in I-2, 13d-14a and in II-1, 34c; and so forth. Rabbinic passages are also treated in this way, as for example B. T. Ḥagigah 11b, which is interpreted differently in I-1, 3b and in II-3, 43d.

51. Bibago differs with Maimonides, for example, on the conventionality of good and bad in I-2, 15b, on the philosophical interpretation of the story of Cain, Abel, and Seth in II-5, 57b-c and 58, and on Rabbi Eliezer's view of creation ex nihilo in III-1, 74c.

52. DE II-6, 67c: Wehanna^{c}ar haqqaṭon ^{c}al ketef ha^{c}anaq yir'eh mah sheyir'eh ha^{c}anaq weyoter. See Robert King Merton, On the Shoulders of Giants: A Shandean Postscript (New York, 1965), especially pp. 193-96, 233-41, and 268.

53. DE I-3, 17c. A partial list of the following sources that Bibago mentions by name in the Derekh 'Emunah can be found in SteAbr, pp. 85-91.

54. On the intermediate nature of the color green in his book Mar'oth ha-Shethen (The Colors of Urine), DE III-3, 88b. On this book, see Moritz Steinschneider, Die Hebräischen Übersetzungen des Mittelalters und die Juden als Dolmetscher (Berlin, 1893), hereafter referred to as SteHU, pp. 757-59 and 840.

55. He is mentioned somewhat frequently. DE I-1, 5b; I-3, 24c, 26a; II-3, 47b; II-5, 57b; and III-2, 79d. Steinschneider, however, says "selten," mentioning as an example only the last reference. SteAbr, p. 89.

56. DE II-3, 47c; III-2, 84a-b; III-5, 100d. Cf. SteAbr, p. 90.

57. DE III-3, 89c.

58. DE I-3, 16d and 24c. See SteAbr, p. 91, where the latter reference is said to come from his book Yeqqavu ha-Mayim (Let the Waters Be Gathered). Samuel is probably also intended in the reference to ibn Tibbon on 23b.

59. He is mentioned very frequently. DE I-2, 12c; II-6, 66a-b; III-2 (on miracles), 79a, 80a, 84c; III-3 (on creation), 86d, 87d, 88c-d, 89a; III-5, 98d, 101c. Bibago usually disagrees with Gersonides.

60. He is also mentioned rather frequently. DE II-2, 38a, 39b-c; II-5, 59a; III-3, 88d; III-4 (on the future world), 90d-91a, 93d, 94b. In 90d-91a, Bibago defends Maimonides against the criticism of Naḥmanides in his Sha^{c}ar ha-Gemul (Chapter on Recompense).

Notable by his absence from the list of Jewish philosophers named by Bibago is Ḥasdai Crescas, who about seventy years earlier was the rabbi in the same city, Saragossa, where Bibago evidently spent his last years. Bibago's failure to mention Crescas by name cannot be due simply to his disagreement with him over certain issues, since Bibago is very critical of Gersonides and yet, as we have seen, he mentions him by name rather frequently. All the Jewish philosophers named by Bibago flourished at least a century before him, so it could be that Crescas, like Joseph Albo, lived too close to Bibago's own generation for Bibago to name him. Abraham Shalom, Bibago's contemporary who also defends Maimonides, discusses Crescas as well as Gersonides frequently by name. Albo, who was Crescas's student, also mentions Crescas by name. Medieval Christian philosophers, however, rarely cite men of their own age. See for example William Kneale and Martha Kneale, The Development of Logic (Oxford, 1962), p. 236.

61. *DE* I-2, 9a; I-4, 33c; II-2, 38a-c; II-4, 53a; II-5, 55d.
62. *DE* II-6, 67b.
63. *DE* II-3, 47c.
64. Ibid.
65. *DE* III-5, 101c, 102b-c. The former citation is almost exactly like a passage on the Rabad in Joseph Albo's *Sefer ha-^{c}Iqqarim*, ed. and trans. I. Husik (Philadelphia, 1929), I-2, p. 53. The passage seems to be a different version of Rabad's well-known, caustic note on Maimonides' contention that one who believes in divine corporeality is a heretic (*min*). See Maimonides' *Mishneh Torah*, "Hilkhoth Teshuvah," 3:7, and Joseph Karo's "Kesef Mishneh" *ad. loc.* According to Bibago's version and to another quote in the same passage in *DE*, Rabad's view was that one who erred in speculation or by taking texts too literally could not be called a heretic. In the second citation, 102b-c, Bibago, unlike Albo, defends Maimonides. Cf. Isadore Twersky, *Rabad of Posquières: A Twelfth-Century Talmudist* (Cambridge, Mass., 1962), pp. 282-86.
This Rabad should be distinguished from the Rabad who wrote *Sefer ha-'Emunah ha-Ramah*.
66. *DE* I-1, 5b.
67. *DE* II-3, 47c. This is the lexicon written by Nathan ben Yeḥiel of Rome around 1101.
68. *DE* II-3, 46d.
69. Ibid.
70. Ibid., also I-4, 30d.
71. Bibago mentions *ha-Zohar* in *DE* I-2, 14d, *Sefer ha-Zohar* in I-1, 5c, *Ba^{c}al ha-Zohar* in II-5, 55d and III-5, 102a, and *Midrash ha-Zohar* in II-2, 39a; II-5, 54b; III-1, 78b; III-4, 92a; III-5, 97c.
72. *DE* I-3, 23d, and III-2, 80a.
73. *DE* I-4, 31d-32a; III-2, 80a-b.
74. For example, *DE* II-2, 39c; II-4, 49d; III-2, 81a-c, 85d; also the school (*kath*) of ibn Rushd in II-6, 63a.
75. *DE* I-3, 17b, 22d; I-4, 28b; II-4, 49c; II-6, 62d; III-1, 75a; III-2, 80d-81a. He also mentions the school (*kath*) of ibn Sīnā in I-4, 31c; II-4, 51d; III-1, 78d.
76. *DE* II-3, 46c.
77. *DE* III-1, 75a. This is the longest of ibn Rushd's works on the subject of conjunction with the Active Intellect. A Hebrew translation of the complete text has been preserved in Narboni's commentary on it, written in 1344, and this was the basis of the two commentaries written over a century later by Joseph ben Shem Ṭov ibn Shem Ṭov. See Moses Narboni, *Be'ur la-"Sefer Moreh Nevukhim,"* ed. J. Goldenthal (Vienna, 1852), p. 20a (on *MN* I-74); Moritz Steinschneider, "Josef b. Schemtob's Commentar zu Averroës' grosserer Abhandlung über die Möglichkeit der Conjunction," *MGWJ* 32 (1883): 460; Ste*HU*, secs. 99-101, pp. 191-97; Abū l-Walīd ibn Rushd, *Des Averroës Abhandlungen: "Über die Möglichkeit der Conjunction," oder "Über den Materiellen Intellekt,"* ed. and trans. Ludwig Hannes (Halle, 1892); idem, *Drei Abhandlungen über die Conjunction des Separaten Intellekts mit dem Menschen von Averroës (Vater und Sohn)*, trans. S. ibn Tibbon, ed. J. Hercz (Berlin, 1869).
In *DE* II-3, 44c, Bibago mentions a *Sefer 'Efsharuth ha-Devequth* (*Book on the Possibility of Conjunction*) without noting its author. Evidently it is the same work by ibn Rushd described above.
78. *DE* II-3, 46c; III-3, 88c.
79. *DE* I-1, 3b, the last line. Steinschneider wonders if these are his *Investigations in Physics* (*Quaestiones*, *Derushim ha-Ṭiv^{c}iyyim*),

a Hebrew collection of articles on physics attributed to ibn Rushd. SteAbr, p. 87; SteHU, sec. 91, pp. 178-82.

In medieval usage, ṭivᶜiyyim may also have meant "medical." SteHU, sec. 211, p. 369, n. 5; Harry A. Wolfson, "The Classification of Sciences in Medieval Jewish Philosophy," Hebrew Union College Jubilee Volume (Cincinnati, 1925), pp. 267-68, reprinted in his Studies in the History of Philosophy and Religion, ed. I. Twersky and G. H. Williams, 2 vols. (Cambridge, Mass., 1973-77), 1:497-98.

80. DE I-3, 18c.

81. DE I-4, 31c; II-7, 69a; III-3, 88b.

82. DE III-3, 88d. See Francis Edwards Peters, Aristoteles Arabus: The Oriental Translations and Commentaries on the Aristotelian Corpus (Leiden, 1968), pp. 19-20; Wolfson, Crescas' Critique, p. 526.

83. DE III-4, 93d. This is ibn Rushd's commentary to Aristotle's Meteorologica. Peters, Aristoteles Arabus, pp. 39-40. Ibn Rushd was also the author of A General Book on Medicine (Kitāb Kullīyāt fī al-Tib). See SteHU, sec. 86, p. 171; sec. 429, pp. 671-76. Bibago mentions a book Kullīyāt in regard to ibn Rushd in DE I-4, 33b. It seems, however, that ibn Rushd is here the author of a commentary to the book, not the author of the book itself. Since, as we shall see, Bibago mentions in another of his works a commentary that he himself had written to the Kullīyāt, Steinschneider suggests that Bibago intended his own commentary here. SteAbr, p. 137.

84. DE I-4, 31c; II-7, 69a.

85. DE II-4, 49d; III-2, 85d.

86. DE III-1, 75a; III-2, 81a.

87. DE III-1, 75a.

88. DE I-3, 19d; I-4, 28d, 29b, 33b; II-3, 44a, 45b.

89. Steinschneider suggests that the references to the works of Aristotle in the Derekh 'Emunah refer to the editions contained in the commentaries of ibn Rushd. SteAbr, p. 87. If so, this would make ibn Rushd's influence even more pervasive.

The articles on Averroes in the Jewish encyclopedias unfortunately say that Bibago was an opponent of his and even imply that Bibago was a sixteenth-century figure. Encyclopaedia Judaica (Berlin, 1929), 3:775; Encyclopaedia Judaica (English, Jerusalem, 1971), 3:952. I. Broyde, in his article on Averroism in The Jewish Encyclopedia (New York, 1902), 2:348b, says that Bibago "abuses Averroism" in his Derekh 'Emunah. This view seems to be based on a passage in Ernest Renan's Averroes et l'averroisme (Paris [1859]), p. 198. Renan, in describing the decline of Averroism in the sixteenth century and the resurgence of Jewish theology, says that Joseph Albo, Abraham Bibago, and Isaac Abravanel defended the doctrines of creation, revelation, and immortality against the philosophers.

90. DE I-4, 37a; II-3, 44c. See Moritz Steinschneider's Al-Fārābī (St. Petersburg, 1869), pp. 94 and 107; Alexander Altmann, "Ibn Bājja on Man's Ultimate Felicity," in his Studies in Religious Philosophy and Mysticism (Ithaca, N.Y., 1969), p. 75, especially note 4.

91. That is, 'Abuḥamid.

92. DE III-2, 81b. "Besifro behappalah," II-5, 55a; III-3, 87d.

93. DE III-1, 75d. This work, which Bibago also mentions in his "Supercommentary on the Metaphysics," is the part of al-Ghazālī's Maqāṣid al-Falāsifah (Intentions of the Philosophers [Egypt, 1936], in Hebrew Kawwanoth ha-Pilosofim) that deals with physics. Bibago's reference to the Tivᶜiyoth in DE II-4, 49c, is evidently to the same work. There, as in his references to the work in his "Supercommentary

on the Metaphysics," Bibago associates al-Ghazālī with ibn Sīnā, whom al-Ghazālī criticizes in his Tahāfut al-Falāsifah. SteAbr, pp. 132-33. Al-Ghazālī's summary of the philosophers' opinions in his Intentions, however, was taken by many medievals to indicate his agreement with those views. Arthur Hyman and James J. Walsh, eds., Philosophy in the Middle Ages (New York, 1967), p. 263; Frederick Copleston, A History of Philosophy, vol. 2, pt. 1 (Garden City, N.Y., 1962), pp. 220-21.

94. DE II-2, 42a; II-1, 36a; II-5, 59b. See Miguel Asín Palacios, "La 'Carta de Adiós' de Avempace," Al-Andalus 8 (1943): 1-87; Arabic text, pp. 15-40; SteHU, sec. 206, pp. 357-61.

95. DE I-3, 20a. Ibrahim Abū Isḥāq al-Zarkali (known in Europe often as Azrachel or Arzachel) was an eleventh-century Spanish astronomer and instrument designer who edited the Toledo Tables of planetary motions. Moritz Steinschneider, "Études sur Zarkali," Bulletino della bibliografia e della storia delle scienze mathematiche e fisiche, vols. 14, 16-18, 20 (Rome, 1881, 1883-85, 1887); Pierre Duhem, Le Système du monde, vols. 2-4 (Paris, 1954).

96. DE II-3, 47b. Bibago evidently knew the Hebrew translation of this classic work. SteAbr, p. 88; SteHU, sec. 535, pp. 872-83; The Encyclopaedia of Islam: New Edition, fasc. 67-68 (Leiden, 1974), pp. 503-06, s.v. "Kalīla wa-Dimna."

97. That is, Ben Daqlis. DE I-2, 16a; I-3, 18d, 27b. This may refer to the medieval Arabic and Hebrew corpus of Neoplatonic writings attributed to the pre-Socratic Greek philosopher Empedocles. See David Kaufmann, "Pseudo-Empedokles als Quelle Salomon ibn Gabirols," Studien über Salomon ibn Gabirol (Budapest, 1899), pp. 1-63; Samuel M. Stern, "Anbaduklis," The Encyclopaedia of Islam: New Edition, vol. 1 (Leiden and London, 1960), pp. 483-84.

98. For example, DE I-2, 10a; I-3, 17b; II-3, 46d; II-6, 62d. Also the references to the "Philosopher," DE I-2, 11b; II-5, 54d; II-6, 61b; II-7, 68d; III-4, 92c; III-5, 98a. See also SteAbr, p. 85.

99. Book on the Syllogism. DE II-7, 68d. See Peters, Aristoteles Arabus, pp. 14-17; SteHU, pp. 46-47.

100. Book of Demonstration. DE II-7, 72d; III-3, 88d. See SteHU, p. 47, and n. 82 above. On Bibago's commentary on this work, see p. 5.

101. Book of Dialectics. DE II-5, 54d; II-7, 69d; III-3, 86c. See Peters, Aristoteles Arabus, pp. 20-23; SteHU, pp. 47-48. On this and the two preceding works on logic, see also Maimonides' Milloth ha-Higgayon (Treatise on Logic), ed. and trans. I. Efros, PAAJR 8 (1938), ch. 10, pp. 47-48 and 118 in the Hebrew texts and p. 53 in the English translation.

102. DE I-2, 8b; I-3, 18c; II-3, 46d; II-6, 61b, 63b; II-7, 69d; III-1, 75a; III-3, 86d. See Peters, Aristoteles Arabus, pp. 30-34; SteHU, pp. 109-15. The full Hebrew title, Ha-Shema^{c} ha-Ṭiv^{c}i, is a translation of the Greek title Phusikés 'Akróāseus (Lectures on Physics). See SteHU, p. 108.

103. On the Heavens and the (Sublunar) World. DE II-6, 60c; III-3, 86d. See Peters, Aristoteles Arabus, pp. 35-36; SteHU, secs. 55-58, pp. 125-29.

104. Meteorologica. DE I-3, 19c, 22d. See n. 83 above and SteHU, secs. 61-62, pp. 132-36.

105. De Anima. DE II-1, 34a; II-2, 38d, 40a; II-6, 61d, 65d; III-2, 81d. See Peters, Aristoteles Arabus, pp. 40-45; SteHU, secs. 68-71, pp. 146-49.

106. DE I-1, 5d; I-2, 11b. In the medieval Arabic tradition, Aristotle's three works on animals were grouped together into one work consisting of nineteen books, i.e., the ten books of the History of Animals, the five books of the Generation of Animals, and the four books of the Parts of Animals. Peters, Aristoteles Arabus, pp. 47-48; SteHU, sec. 67, pp. 143-46.

107. Very frequently. For example, DE I-1, 2c, 4a; I-2, 11d, 12d; I-3, 16c-d; I-4, 32c; II-1, 34a; II-2, 38b, 40b; II-5, 54d; II-7, 67c; III-2, 80c-d; III-4, 92c. See Peters, Aristoteles Arabus, pp. 49-52; SteHU, secs. 76-77, pp. 156-58.

108. DE I-2, 9c, 12a, 15a; II-1, 34b; II-2, 41c; II-6, 63c, 65a; II-7, 68d; III-4, 89c; III-5, 98a. See Peters, Aristoteles Arabus, pp. 52-53; SteHU, sec. 110, pp. 209-12.

109. DE II-3, 45d, 47a.

110. DE I-2, 8a.

111. In DE II-3, 46b, Bibago describes the theorem in geometry that is usually cited in the name of Pythagoras.

112. DE III-5, 98a.

113. DE III-3, 87d, 88a.

114. DE I-2, 8a.

115. DE II-3, 46c.

116. DE I-3, 17b; II-3, 43b, from MN III-17 (2) and I-31, p. 49, respectively.

117. DE I-2, 9b; II-3, 44b. See Eduard Zeller, Die Philosophie der Griechen in ihrer Geschichtlichen Entwicklung (Leipzig, 1881), vol. 3, pt. 2, pp. 739-42.

118. DE III-4, 92c. Themistius's "Commentary on Aristotle's De Anima" is frequently quoted by ibn Rushd in his "Great Commentary" and his "Middle Commentary." Peters, Aristoteles Arabus, p. 42.

119. DE I-4, 33b; II-6, 63b.

120. DE II-3, 46b.

121. DE I-2, 8a.

122. DE I-2, 10a.

123. DE I-4, 29b.

124. DE I-4, 33d. See SteAbr, p. 86.

125. DE I-2, 12a; II-1, 35d; II-7, 67c, 68c. See also III-1, 76c-d; III-2, 86b.

126. DE II-3, 47a. It was also in his "youth" (baḥaruth) that Bibago engaged in a discussion with a sage, evidently a Christian, at the court of King John II of Aragon. DE III-5, 99b. See p. 1 above. The sage is obviously Christian because he asks why Bibago does not accept the doctrine of the incarnation since he accepts such an unphilosophical doctrine as creation.

127. DE II-3, 46c.

Cf. Eusebius's Praeparatio Evangelica, ed. K. Mras (Berlin, 1954), 9:5, pp. 491-92. On Eusebius and the Jews, see Samuel Krauss, "The Jews in the Works of the Church Fathers: IV Eusebius," in JQR 6 (1894): 82-88; Encyclopaedia Judaica (English), 6:977-78. Eusebius, bishop of Caesarea at the beginning of the fourth century, shows the superiority of Judaism over Greek paganism as a proper foundation for Christianity at the end of his Praeparatio Evangelica, but in his Demonstratio Evangelica he severely criticizes Judaism in relationship to Christianity.

The story about Aristotle and the Jew from Clearchus's lost treatise on sleep is also reproduced in Josephus's Contra Apionem, 1.22.176-82. See Hans Lewy, "Aristotle and the Jewish Sage According to Clearchus of Soli," HTR 31 (1938): 205-35. Clearchus had been a pupil of Aristotle.

128. See The Jewish Encyclopedia, 2:99a; Encyclopaedia Judaica, 3:339; Encyclopaedia Judaica (English), 3:449.

129. DE II-3, 46c. Azariah de Rossi (1513-1578) brings a report in the name of Joseph ben Shem Ṭov ibn Shem Ṭov that Aristotle had converted in his old age. Sefer Me'or ᶜEnayim, ed. D. Cassel (Vilna, 1866), p. 91b.

Gedalya ibn Yaḥya (1515-1587) quotes de Rossi's story from Joseph ben Shem Ṭov ibn Shem Ṭov and also brings Bibago's story from Eusebius about Aristotle's being Jewish. Shalsheleth ha-Kabbalah (Jerusalem, 1962), p. 241. The Italian rabbi Judah Moscato (1530-1593), in his commentary "Qol Yehudah" to the Sefer ha-Kuzari (Israel, 1958-59), II-66, brings Bibago's story from Eusebius about Aristotle's being Jewish. He notes that it is also found in Josephus and that Bibago's version has many errors in it. Moscato refers to Bibago here and elsewhere simply as the author of the Derekh 'Emunah. See also SteAbr, pp. 89 and 143.

130. Chaim Wirszubski, "Appendix VI: Aristoteles Iudaeus," in his edition of Flavius Mithridates, pp. 72-75. Wirszubski argues that Bibago's assertion that Aristotle was Jewish is not a deliberate Jewish distortion of the account since at least two other contemporary authors, Marsilio Ficino, a Christian, and Flavius Mithridates, a convert to Christianity, also assert that Aristotle was Jewish in their versions of the account. Wirszubski concludes that, in the defective Latin translation of Eusebius's Praeparatio Evangelica published in 1470, a misleading full-stop before "Aristoteles" makes the name go with "iudaeus" after it. I wish to thank Professor Wirszubski for kindly calling my attention to this note while I was in Jerusalem in 1970.

131. SteAbr, p. 95, no. 2. Copies of this very rare edition can be found in the Bodleian Library, the Library of the British Museum, the New York City Public Library, and Leningrad's Asiatic Museum. See Steinschneider, Catalogus Liborum Hebraeorum, p. 670; Joseph Zedner, ed., Catalogue of the Hebrew Books in the Library of the British Museum (London, 1867), p. 28; and Israel Zinberg, A History of Jewish Literature, trans. and ed. B. Martin (Cleveland, 1973), 3:256. The National and Hebrew University Library in Jerusalem has a photograph of the copy in the Bodleian Library.

The sermon in this volume was delivered by Bibago at the request of the congregation after his attempt to deliver it the preceding Sabbath was disrupted by a Christian mob attacking the synagogue. See Zinberg, Jewish Literature, 3:256.

132. Paris 995.3 (ZotCatP, p. 178) and Rab. 80, Jewish Theological Seminary, New York (originally Adler 28), fols. 121-42.

133. DE III-3, 88c.

134. Steinschneider, Die Hebräischen Handschriften, pp. 25, 167-68; SteAbr, pp. 127-37. SteHU, sec. 86. pp. 168-71, repeats the latter with abbreviated notes.

135. SteHU, secs. 79-80, pp. 160-61; Peters, Aristoteles Arabus, p. 51.

136. SteAbr, pp. 127, 129-30.

137. Ibid., p. 131.

138. Ibid., pp. 138-41.

139. Ibid., pp. 132-35. Some of the works that are mentioned here and are not mentioned in the Derekh 'Emunah are Apollonius's Conic Sections (Sefer he-Ḥaruthim, see MN I-73 [10], p. 123), al-Fārābī's Book of the Principles of Beings (Sefer Hathḥaloth ha-Nimṣa'oth), ibn Tufayl's Ḥayy ben Yaqẓan, and ibn Rushd's Treatise on the Substance of the Celestial Sphere (Ma'amar be-ᶜEṣem ha-Galgal).

140. SteAbr, pp. 133-34. On Nicolas Bonet (d. 1343), see Études Franciscaines 37 (1925): 638-57; Dictionnaire d'histoire et de géographie ecclesiastiques (Paris, 1937) 9:849-52. One of his works on metaphysics was published in Barcelona in 1483.

141. SteAbr, pp. 134-35, 141-42. See Shlomo Pines, "Ha-Ṣuroth ha-'Ishiyoth be-Mishnatho shel Yedaᶜyah Bedershi," Harry Austryn Wolfson Jubilee Volume, Hebrew section (Jerusalem, 1965), 3:187, n. 2, and 198, n. 30; idem, "Scholasticism," pp. 4-5.

142. That is, his commentaries on Aristotle's Posterior Analytics and Physics and on ibn Rushd's Kullīyāt. See SteAbr, p. 135. The "Supercommentary on the Metaphysics" is in turn mentioned twice by Bibago in the Derekh 'Emunah. DE II-7, 67c, 69a. It was thus written before the Derekh 'Emunah.

143. ZotCatP, p. 178. The beginning section of the manuscript is missing.

144. "ᶜEṣ Ḥayyim," Derekh 'Emunah, and Zeh Yenaḥamenu are the first three parts respectively of Paris 995. They are also the three works of Bibago that are mentioned by Shabbethai Bass in his Sifte Yeshenim, pp. 17b, 19a, and 59a.

145. DE II-6, 60c; III-3, 87c, 88c. In III-3, 86d, Bibago mentions two works that he wrote on creation, the reference evidently being to the "ᶜEṣ Ḥayyim" and Zeh Yenaḥamenu, which are mentioned together in 88c. SteAbr, p. 125, no. 9.

146. DE III-3, 87c. In his 'Or ha-Ḥayyim, pp. 123-24, Ḥayyim Michal argues that this work "ᶜEṣ Ḥayyim" is concerned not just with creation but with other areas as well in which the Torah goes beyond what reason can prove. See DE II-6, 60c. He contends that Zeh Yenaḥamenu is not another treatise on creation but rather that chapter of "ᶜEṣ Ḥayyim" that treats of creation. See DE III-3, 88c. Also said by Michal to be chapters of "ᶜEṣ Ḥayyim" are three other works mentioned by Bibago in the Derekh 'Emunah but no longer extant: an essay on sacrifices, a defense of Maimonides against Moses Naḥmanides' criticisms in his Perush ha-Torah, and an essay on resurrection called "Maḥazeh Shaddai." The "ᶜEṣ Ḥayyim" is thus according to Michal a major collection of Bibago's essays. Michal had evidently noticed that the "ᶜEṣ Ḥayyim" is always called a book (sefer) in the Derekh 'Emunah, whereas these other works that are said to be its chapters are each called an article (ma'amar). Michal, however, does not seem to have been aware of Paris 995.1.

Michal's collection of books was bought by the British Museum in 1848. The Catalogue of the Hebrew Books in the Library of the British Museum (1867), p. 28, lists two copies of the Derekh 'Emunah and adds that one of them has copious notes. This is most likely Michal's copy.

Moritz Steinschneider, in SteHU, sec. 38, p. 90, n. 312, mentions a MS. Zunz 4 that is called "ᶜEṣ Ḥayyim." It is a commentary on the Torah and one of its owners had noted that its author was Bibago. Steinschneider points out, however, that the author of the manuscript calls himself Moses and refers to another of his works, "Ma^{c}yan Gannim." This manuscript is now Montefiore 17.1. See Hartwig Hirschfeld, Descriptive Catalogue of the Hebrew MSS. of the Montefiore Library (London, 1904), pp. 4-5. The manuscript is there described as having been written in the fifteenth century in Italian rabbinic characters. It is further said to be an autograph of the author and so wrongly ascribed by a later owner to Abraham ben Shem Ṭov Bibago.

147. That is, the Book of Demonstration. See nn. 82 and 100 above.

148. SteAbr, pp. 126-27; SteHU, sec. 38, pp. 89-91; ZotCatP, p. 169; Stefano Evodio Assemani and Guiseppe Simone Assemani, eds., Bibliothecae Apostolicae Vaticanae Codicum Manuscriptorum Catologus, vol. 1, Codices Ebraicos et Samaritanos (Rome, 1756), p. 333.

149. See p. 1 and n. 6 above.

150. The other dated work is the two letters to Moses Arondi written in 1470. SteAbr, p. 84.

151. There was a Hebrew translation. SteAbr, p. 126, n. 22.

152. SteAbr, p. 135.

153. Ibid., p. 125; ZotCatP, p. 180. The topic is mainly matter and form.

154. DE I-4, 33a. See SteAbr, p. 95; ZotCatP, p. 180.

155. SteAbr, p. 125, no. 7; G. B. de Rossi, MSS. Codices, 2:49-50. The topic of the letters is motion. Moses Arondi was one of those associated with Abram Bivagch in the circumcision of the converso at Huesca in 1465. Baer, Die Juden, 2:488. See p. 1 above.

156. DE I-3, 24d-25b. In the course of his summary of this work, Bibago compares the four major types of sacrifices with the four parts of existence. See also SteAbr, p. 125.

157. DE II-2, 38a. Also SteAbr, p. 125.

158. The reference is to Num. 24:4 and 16, verses from Balaam's third and fourth prophecies.

159. DE III-5, 102c-d. It should be noted, however, that Bibago on the other hand also denies that resurrection and redemption take place in time. They are rather atemporal but spiritual processes. It was to refute these naturalistic philosophers, Bibago argues, that Maimonides seems to say that resurrection is in time.

160. See n. 145.

161. SteAbr, p. 127, 134-35; SteHU, sec. 54, p. 124; sec. 86, p. 171. See n. 142.

162. SteAbr, pp. 135, 137; SteHU, sec. 86, p. 171; sec. 429, pp. 675-76. See nn. 83 and 142.

163. Isaac ben Judah Abravanel and Saul ben Moses ha-Kohen Ashkenazi, She'eloth leha-Hakham . . . Shaul ha-Kohen . . . : Shesha'al me'eth he-Ḥakham . . . Yiṣḥaq Abravanel. . . . (Venice, 1574; reprinted as Teshuvoth R. Yiṣḥaq Abravanel ^{c}al She'eloth Shesha'alu R. Shaul ha-Kohen, Jerusalem, 1966-67), the end of the tenth question [p. 10b]. Steinschneider suggests that Saul ha-Kohen Ashkenazi is here referring to Bibago's "Ma^{c}amar beribuy ha-Ṣuroth" (Paris 1004.1). SteAbr, p. 95.

164. David Solomon Sassoon, ed., 'Ohel Dawid: Descriptive Catalogue of the Hebrew and Samaritan Manuscripts in the Sassoon Library (London, 1932), pp. 671-75. This is no. 9649 in the Hebrew University Microfilm Room.

165. ZotCatP, p. 217. This work in Florence MS. 530 is anonymous.

166. Johann Christoph Wolf, Bibliotheca Hebraea, vol. 3 (Hamburg, 1727), no. 60, p. 23.

167. Adolf Neubauer, "Documents inédits," Revue de études juives 5, no. 9 (July-September 1882): 45, n. 1. Steinschneider, in Hebräische Bibliographie 21 (1881): 82, had said that Bibago was most likely the author of this medical manual because Bibago, as we have seen, refers to another medical work of his, a commentary on ibn Rushd's Kullīyāt. In SteAbr (1883), pp. 125-26, Steinschneider wavers in the face of Neubauer's note. Paris 1181 and 1182 are indeed said to have been written in the fourteenth century and Bibago lived in the fifteenth century, but Steinschneider did not consider this to be determinant. In SteHU (1893), however, secs. 415 and 581, pp. 657 and 972, Steinschneider seems to accept Neubauer's view.

168. See Eliakim Carmoly, "Analecten: 8. Plagiate," Israelitische Annalen, 29 March 1839, p. 101; idem, "Toldoth Don Yiṣḥaq Abravanel," 'Oṣar Neḥmad, ed. I. Blumenfeld (Vienna, 1857), 2:54-55.

Carmoly's charge of plagiarism is considered too harsh in an article signed "Tsarphati" in the same volume of the Israelitische Annalen, p. 181. Abravanel, after all, was too prolific an author to have to resort to such devices. In another response, Samuel David Luzzatto not only rises to Abravanel's defense but also uses the occasion to attack Bibago for his excessive dependence upon Maimonides and Aristotle. Luzzatto praises Abravanel as an anti-Maimonist whose true views appear finally in the last two chapters of the Rosh 'Amanah. Bibago, Luzzatto concludes, was not worthy of mention by Abravanel. "Über die angeblichen Plagiate Abrabanel's und Moscato's," Israelitische Annalen, 10 and 17 January 1840, pp. 17 and 25. Both "Tsarphati" and Luzzatto consider it coincidental that both Bibago and Abravanel mention a work that they wrote called "Maḥazeh Shaddai."

On Abravanel's discussion of Maimonides' thirteen principles of faith in the Rosh 'Amanah, see Eugene Mihaly, "Isaac Abravanel on the Principles of Faith," HUCA 26 (1955): 481-502. Abravanel's Rosh 'Amanah was first published in Constantinople in 1505 and recently in Tel Aviv in 1958. The following passages in Abravanel's Rosh 'Amanah correspond to the designated passages in the Derekh 'Emunah:

- ch. 10, pp. 55-56 (in the 1958 edition of Rosh 'Amanah) corresponds to DE III-5, 99c on attributes as either negations or deeds.
- p. 56 corresponds to DE III-5, 101d on the second, third, and fourth principles.
- p. 57 corresponds to DE III-5, 100a on eternal and future deeds.
- pp. 57-58 corresponds to DE III-5, 101b on R. Eliezer b. Pedath.
- ch. 12, p. 64 corresponds to DE III-5, 101b on Rabad's defense of unintentional heresy, which Bibago in turn had borrowed from Albo (see n. 65 above). Abravanel does mention Albo here.
- p. 64 corresponds to DE III-5, 102b-c on the defense of Maimonides against Rabad's criticism. In this latter instance, Abravanel quotes Bibago almost verbatim. The interesting exception is that, whereas Bibago cites the Christians as an example of those who would not be called heretics by the Rabad, Abravanel substitutes Ṣadoq and Baythus. On the top of p. 65, Abravanel also quotes DE III-5,

102c verbatim, on 'Aḥer's materialism. See Jakob Guttmann, Die Religionsphilosophischen Lehren des Isaak Abravanel, (Breslau, 1916).

169. Abravanel and Ashkenazi, She'eloth, pp. 18b-20c. Abravanel also mentions contemporaries, such as Shem Ṭov and Eli Habillio, so that one could not argue that Bibago was excluded because he was a contemporary. In his comments on Numbers, ch. 20, Abravanel mentions the opinion of "one of the sages of the generation" ('eḥad me-ḥakhme haddor) that Moses did not sin. Although the reference is clearly to Bibago, Abravanel still does not name him. See Abravanel's Perush ha-Torah: Sefer Bemidbar (Warsaw, 1862; Reprint, Jaffa and Jerusalem: Sefarim Torah Wada^{c}ath, n.d.), p. 20c.

170. See n. 163 above.

171. Joseph Solomon Delmedigo, Maṣref le-Ḥokhmah (Basel, 1629), p. 8b; "'Iggereth 'Aḥuz" in Melo' Hofnayim, ed. A. Geiger (Berlin, 1840), p. 22. A note at the beginning of Montefiore 289 also points out that Bibago was Isaac Arama's guide. See the end of this chapter, p. 7, and n. 186. Hayyim Michal suggests that Delmedigo's statement may apply to Abravanel instead of Arama since Abravanel borrowed whole paragraphs from Bibago in his Rosh 'Amanah. Michal adds that Abravanel's dependence upon Bibago was noted by Wolf Heidenheim in his copy of the Derekh 'Emunah. 'Or ha-Ḥayyim, pp. 122-23. Thus Heidenheim, who died in 1832, was the first to notice this relationship between Abravanel and Bibago, although Carmoly was the first to publish an article on it in 1839. Heidenheim's copy of the Derekh 'Emunah is now in the National and Hebrew University Library in Jerusalem.

172. ^{c}Aqedath Yiṣḥaq (Bialystok, 1911), "Parshath Ḥuqqath," ch. 80.

173. Michal, 'Or ha-Ḥayyim, sec. 255, p. 123, note; Sarah Heller Wilensky, R. Yiṣḥaq Arama u-Mishnatho (Jerusalem, 1956), pp. 44-45, 201-02.

174. Solomon ibn Verga, Sefer Shevet Yehudah, ed. Y. Baer, notes by A. Shoḥeṭ (Jerusalem, 1947), p. 88.

175. That is, DE III-5, 99b. See ibn Verga, Sheveṭ Yehudah, p. 194, and also pp. 175 and 178.

176. Me'or ^{c}Enayim, pp. 31a, 182b.

177. Ibid., p. 91b.

178. See n. 129 above.

179. "Qol Yehudah" on Sefer ha-Kuzari, 2:6, 2:66.

180. Maṣref le-Ḥokhmah, pp. 8b-9a.

181. Sefer ^{c}Avodath ha-Qodesh (Warsaw, 1883), pt. 3, chs. 16-17.

182. ^{c}En Ya^{c}aqov at the end of Berakhoth (Venice, 1546), pp. 51b-52a.

183. For example, Manoth ha-Levi (Venice, 1585), p. 180. Bibago is also mentioned by Alkabeṣ in 'Ayeleth 'Ahavim (Venice, 1552) and in his "Beth ha-Shem." See n. 49 in ch. 2. I wish to thank Mrs. Berakha Zak for informing me of the frequency with which Alkabeṣ refers to Bibago.

Bibago, along with Maimonides, Isaac Arama, and Jacob ibn Ḥabib, is also cited frequently in a manuscript in an oriental hand attributed to R. Ḥiyya Rofe (d. 1620) of Safed. See Carlo Bernheimer, Catalogue des manuscrits et livres rares hébraïques de la bibliothèque du talmud torah de Livourne (1914), no. 36, p. 70.

184. Sassoon, ed., _'Ohel Dawid_, vol. 2, no. 919, pp. 1010-17. The only other philosophic source represented in this Kabbalistic collection is Simon b. Ṣemaḥ Duran's, _Magen 'Avoth_ (Livorno, 1785).

185. Fraenkel-Goldschmidt, ed., _Sefer ha-Miqnah_. See especially pp. 34-42 and 73-75 in the Introduction. An earlier version of this work was submitted to the Hebrew University in 1964 as a Master's thesis. On Josel of Rosheim, see also Selma Stern, _Josel of Rosheim_, trans. G. Hirschler (Philadelphia, 1965), especially pp. 225-34 on the _Sefer ha-Miqnah_. Stern, however, was unaware of the relationship of this work to Bibago's _Derekh 'Emunah_.

On p. 74 of her Introduction, Fraenkel-Goldschmidt asks why Rosheim should have chosen to reproduce a large portion of Bibago's work in particular. It should become clear in the course of this study that the major theme of the first third of the _Derekh 'Emunah_ is divine providence. This emphasis was obviously important for the Jews of Spain in the decades before their expulsion in 1492. I would suggest that it was this same emphasis upon divine providence that led Rosheim to append selections from especially the first third of the _Derekh 'Emunah_ to his description in the first section of the _Sefer ha-Miqnah_ of the expulsions of the Jews from the various areas of Germany in the fifteenth century. This seems to be the primary connection between the two works that Fraenkel-Goldschmidt is seeking.

186. Hirschfeld, _Descriptive Catalogue_, p. 91. See n. 171 above.

On the influence of Spanish-Jewish philosophy in sixteenth-century German-Jewish thought, see Ḥaim Hillel Ben-Sasson, "Jewish-Christian Disputation in the Setting of Humanism and Reformation in the German Empire," _HTR_ 59 (1966): 369-90. The connection between Bibago and Rosheim is dealt with on pp. 369-71.

187. Ste_Abr_, pp. 79-96, 125-44, 239-40. See n. 1 above. The article on Bibago in the _Jüdisches Lexikon_, vol. 1 (Berlin, 1927), pp. 961-63, was written by Max Joseph, a rabbi in Stolp, Germany. The bibliography at the end of the article contains the following entry: M. Joseph, Abraham Bibago's Religionsphilosophie, 1901, nur handschriftlich in der Bibliothek der Hochschule für Wissenschaft des Judenthums, Berlin. This dissertation is also listed in the bibliography at the end of the article on Bibago in the German _Encyclopaedia Judaica_, 4:483. The dissertation is evidently no longer extant, but Joseph's article in the _Jüdisches Lexikon_ is most likely a summary of it. The article, translated into English, serves as the entry for Bibago in the _Universal Jewish Encyclopedia_ (New York, 1940), 2:279. Judging from this article, the dissertation does not seem to have been especially significant. Joseph says that Bibago's closest affinity is with Albo, but the similarities he mentions would include a host of other Jewish philosophers as well.

At the Fifth World Congress of Jewish Studies in Jerusalem on August 6, 1969, Yosef Hakker delivered a paper on "The Role of Rabbi Abraham Bibago in the Polemic on the Place of Philosophy in Jewish Life in Spain in the 15th Century." Hakker's paper, in Hebrew, appeared in 1972 in the _Proceedings of the Congress_, 3:151-58 (English abstract, pp. 94-95). Hakker emphasizes Bibago's moderation in the dispute over philosophy.

The present study is a revised version of the doctoral dissertation that I submitted to the Department of Near Eastern and Judaic

Studies at Brandeis University in 1973. As I was completing the preparation of the manuscript for the press, I saw a copy of the doctoral dissertation that Avraham Nuriel submitted to the faculty of the Hebrew University in Jerusalem in 1975. His work is entitled "Mishnatho ha-Pilosofith shel R. Avraham ben Shem Ṭov Bibago." Nuriel's work is more comprehensive than the present one. It attempts to present all aspects of Bibago's philosophy as it appears in all his works.

188. In Jews in Christian Spain, 2:489, n. 34.

Chapter Two
The Existence of God

1. Gordon Leff, Bradwardine and the Pelagians: A Study of His "De Causa Dei" and Its Opponents (Cambridge, 1957), pp. 8-10.

2. For example, DE II-5, 53d: meṣi'uth hashem we'aḥdutho hem niqnim lanu ᶜal ṣad ha'emeth weᶜal ṣad ha'emunah. In DE II-4, 52c, Abraham is said to have taught people about God's existence through inquiry and speculation, whereas Jacob did so through faith.

3. DE II-4, 49a-b; II-7, 68b, 70c. In II-5, 59a-b, five similarities are described between faith and rational knowledge. Abraham Shalom, Sefer Neweh Shalom (Venice, 1575), pp. 87b-89a, says that prophecy yields knowledge without its premises. His view is in opposition to that of Gersonides in MH II-4. Thus the similarity that Bibago draws between knowledge and faith, Shalom draws between knowledge and prophecy. This then is an instance of Bibago speaking of faith where other philosophers spoke of prophecy.

4. DE I-3, 17d; II-4, 49b; and II-5, 53d, referring to Exod. 20:2 and Deut. 5:6. Cf. Maimonides, MT "Hilkhoth Yesode Torah," I-6, Ḥasdai Crescas, OH Introduction, p. 3a, and Shalom, Neweh Shalom, VIII-6, p. 133a.

5. DE III-1, 73a. Cf. Thomas Aquinas, ST I-i-7.

6. DE II-4, 49d: ha'emunah ha'amithith 'asher hi' ḥokhmah sheminith. Also 50b. Cf. Thomas Aquinas, ST I-i-2 and 6.

7. DE III-1, 73d. On Aristotle's statement (Posterior Analytics I-9, 76a16-17) that no master of any art can demonstrate the proper principles of his own art, ibn Rushd comments that this refers to "an absolute demonstration which shows cause and existence. For the master of particular arts can demonstrate the causes of his own subject through signs, or a posteriori, . . ." Harry A. Wolfson, "Averroes' Lost Treatise on the Prime Mover," HUCA 23, pt. 1 (1950-51):692. Cf. also pp. 695-96. Reprinted in his Studies in the History of Philosophy and Religion, ed. I. Twersky and G. H. Williams (Cambridge, Mass., 1973-77), 1:411, 414. See also Thomas Aquinas, ST I-i-8.

8. DE III-3, 86c. Joseph ibn Kaspi (1297-1340) similarly speaks of two types of demonstration, one a priori and one a posteriori, and like Bibago he uses the example of the deduction of fire from smoke. The a priori proof, however, he calls a "demonstration of existence and cause" (mofeth meṣi'uth wesibbah) or simply a "demonstration" (mofeth), and the a posteriori proof he calls a "demonstration of existence" only (mofeth meṣi'uth) or a "demonstration and sign" (mofeth we'oth) or simply a "sign" ('oth). Mishneh Kesef: Shene Be'urim ᶜal ha-Torah, ed. I. Last, vol. 1, Ṭirath Kesef (Pressburg, 1904), pp. 11-12. Cf. ᶜAmude Kesef u-Maskiyoth Kesef: Shene Perushim ᶜal sefer

ha-"Moreh" leha-RaMBaM, ed. S. Werbluner (Frankfurt a. M., 1848), p. 88 (on MN II-1), and also the passage from ibn Rushd in the preceding note.

In DE III-2, 84a-b, Bibago mentions Kaspi's interpretation of the biblical "sign" ('oth) as an a posteriori demonstration and the biblical "wonder" (mofeth) as an a priori demonstration. As for a "demonstration of cause and existence" (mofeth meṣi'uth wesibbah), in III-3, 86d, Bibago refers to this as a rare third type of demonstration.

Moses Narboni (d. after 1362), in his Be'ur la-"Sefer Moreh Nevukhim," ed. J. Goldenthal (Vienna, 1852), p. 16a, on MN I-71, and Efodi (Profiat Duran, d. about 1414), in his "Commentary" on the Sefer Moreh Nevukhim (Jerusalem, 1959), p. 17a, on MN II-1, call the a posteriori demonstration mofeth re'ayah, as Bibago does, and say that only by this kind of demonstration can God's existence be proved.

On these two types of demonstrations, see also Thomas Aquinas, ST I-ii-2. The terms used there, demonstratio quia (demonstration of fact, a posteriori) and demonstratio propter quid (demonstration of reasoned fact, a priori) go back to Aristotle's Posterior Analytics I-13. Allan B. Wolter, ed. and trans., Duns Scotus: Philosophical Writings (Edinburgh, 1962), p. 179, n. 9. On the development of these terms in medieval Jewish logic, see Shalom Rosenberg, "Logiqa we-'Ontologiyah be-Filosofiyah ha-Yehudith be-Me'ah ha-14" (Ph.D. diss., Hebrew University, Jerusalem, 1973), pp. 4, 240-44, 297-98. It should be noted that the terms "a priori" and "a posteriori" are used in a somewhat different sense in modern philosophy.

9. H. A. Wolfson, "Notes on Proofs of the Existence of God in Jewish Philosophy," HUCA 1 (1924): 575, 584-86, reprinted in his Studies, 1:561, 570-72; idem, The Philosophy of Spinoza (Cambridge, Mass., 1934), 1:192.

10. Ibid. For versions of the creation proof in early Jewish philosophy, see Saadia Gaon, Sefer ha-'Emunoth weha-De^c^oth, I, 1-2; Baḥya ibn Paquda, Sefer Ḥovoth ha-Levavoth I, 4-6; and Joseph ibn Ṣaddiq, Sefer ha-^c^Olam ha-Qatan, ed. S. Horovitz (Breslau, 1903), ch. 3, p. 51. Cf. also Judah Halevi, Sefer ha-Kuzari, II-50 (trans. J. ibn Tibbon; ed. A. Ṣifroni [Tel Aviv, 195?], p. 109). Halevi, in V-18, the first three axioms, and Maimonides, in MN I-74, describe the Kalām proofs for creation.

See also H. A. Wolfson, "Patristic Arguments Against the Eternity of the World," HTR 59 (1966): 351-67, reprinted in his Studies, 1:182-98; idem, "The Kalām Arguments for Creation in Saadia, Averroes, Maimonides, and St. Thomas," in Saadia Anniversary Volume, ed. B. Cohen (New York, 1943), 2:197-245; and H. A. Davidson, "John Philoponus as a Source of Medieval Islamic and Jewish Proofs of Creation," JAOS 89 (1969): 357-91.

11. MN I-71, p. 109a (Arabic, p. 124); II, 15-18, 25. In DE III-5, 99b, Bibago points out that the students of Maimonides believe that Aristotle did not demonstrate the eternity of the world and that creation is therefore a possibility. Also in II-3, 44a, Bibago says that, according to Maimonides, neither the eternity nor the creation of the world can be demonstrated. Gersonides, however, departed from Maimonides in this regard and said that it could be proved from teleology that the world was created, although matter was not created. MH VI-i-6 to 8. See also Yiṣḥaq Julius Guttmann, Ha-Pilosofiyah shel

ha-Yahaduth, trans Y. L. Barukh, ed. Ṣ. Wislavski (Jerusalem, 1963), p. 194, and Seymour Feldman, "Gersonides' Proofs for the Creation of the Universe," *PAAJR* 35 (1967); 113-37.

12. *DE* III-3, 86c-d; also II-3, 43d-44a and II-4, 49c. On creation being known only by tradition and faith, see I-3, 17d and II-6, 63a. Thomas Aquinas also said that neither the eternity nor the creation of the world can be proved. Whereas Maimonides, however, said that creation should be accepted through prophecy (*MN* II-16, p. 35a; Arabic, p. 204), Aquinas says it should be held on faith. *ST* I-xlvi-1, 2. Like Aquinas, Bibago uses the term "faith" (*'emunah*) in this regard. See n. 3 above.

13. *DE* II-4, 49c: bereshith bara' . . . hu' mofeth memuṣṣa[c] beyn haḥakhamah weha-emunah.

14. Bibago's rehearsals of the creation proof in terms of the principle of causality are in *DE* I-1, 5b; I-3, 17d; II-4, 49c; and II-6, 61a. In *ST* I-i-8, Thomas Aquinas says that one can construct valid proofs on premises known from faith and authority.

15. *DE* II-4, 49c: memmeṣi'u' hammeḥudash beqalluth nimraṣ navo' 'el meṣi'u' hammeḥadesh. For Isaac Arama (1420-1494), the proof of God's existence from the Torah principle of creation is so good that there is no further need for a philosophic proof. Sarah Heller Wilensky, *R. Yiṣḥaq Arama u-Mishnatho* (Jerusalem, 1956), pp. 90, 102.

16. *MN* II-31, pp. 65b-66a (Arabic, p. 253).

17. *MN* I-71, p. 109b; II-2, p. 17a (Arabic, pp. 125, 175). For a criticism of this latter passage, see Ḥasdai Crescas, *OH* I-ii-20, p. 21a. The conclusion is so obvious, in fact, that proofs for creation were usually taken by themselves as proofs for the existence of God. See Wolfson, "Kalām Arguments," pp. 230-31, 234.

In his review of Kalām theology in *Sefer ha-Kuzari*, V-18, third axiom, Judah Halevi interprets this principle of causality in terms of the Kalām principle of specification or determination.

18. *MN* I-35; I-72, p. 115b; II-16, 35a (Arabic, pp. 134, 204). Further, the phrase "at the first chance thought" is used to describe how quickly the doctrine of creation yields the conclusion that God exists. See n. 16 above. The same phrase, however, is used pejoratively in *MN* I-2, p. 15a (Arabic, p. 16), where Maimonides says that things are not as the vulgar first think them to be.

Bibago thus elevates tradition and calls it faith (*'emunah*), which is what Thomas Aquinas spoke about (see nn. 12 and 14). Bibago further describes this faith in terms that other Jewish philosophers usually reserved for prophecy (see nn. 3 and 12.) He is less concerned with the prophecy that accrues to the few and more concerned with the faith that is available to the entire people. While he has no specific discussion of prophecy in general, however, Bibago does devote a chapter to the unique character of Moses' prophecy, on which the faith is based. See II-6, 60b-67c. Bibago's concept of faith does seem to have a certain kinship to Judah Halevi's notion of prophecy in that both are the result of the divine influence upon the Jewish people. See, e.g., *DE* II-4, 49b, *Sefer ha-Kuzari*, I-95.

19. *DE* II-6, 61a. These three divine attributes mentioned here are the topics of the first three chapters in the *Derekh 'Emunah*. Isaac Arama also said that the Torah doctrine of creation teaches us the existence of the God of the Torah. Wilensky, *R. Yiṣḥaq Arama*, p. 90.

20. DE III-1, 73d.
21. That is, the First Commandment, Exod. 20:2 and Deut. 5:6.
22. DE I-3, 17d.
23. DE I-1, 6c; II-4, 52c; II-5, 56b; II-6, 62c; and III-4, 95b.
24. DE II-5, 53d and II-6, 62d.
25. DE II-4, 49b; mehathmadath hatenu[c]o' hashamayimiyo' hammoro' [c]al meṣi'utho.
26. DE III-2, 82d.
27. MN II-1(1), pp. 12b-14a (Arabic, pp. 169-71). In referring to this proof, Bibago usually mentions only the heavenly motions because it was generally accepted that motion and change in this lower world were caused by the motion of the spheres. The problem was to trace the celestial motion back to an immaterial, unmoved mover. Thomas Aquinas, who also used this as his first proof of God's existence, calls it a proof from motion. ST I-ii-3.
28. Wolfson, "Averroes' Lost Treatise," pp. 684-85, reprinted in his Studies, 1:403-04; idem, "Notes on Proofs of the Existence of God," pp. 588-90, reprinted in his Studies, 1:574-76. For a review of the various arguments on whether or not God moves the first sphere directly, see Gersonides, MH V-iii-12, pp. 45d-46a; Ḥasdai Crescas, OH IV-12, p. 91; Shalom, Neweh Shalom, II-8, pp. 35a-36a.
29. For example, DE II-5, 53d. See n. 24 above.
30. DE I-4, 31c.
31. DE I-4, 31b-c; III-1, 75c; and III-2, 80b. See also II-5, 57a.
32. DE II-4, 50b. Abraham Shalom, in his discussion of the question (see n. 28), also agrees that God moves the first sphere directly and says that this was Aristotle's opinion.
33. See n. 28. Agreeing with ibn Sīnā are al-Fārābī, according to Crescas and Albo (Sefer ha-[c]Iqqarim, ed. and trans. I. Husik [Philadelphia, 1929], III-3, p. 31), and al-Ghazālī, according to Shalom.
34. See al-Ghazālī, Tahāfut al-Falāsifah, ed. M. Bouyges (Beirut, 1927), IV-11, p. 138; referred to by Wolfson, "Averroes' Lost Treatise," p. 687, reprinted in his Studies, 1:406. See also Wolfson, Spinoza, 1:193-96.
35. DE I-4, 31c. See n. 31 above. Abraham Shalom notes that in MN I-70, I-72, and II-1 Maimonides says that God moves the highest sphere, whereas in II-4 he says that it is impossible that the Necessary Existent should move the highest sphere. MN I, pp. 104b, 114b; II, 13b-14a, 20b-21b (Arabic, pp. 119, 132-33, 171, 180), and Neweh Shalom, II-8, p. 35a. In the passage in I-70, Maimonides refers to the same verses to which Bibago refers, Ps. 68:5 and Deut. 33:26.
36. MN II-1(3), pp. 14b-15b (Arabic, pp. 172-73). Wolfson agrees that Maimonides did not believe God to be the proximate mover of the outermost sphere. Maimonides was nevertheless able to use the proof from motion, Wolfson explains, because of his unique theory that the celestial intelligences are not immovable and separate but are within the sphere and movable. H. A. Wolfson, "Notes on Proofs of the Existence of God," pp. 591-94, reprinted in his Studies, 1:578-80. An anonymous medieval Christian criticizes Maimonides for believing the intelligences to be within the spheres rather than external to them, as Thomas Aquinas thought. Isaac Husik, "An Anonymous Medieval Christian Critic of Maimonides," JQR, n.s. 2 (1911): 180-81.

37. OH I-iii-2.
38. Sefer ha-[c]Iqqarim, II-5, pp. 29-33. Abraham Shalom refers to both Maimonides' first proof, the Aristotelian one from motion, and his third proof, the one drawn from ibn Sīnā's demonstration of a necessarily existent Being. H. A. Davidson, The Philosophy of Abraham Shalom (Berkeley and Los Angeles, 1964), pp. 18-23.
39. DE II-6, 60d.
40. Wolfson, "Averroes' Lost Treatise," pp. 688-97, reprinted in his Studies, 1:407-16.
41. Ibid., pp. 688, 698-99.
42. MN I-34, p. 53; I-71, p. 110a (Arabic, pp. 50, 126).
43. DE III-2, 83a.
44. Ibid., 82d. See MN I-71, p. 110a.
45. DE I-4, 31b and III-1, 76b.
46. DE III-4, 95c.
47. DE I-1, 5b-c.
48. DE II-5, 57a.
49. Wolfson, Spinoza, 1:203.
50. DE I-1, 5b-c. This conservation argument was admitted by Ockham as a proof for God's existence. I Sent. ii-10, O. Also Étienne Gilson, History of Christian Philosophy in the Middle Ages (New York, 1955), pp. 497, 789.
51. DE I-3, 17b.
52. DE I-1, 7b.
53. Cf. DE I-3, 23c.
54. DE I-3, 17d.
55. Alexander Altmann, "The Delphic Maxim in Medieval Islam and Judaism," in his Studies in Religious Philosophy and Mysticism (Ithaca, N.Y., 1969), pp. 24-25.
56. DE I-3, 23c. See Altmann, "Delphic Maxim," in idem, Studies, pp. 1-6, 38.
57. DE I-3, 26c.
58. DE II-6, 63d.

Chapter Three
The Divine Attributes

1. Harry A. Wolfson, "Albinus and Plotinus on Divine Attributes," HTR 45 (1952): 118-19, 122, reprinted in his Studies in the History of Philosophy and Religion (ed. I. Twersky and G. H. Williams [Cambridge, Mass., 1973-77]), 1:117-18, 122.
2. Ibid., p. 117.
3. Harry A. Wolfson, Philo (Cambridge, Mass., 1962), 2:157. Maimonides differed from his predecessors in distinguishing the divine actions from God's causal relations to the world and in asserting of God only the actions (his fifth class of attributes), not the relations. MN I-52; Harry A. Wolfson, "The Aristotelian Predicables and Maimonides' Division of Attributes," in Essays and Studies in Memory of Linda R. Miller, ed. I. Davidson (New York, 1938), p. 227, reprinted in his Studies, 2:186-87.
4. Harry A. Wolfson, "Philosophical Implications of the Problem of Divine Attributes in the Kalām," JAOS 79 (1959): 74. Although Philo had derived the principle of the incomprehensibility of God from the scriptural concepts of God's unnamability and His unlikeness to

the world (Wolfson, *Philo*, 2:117-24), the first formal classification of negative attributes and the first use of them to reinterpret positive attributes all occur in Albinus and Plotinus. Wolfson, "Albinus," pp. 117, 129; idem, "Negative Attributes in the Church Fathers and the Gnostic Basilides," *HTR* 50 (1957): 147, reprinted in his *Studies*, 1:132-33.

5. *MN* I, 52-53, 58-59. On Maimonides' logical development of the theory of negative attributes, see Harry A. Wolfson, "Maimonides on Negative Attributes," in the *Louis Ginzberg Jubilee Volume on the Occasion of his Seventieth Birthday* (New York, 1945), p. 411, reprinted in Wolfson's *Studies*, 2:195.

6. Thomas Aquinas, *ST* I-xiii-1; Crescas, *OH* I-iii-3; Yiṣḥaq Julius Guttmann, *Dath u-Mada^{c}*, ed. S. Bergman and N. Rotenstreich; trans. S. Esh (Jerusalem, 1956), p. 186. Shlomo Pines notes a similar reaction in the east to ibn Sīnā's theory of negative attributes on the part of Abu'l-Barakāt, who also advocates essential attributes. "Studies in Abu'l-Barakāt al-Baghdadi's Poetics and Metaphysics," *Scripta Hierosolymitana* 6 (1960): 169-71.

7. Abraham Shalom, *Sefer Neweh Shalom* (Venice, 1575), XII-i-3; Isaac Abravanel, *Rosh 'Amanah* (Tel Aviv, 1958), ch. 10, pp. 55-56. See also Herbert A. Davidson, *The Philosophy of Abraham Shalom* (Berkeley and Los Angeles, 1964), pp. 36-37; Alexander Altmann, "The Divine Attributes," *Judaism* 15 (1966): 57.

8. *DE* I-4, 29a.

9. Ibid.: lefi shehatto'ar wehammetu'ar ra'uy sheyihyu b' devarim. Also III-5, 99c. As part of his denial of essential attributes, Maimonides says that the attribute is not the essence of what it describes but something added to the essence, "shehatto'ar biliti ^{c}eṣem hammetu'ar weshehu' ^{c}inyan nosaf le^{c}eṣem." *MN* I-51, p. 71a.

Further, Maimonides affirms later that "if you say that God, may He be exalted, is a certain substratum upon which certain borne things are superposed and that this substratum is not like these borne things, the utmost of our apprehension would be, on the basis of this belief, polytheism and nothing else. For every substratum bearing things is undoubtedly, according to its definition, a duality, even if it be one in its existence. For the notion of the substratum is different from that of the adjunct borne by it." *MN* I-60 (p. 145 in the Pines translation).

10. *DE* III-5, 99c. On Bibago's phrase "ne^{c}elam mimmenu takhlith hahe^{c}elam," cf. Crescas, *OH* I-iii-5, 26b: mahutho yith' betakhlith hahe^{c}elam. This is from one of the passages taken over almost intact from Bibago by Abravanel in his *Rosh 'Amanah*, ch. 10, pp. 55-56.

11. *DE* I-4, 29a. Crescas also singles out these two attributes, in addition to existence and unity, as negations of their privations. Crescas concludes, however, that as opposites of privations these are positive, affirmative attributes, not negative attributes. *OH* I-iii-3, 25a.

For an attempt to resolve the inconsistencies in Crescas's theory of the divine attributes, see Harry A. Wolfson, "Crescas on the Problem of Divine Attributes," *JQR*, n.s. 7 (1916-17): 200-210, reprinted in his *Studies*, 2:316-26. For a presentation of the problem, see Yiṣḥaq Julius Guttmann, *Ha-Pilosofiyah shel ha-Yahaduth*, ed. S. Wislavski, trans. Y. L. Barukh (Jerusalem, 1963), pp. 211-13.

12. *DE* III-5, 99c-d.

13. Cf. MN I-58, 86a (Arabic, p. 92); Crescas, OH I-iii-1, end, 22a; iii-3, 24b. On the latter, however, see n. 11 above.

14. DE III-5, 99c. This is Bibago's only reference in the Derekh 'Emunah to the theme of essence and existence.

15. Cf. Abravanel, Rosh 'Amanah, ch. 20, p. 120. Abravanel, however, uses the word 'emeth for truth instead of ṣodeq, and the identification of truth and existence seems to be in a context different from what we find in ibn Rushd.

16. "Existence in the nature of things is a logical concept which affirms the conformity of a thing outside the soul with what is inside the soul. Its meaning is synonymous with the true, . . . [Cf. Aristotle, Met. IV-7, 1011b26.] The term 'existence' is used in two senses; the first synonymous with the true, . . . The second sense stands in relation to the existing things as their genus, in the way the existent is divided into the ten categories, and into substance and accident. . . . For the term 'existence' is used in two meanings, the former signifies the true and the latter the opposite of non-existence, and in this latter sense it is that which is divided into the ten categories and is like their genus. This essential sense which refers to the things which exist in the real world outside the soul is prior to the sense it has in the existents of second intention, . . . the existent which has the meaning of the 'true' is something in the mind, namely that a thing is outside the soul in conformity with what it is inside the soul, . . ." Tahāfut al-Tahāfut: The Incoherence of the Incoherence, trans. S. van den Bergh (London, 1954), 1:179-80. See also TAT VIII, 392:8-393:3, and Die Metaphysik des Averroes, trans. M. Horten (Halle, 1912), I-1, p. 9.

These two senses of "existence" in ibn Rushd are two of the three or four senses of "being" in Aristotle's Metaphysics. "The terms 'being' and 'non-being' are employed firstly with reference to the categories, and secondly with reference to the potency or actuality of these or their non-potency or non-actuality, and thirdly in the sense of true and false. . . . he who thinks the separated to be separated and the combined to be combined has the truth, while he whose thought is in a state contrary to that of the objects is in error." Met. IX-10, 1051a34-b5. (Trans. W. D. Ross, second edition, in The Works of Aristotle, ed. W. D. Ross, vol. 8 [Oxford: Clarendon Press, 1928].) In Met. V-7, 1017a7-b9, Aristotle lists four usages of the word "being." See Wolfson, "Crescas on Divine Attributes," p. 192, n. 86, reprinted in his Studies, 2:308.

The second of the three Aristotelian usages of "being" in the above quote, i.e., potency or actuality, is referred to by Joseph Albo in his Sefer ha-ᶜIqqarim, IV-43, ed. and trans. I. Husik (Philadelphia, 1929), pp. 430-32. The first and the third are, as we have seen, the two senses of "existence" adopted by ibn Rushd and his followers. Albalag, for example, refers to these two senses of "existence." Georges Vajda, Isaac Albalag (Paris, 1960), pp. 37-38. Aquinas also uses this twofold meaning of "existence." See De Ente et Essentia, nos. 3-6; ST I-iii-4.

Concerning the expression of this distinction in Hebrew, Salomon Munk brings the following quote from a Hebrew version of ibn Rushd's Epitome of Metaphysics: shem hannimṣa' shav 'el shene 'elu haᶜinyanim levad . . . 'el haṣṣodeq we'el mah shehu' nimṣa' ḥuṣ lasekhel. Le guide des égarés (Paris, 1856-66), 1:231, on MN I-57. Albalag says that the second reference of "existence" is to "^{c}eṣem haddavar mammash." Vajda, *Albalag*, pp. 37-38.

17. *TAT* V, 304:13-305:5. Narboni, in his *Be'ur la-"Sefer Moreh Nevukhim,"* ed. J. Goldenthal (Vienna, 1852), p. 9a, on *MN* I-57, asserts the identity of essence and existence and brings this opinion in the name of ibn Rushd. Cf. Aristotle, *Met*. IV-2.

18. Narboni, *Be'ur* on *MN* I-57. See the analysis of Narboni's criticism in Alexander Altmann, "Essence and Existence in Maimonides," in his *Studies in Religious Philosophy and Mysticism* (Ithaca, N.Y., 1969), pp. 121-22, originally published in the *Bulletin of the John Rylands Library*, vol. 35, no. 2 (Manchester, 1953).

19. *DE* III-5, 101d.

20. *DE* III-5, 99d: shenishlol mimmenu haribuy hammispari . . . ki 'eyn ha'aḥduth davar te'ori 'elaw u-lazeh hu' 'eḥad welo' be'aḥduth. Also 101c. Crescas referred to unity as the absence of plurality. *OH* I-iii-3, 22b. Cf., however, n. 11 above. Bibago's denial that unity is adjectival may refer to Crescas's description of it as essential. Maimonides says that only "one" can express the negation of the many, and in describing the divine unity, the ibn Tibbon Hebrew translation of Maimonides uses the phrase "'eḥad welo' be'aḥduth." *MN* I-57, 85a. On the origin of phrases such as this in al-Naẓẓam, see Wolfson, "Philosophical Implications," pp. 76-77. Joseph Albo also gives a negative meaning of unity in *Sefer ha-^{c}Iqqarim*, II-10, p. 58.

21. *DE* III-5, 101d: she'eyno nofel taḥat hammispar. Although Maimonides says that, because of the limitations of language, we can express the negation of many only by "one," neither "many" nor "one" can in fact be attributed to God. *MN* I-57, 84b-85a (Arabic, p. 90).

22. *DE* III-1, 74a. On the dual meaning of "one" as both uniqueness and simplicity in Philo, al-Fārābī, ibn Sīnā, and al-Ghazālī, see Harry A. Wolfson, "Avicenna, Algazali and Averroes on Divine Attributes," *Homenaje a Millas-Vallicrosa*, vol. 2 (Barcelona, 1956), pp. 545-47, reprinted in his *Studies*, 1:143-45. Crescas also describes this dual meaning of "one" in *OH* I-iii-4, 26a.

23. *DE* II-6, 60d-61a.

24. *DE* II-6, 60d: hahekhraḥi hammeṣi'uth hu' haddavar 'asher 'i 'efshar sheyimaṣe' ^{c}al zulat haṣṣad 'asher hu' bo. This passage is the only one in the *Derekh 'Emunah* in which Bibago refers to God as the Necessary Existent. At first he uses the term *hahekhraḥi hammeṣi'uth* to refer to necessary existence, and then he uses *hammeḥuyyav hammeṣi'uth*. Moses al-Lawi uses the word *hekhraḥi* to refer to ibn Rushd's description of anything already in existence as a "compulsory" existent. Its opposite, the possible (*'efshari*), is what is not yet existent and so may or may not be. Harry A. Wolfson, "Averroes' Lost Treatise on the Prime Mover," *HUCA* 23, pt. 1 (1950-51): 700-701, reprinted in his *Studies*, 1:419-20.

Bibago's proof for the divine unity from the concept of necessary existence is somewhat like the first half of a proof from necessary existence referred to by ibn Rushd in the name of ibn Sīnā and al-Ghazālī. It argues that if necessary existence is a peculiar characteristic specifying the existent like a proper name, there cannot then be two of them, just as if Amr is a man because he is Amr, Zaid cannot also be a man. *TAT* V, 287:5-12, 292:1-8. The second half of ibn Rushd's proof, which deals with the possibility that necessary existence might be a general characteristic, is listed by

Bibago as his fourth proof. Moses Narboni and Shem Ṭov ben Joseph ibn Shem Ṭov, in their commentaries on MN II-1 (pp. 25b-26a and 15b, respectively), refer to this proof of ibn Rushd.

25. In MN I-75 (p. 223 in the Pines translation), Maimonides calls this "the method of differing from one another," which, he adds, is a "philosophic and demonstrative method" that he himself uses later in II-1, p. 16a. Cf. the paraphrase from al-Fārābī's Sefer Hathḥaloth in ibn Kaspi's commentary on MN II-1 (p. 90). The proof usually argues that, since two deities must have something in which they differ and something in common, each would have to be composite and neither could therefore be the first being. Bibago, however, asserts only that a second deity must differ somehow from the first.

26. Bibago here seems to mean that the necessarily existent would not be necessarily existent in respect of its essence if its necessary existence were not a peculiar characteristic but were common to itself and a second necessarily existent. Maimonides uses the concept of the necessary of existence in virtue only of itself in MN II-1, p. 15b (Arabic, p. 173).

27. DE II-6, 60d. See n. 24 above.

28. Deut. 6:4.

29. MN I-61, 92a; I-63, 95b (Arabic, pp. 101, 106).

30. DE II-6, 60d. Cf. MN I-72, 110b, 112b; II-1, 16a (Arabic, pp. 127, 130, 174). Crescas, OH I-iii-4, 26a, also has a proof for the divine unity based on the world being like one individual.

31. Bibago in this second proof switches back from the terminology of the "necessarily existent" that he had used in the first proof to the Aristotelian terminology of the "mover" that he more frequently uses.

32. On the difference in the matters of the upper and lower worlds, see MN I-72, 111a; II-26, 52b (Arabic, pp. 128, 232). In II-19, 43b (Arabic, p. 215), Maimonides further distinguishes the matter of the spheres from that of the stars, so that there are for him three matters altogether.

33. MN I-75, 129b (Arabic, p. 156). Ibn Khaldun also refers to the well-known Kalām proof of the divine unity from "mutual antagonism." See Harry A. Wolfson, "Ibn Khaldun on Attributes and Predestination," in Wolfson's Religious Philosophy: A Group of Essays (New York, 1965), pp. 180-81.

34. DE II-6, 61a.

35. Ibid. The assumption of a characteristic common to two deities often leads to the conclusion that both deities would then have to be composite instead of simple. See for example MN II-1. 15b, 16a (Arabic, p. 173), TAT 292:1-8, and al-Fārābī's Sefer Hathḥaloth as paraphrased by ibn Kaspi in his commentary on MN II-1, p. 90. In MN II-1, 15b, and TAT 292:1-8, the characteristic posited as common to two deities is necessity of existence, so that in these two cases the proof for the divine unity that posits a common characteristic is combined with the proof for the divine unity based on the divine necessity of existence. See n. 24 above. In MN II-1, 16b, and in al-Fārābī, this proof for the divine unity that posits a common characteristic is combined with what Maimonides called "the method of differing from one another." See n. 24 above. In MN II-1, 16b, as here in Bibago's fourth proof for the divine unity, the characteristic common to the two deities is that of being a deity.

36. DE III-5, 100c: 'Eyno geshem ki kol geshem 'amnam bamaqom. . . . Also DE III-5, 101d. Bibago follows Aristotle's definition of place as the boundary of the containing body at which it is in contact with the contained body. Physics IV-4, 212a5-8. Cf. Albo, Sefer ha-ᶜIqqarim, II-17, pp. 101, 104.

37. DE III-5, 99d: Be'amarnu she'eyno geshem hu' shelilath haharkavah. . . . Also 101c. In medieval philosophy, simplicity, indivisibility, incorporeality, and unity all came to mutually imply one another. Wolfson, Philo, 2:98-101, 149.

38. MN II-1, 16b (Arabic, p. 175). S. Munk calls attention to this twofold nature of Maimonides' proof in his comments to this passage in his Le guide des égarés, 2:46. It should be noted that two of the five kinds of plurality mentioned by ibn Rushd (TAT 296-302) are the divisibility of body into matter and form and the plurality of attributes, accidental or otherwise. See also Wolfson, Philo, 2:125.

39. MN I-76, the second method, p. 132 (Arabic, p. 160); II-intro., prop. 22, p. 9b (Arabic, p. 167). This was also the view attributed to ibn Sīnā. See DE I-4, 29b, and Munk, ed., Le guide, 2:20, on prop. 22.

40. DE I-4, 29b; Munk, ed., Le guide, 2:20; and the "Commentary" of Shem Ṭov ben Joseph ibn Shem Ṭov on MN II-introduction, p. 9b (on prop. 22) and II-1, p. 16b.

The dimensions of body were considered accidents of body. See the "Commentary" of Shem Ṭov ben Joseph ibn Shem Ṭov and the "Commentary" of Efodi on MN I-76, the second method, p. 132b. This is why Maimonides concludes that the divisibility of body into dimensions implies that it has accidents.

41. DE III-5, 99d: Be'amarnu shehu' qadmon hu' shelilatho min hahawayyah wehahefsed. Also 101c. Cf. MN I-57, 85a (Arabic, p. 90) and Crescas, OH I-iii-3, 24b.

42. DE III-5, 100c. On the other hand, Bibago had said at the beginning of his book that, in contrast to the transience of beings in this world, it is the permanence of the celestial beings that indicates the divine power. DE I-1, 3c.

43. DE III-5, 101d: U-ve'ama' shehu' qadmon lekhol qadmon be'er she'eyno nofel taḥath hazzeman we'eyno mugbal bo. . . . Cf. MN I-57, 85a: Lo' shehu' yithᶜaleh nofel taḥath hazzeman.

Immediately preceding this Maimonides says that we speak loosely when we predicate qadmon of God because it should be predicated only of things to which time attaches. See also MN II-1, 14a (Arabic, p. 171), the end of the first proof for the existence of God. See also Shalom, Neweh Shalom, VII-ii-7, p. 119b. Wolfson calls this concept of eternity as beyond time Platonic, as opposed to the Aristotelian concept of eternity as endless time. Harry A. Wolfson, The Philosophy of Spinoza (Cambridge, Mass., 1934), 1:358-69. On qadmon and neṣaḥ as eternal a parte ante and a parte post, see Judah Halevi, Sefer ha-Kuzari, V-18, fourth and fifth axioms; Albo, Sefer ha-ᶜIqqarim, II-18, pp. 109-10; Abravanel, Rosh 'Amanah, ch. 16, pp. 93-94. In DE III-5, 99d, 100c, and 101d, Bibago uses qadmon; in III-1, 74a, and III-5, 100c, he uses neṣaḥ.

44. DE III-5, 99d-100a.

45. DE III-5, 99d.

46. DE III-5, 100a.

47. DE I-4, 29a. On the threefold division of the divine attributes in Bibago, see Avraham Nuriel, "Mishnatho ha-Pilosofith shel R. Avraham ben Shem Ṭov Bibago," (Ph.D. diss., Hebrew University, 1975), pp. 45-47. For another threefold division of the divine attributes, cf. Judah Halevi, Sefer ha-Kuzari, II-2.

48. DE I-3, 17c.

49. MN I-52, 74b; I-53, 77b; I-60, 90a; III-20, 31a (Arabic, pp. 80, 83, 98, 350). Bibago had also said in DE I-2, pp. 9c, 11c-d, that God's attributes are not additional to His essence. The sixteenth-century Kabbalist Solomon Alkabeṣ also emphasized that God's attributes are nothing added to His essence. He said that this doctrine is one of the approaches of the Kalām to divine attributes and that the doctrine can be found in Bibago's Derekh 'Emunah. See his 'Ayeleth 'Ahavim (Venice, 1552), p. 49a. (I wish to thank Mrs. Berakha Zak for calling my attention to this reference by Alkabeṣ to Bibago.)

50. See the beginning of this chapter.

51. DE I-3, 17c: Mehadderakhim hashelemi' 'asher lo yith' hekhraḥ sheyavo'u pe^{c}ulo' shelemoth wehadderakhim hen hemmah hatte'arim ha^{c}aṣmutiyyim. . . . See also DE I-3, 26c and I-1, 4b.

52. MN I-54, p. 80a-b: Happe'uloth . . . hem hem hadderakhim. . . .

53. DE I-2, 9b-c: Wehadderakhim hem haqqinyanim wehaṣṣuroth hanniqnoth banefesh. Also DE III-4, 89d-90a: Hadderakhim hem hammidoth wehatte'arim. . . . See ch. 6, n. 89, on whether God is a soul.

54. DE I-3, 26a; III-4, 90a.

55. OH I-iii-3. See nn. 5 and 6 above. In his commentary on MN I-51, pp. 71b-72a, Isaac Abravanel identifies Crescas's position on essential attributes with the position, also rejected by Maimonides, of those who say that the divine attributes are neither the divine essence nor something added to this essence.

56. Sefer ha-^{c}Iqqarim, II-30. See also Y. J. Guttmann, Ha-Pilosofiyah, pp. 228-29; Altmann, "Divine Attributes," p. 57. Bibago's contemporary Abraham Shalom, in his defense of Maimonides' theory of the divine attributes, utilizes the view of ibn Rushd and Gersonides. H. A. Davidson, Abraham Shalom, p. 32.

57. DE I-3, 17c; OH I-iii-3, pp. 23, 24b-26a.

58. OH I-iii-3, 24b; MN I-54, 80a-b (Arabic, p. 84). See n. 52 above. Crescas's pupil Joseph Albo also followed Maimonides in referring the derakhim of Exod. 33:13 to the divine actions. Sefer ha-^{c}Iqqarim, II-22, pp. 134-35.

59. OH I-iii-3, 24b; MN I-54, 79b-80a (Arabic, pp. 83-84).

60. DE I-3, 17c. See n. 51 above.

61. DE I-3, 26a; OH I-iii-3, 22b.

62. DE I-3, 26a; MN I-54, 79b-80a (Arabic, pp. 83-84).

63. DE II-7, 70d: Haṭṭov wehannimṣah yithhafkhu ki mah shehu' nimṣah hu' ṭov u-mah shehu' ṭov hu' nimṣah. . . . Also DE I-1, 4a: Haṭṭov wehammeṣi'uth yithhafkhu. Cf. MN III-10, 13b: kol meṣi'uth ṭov. Also 14a.

64. OH I-iii-3, 24b. Also Y. J. Guttmann, Ha-Pilosofiyah, p. 213.

65. DE I-3, 27c: Hu' haṭṭov hahehlaṭi. Cf. OH II-vi-4, 60b: Haṭṭov hammuḥlaṭ. In DE II-6, 63d, Bibago speaks of three types of "good": Hari'shon ṭov mo^{c}il . . . wehasheni ṭov ^{c}arev . . . wehashelishi . . . ṭov beheḥleṭ.

66. DE I-1, 7c: Ṣedqo weṭovo 'asher hem ᶜaṣmutho. Also DE III-1, 73b. Cf. OH III, introduction, 61b.

67. DE I-2, 8c. Cf. OH III-i-5, 69a.

68. DE III-5, 100b; Sefer ha-ᶜIqqarim, II-22, pp. 130-33.

69. In his "Beth ha-Shem": Ki midothaw wete'araw . . . hem ᶜaṣmutho yith' wekhen ra'ithi bedivre har' Avraham. . . . See also DE III-1, 73b.

70. Pines, "Scholasticism," pp. 38-39. Crescas's emphasis upon the infinite in the divine nature may in turn reflect the influence of Duns Scotus or one of his disciples. Ibid.; also idem, "Studies in Abu'l Barakāt al-Baghdadi's Poetics and Metaphysics," Scripta Hierosolymitana 6 (1960): 170. Infinity, originally a negative concept for the Greeks, became a positive perfection of transcendent being in the philosophy of Henry of Ghent. Étienne Gilson, History of Christian Philosophy in the Middle Ages (New York, 1955), pp. 448-49.

71. OH I-iii-3, pp. 23b-24b. Also Pines, "Scholasticism," p. 38; Wolfson, "Crescas on Divine Attributes," p. 204, reprinted in his Studies, 2:320.

72. MN III-20, 30b-31a (Arabic, p. 340).

73. DE I-2, 11c, 12d. Bibago's contemporary Abraham Shalom also adds an emphasis upon infinity to his Maimonidean philosophy. He lists three problems in the assertion of essential divine attributes. Two of them, the problem of plurality in the divine nature and the problem of similarity to creatures, are found in Maimonides. The third problem, how infinite divine attributes can be comprehended by finite minds, is not in Maimonides. Neweh Shalom, XII-i-3, 201a. Also Wolfson, "Crescas on Divine Attributes," p. 10, reprinted in his Studies, 2:256. In V-7, 73b, Shalom quotes a Hermetic source on the impossibility of the finite describing the infinite deity.

In a similar vein, Shalom in I-vii, 7a, reformulates the proof from motion and says that the infinite motion of the celestial spheres points to an infinite mover. In IX-i, 152b, he says that Maimonides explains that we can infer an infinite cause from the continued ordering of the sphere. See also H. A. Davidson, Abraham Shalom, pp. 18-19.

74. OH I-i-12; Harry A. Wolfson, Crescas' Critique of Aristotle (Cambridge, 1929), p. 272. Also OH I-ii-15, 20a and II-iii-2, 40b.

75. DE I-i, 3c. Bibago also uses the terms yekholeth and ᶜoṣem to describe the divine infinity of power. He at great length interprets all of Ps. 145 in terms of these two senses of the divine infinity. Wolfson, Crescas' Critique, p. 613; Albo, Sefer ha-ᶜIqqarim, II-25 and 26, pp. 149-53, 163.

76. Wolfson suggests that the distinction is borrowed from ibn Rushd. Crescas' Critique, p. 613. Bibago's most frequent Hebrew expression for the infinite is bilti baᶜal takhlith. He uses the phrase 'eyn sof adverbially. DE I-2, 13c-d, 14a; I-4, 30d, 31d; II-7, 68a-b. Avraham Nuriel interprets Bibago's entire theory of divine attributes in terms of infinity and finitude. "Mishnatho ha-Pilosofith, p. 40.

Chapter Four
The Divine Will

1. Gordon Leff, Bradwardine and the Pelagians (Cambridge, 1957), pp. 8-11. In this regard it is interesting to note that Étienne Gilson

detects in the work of Gregory of Rimini, the early fourteenth-century thinker, a possible collusion between nominalism and a certain Augustinianism. See Étienne Gilson, History of Christian Philosophy in the Middle Ages (New York, 1955), p. 502.

2. Leff, Bradwardine, p. 17.

3. Yiṣḥaq Julius Guttmann, Ha-Pilosofiyah shel ha-Yahaduth, ed. Ṣ. Wislavski, trans. Y. L. Barukh (Jerusalem, 1963), pp. 180, 187, 221, 229.

4. Ben Zion Netanyahu, The Marranos of Spain from the Late XIVth to the Early XVIth Century According to Contemporary Hebrew Sources (New York, 1966), pp. 113-14, 115-16. In addition to Crescas's 'Or ha-Shem, the authors and works discussed by Netanyahu are Shem Ṭov ibn Shem Ṭov's Sefer ha-'Emunoth, Simon ben Ṣemaḥ Duran's 'Ohev Mishpaṭ, and Joseph Albo's Sefer ha-ᶜIqqarim.

5. Netanyahu says that in the last third of the fifteenth century, the topic of creation had replaced divine providence as a major issue in the work of Spanish-Jewish thinkers such as Abraham Shalom, Isaac Arama, and Bibago. Marranos, p. 136, n. 2. For Bibago at least this would not seem to hold true, for only a small chapter of the Derekh 'Emunah is devoted to the topic of creation (III-3, 86b-89c), whereas the entire first third of the book deals with the divine providence.

6. MN III-20, 31a (Arabic, p. 350). In MN III-23, 36a (Arabic, p. 360), Maimonides refers to governance, providence, and purpose, governance having replaced knowledge in the triad. On numerous occasions, however, Maimonides says that governance requires knowledge. See MN II-5, 22b; III-17, 23b; and III-19, 28b (Arabic, pp. 181, 336, and 346). In the third book of the Moreh Nevukhim, chapters 13, 14, and 25 deal with the divine purpose, chapters 16, 19, 20, and 21 with the divine knowledge, and chapters 15, 17, 18, 23, and 24 with the divine providence.

7. These three topics are also three of the six topics that are discussed by Crescas and that show, according to Netanyahu, that Crescas's system is centered around the theme of the divine providence. Netanyahu, Marranos, pp. 113-14.

8. DE, I-1, 2c.

9. Ibid. Bibago spells out the logic of his arguments with numerous syllogisms. A similar emphasis upon logic as opposed to metaphysics seems to have been characteristic of fourteenth-century Christian scholasticism. Leff, Bradwardine, pp. 8, 16-18.

10. This is noted by Ḥava Fraenkel-Goldschmidt in her edition of Josel of Rosheim's Sefer ha-Miqnah (Jerusalem, 1970), pp. 47-48, nn. 16, 18. Written originally in Regensburg in 1546 by the lay head of German Jewry, this work incorporates large sections of Bibago's Derekh 'Emunah.

11. For example, Saadia Gaon, Sefer ha-'Emunoth weha-Deᶜoth, IV-introduction, 1, and 2; IX-1.

12. Enneads, III-i-7, 9; ii-1, 2.

13. Enneads, V-iii-12, ed. P. Henry and H. R. Schwyzer (Paris, 1959), 2:320. S. MacKenna's English translation (London [1962], 3rd ed. rev.) has a slightly different rendering here, evidently reading "proumethēthe" instead of "prouthumēthe." Although MacKenna's translation is based on the text edited by R. Volkmann (Leipzig, 1884), the latter has the same reading in this passage as Henry and Schwyzer.

Henry and Schwyzer quote in English translation a parallel text from the Epistola de Scientia Divina also indicating that the First Agent would be defective if volition came between Him and His actions.

14. Enneads, V-viii-7. Also III-ii-1 and the note thereon by A. H. Armstrong in the Loeb Classical Library edition (Cambridge, Mass.: Harvard University Press, 1967), pp. 44-45.

15. Abū Naṣr Muḥammad al-Fārābī, Kitāb al-Siyāsat al-Madaniyyah (Hyderabad, 1927), p. 23; Abū ᶜAlī al-Ḥusain ibn Sīnā (Avicenna), Kitāb al-Shifā': al-Ilāhiyyāt, ed. G. C. Anawati et al. (Cairo, 1960), VIII-7, p. 366.

16. Ibn Sīnā, Kitāb al-Shifā', pp. 363-64.

17. Sefer ha-Kuzari, I-1.

18. TAT III, p. 148, XI, p. 426. Cf. ST I-xix-1, obj. 2; also the appendix to pt. 1 of Spinoza's Ethics on the implication of an imperfection in God if He works to obtain an end.

19. For a presentation of the view that Maimonides agrees with the philosophers, see Shlomo Pines's "Introduction" to his translation of Maimonides' Guide of the Perplexed (Chicago, 1964), pp. cxxvii-cxxix.

20. Aristotle, Nicomachean Ethics III-1, 1109b35-1110a2, 1111a22-24. See Harry A. Wolfson, Philo (Cambridge, Mass., 1962), 1:434-35, or "Philo on Free Will and the Historical Influence of His View," HTR 35 (1942): 148-49.

21. Aristotle, Metaphysics V-5, 1015a26-b3, 9-11. The Greek word is ánagkaîon.

22. This has been called the relative concept of freedom. Harry A. Wolfson, "St. Augustine and the Pelagian Controversy," reprinted in his Religious Philosophy: A Group of Essays (New York, 1965), pp. 159-60, 172-75.

23. Enneads, VI-viii-13. Plotinus uses thélema and boúlesis to refer to the will. Spinoza also associates will and necessity, although not in exactly the same sense. Ethics, pt. 1, prop. 32.

24. TAF V, p. 157.

25. MN II-20, p. 46a (Arabic, p. 219).

26. Georges Vajda, Isaac Albalag (Paris, 1960), p. 68.

27. TAT III, p. 160; XI, pp. 438, 441, 444.

28. Kitāb Nihāyat al-Iqdām fi ᶜIlm al-Kalām, ed. and trans. A. Guillaume (London, 1934), ch. 18, p. 397 (English section, pp. 126-27).

29. MN III-17, the third opinion, pp. 23b-24a (Arabic, pp. 336-37); III-23, Ṣophar's opinion, attributed by Maimonides to the Ashᶜariyya, p. 35a (Arabic, p. 358); III-25, p. 38a (Arabic, p. 366); III-26, p. 39b (Arabic, p. 368).

30. MN II-20, p. 46a (Arabic, p. 219). "Purpose" is used here as the English translation for the Arabic qaṣd, usually translated into Hebrew as kawwanah.

31. MN III-17, pp. 23b-24a (Arabic, pp. 336-37); III-25, p. 38b (Arabic, p. 366). Maimonides does not identify the group about which he is speaking in III-25 as the Ashᶜariyya, but it is clear from his description of the Ashᶜariyya in III-17 that it is this sect that he has in mind in III-25. "Final end" is used here as the English translation for the Arabic ghāyat, usually translated into Hebrew as takhlith.

32. MN III-17, p. 24a (Arabic, p. 337).

33. Al-Shahrastānī, Kitāb Nihāyat, p. 397.

34. For example, MN II-19, p. 39a (Arabic, p. 210); II-20, p. 46a (Arabic, p. 218); II-21, p. 47b (Arabic, p. 221).

35. P. 104a (Arabic, p. 117).

36. P. 38 (Arabic, pp. 365-66).

37. Pp. 18b-19a (Arabic, p. 326). On the apparent contradiction between Maimonides' espousal of an ultimate end to existence in I-69 and III-25 and his denial of the same in III-13, see Z. Diesendruck, "Die Teleologie bei Maimonides," HUCA 5 (1928): 415-534.

38. P. 16b (Arabic, p. 323).

39. DE I-1, 7b.

40. For example, I-1, 7c: shegazrah ḥakhmatho bireṣono.

41. DE I-1, 2c.

42. DE I-1, 2d.

43. Ibid.: po^{c}el beṭeva^{c}, po^{c}el beraṣon.

44. Ibid.; also 3a.

45. DE I-1, 3a: po^{c}el beḥiyyuv.

46. Ibid.

47. DE I-1, 4d: lihyoth happo^{c}el beṭeva^{c} po^{c}el ḥaser.

48. DE I-1, 5a, 5b. On 4b Bibago interprets Ps. 145:14 as a proof that God is not a natural agent because He is said there to raise up those fallen and bowed by nature.

49. DE I-1, 4c: geder haraṣon sheyukhal ^{c}al davar we^{c}al ḥilufo.

50. DE I-1, 4d. On the "now," see Aristotle, Physics IV, 10-11, 13; MH VI-i-21; Pines, "Scholasticism," pp. 9-12. Bibago returns to the concept of the "now" in I-2, 10a-b; II-6, 61b; and III-3, 87b, d.

51. DE I-1, 4d; I-3, 18c. Saadia Gaon had said that the dualist heresy arose because of the denial of the possibility that two opposing acts could originate from one author. In his answer to this contention of the dualists, Saadia cites examples of persons performing opposite acts. Sefer ha-'Emunoth, I-3, the beginning of the fifth theory about the origin of the universe. Persons, of course, are voluntary agents in Bibago's classification. Spinoza, in Ethics, I-33, argues that things could not have been produced by God in any other manner because if they had been different, having been produced necessarily, there might be two or more gods, which is absurd.

52. DE I-1, 4d. Simon ben Ṣemaḥ Duran (1361-1444), in his Sefer Magen 'Avoth (Livorno, 1785), I-2, p. 4b, also records a story, with some different details, about King Shabur of Persia executing a dualist heretic Minai. Duran does not say that this dualism arose because of the belief that one agent cannot produce opposite effects, but he does specify that one of the deities produced good and the other evil. Like Bibago, he also concludes that it is because of this heretic that those who believe in two deities are called minim, just as other heretics are called 'epiqursim because of the man Epicurus.

Joseph Albo, in his Sefer ha-^{c}Iqqarim, ed. and trans. I. Husik (Philadelphia, 1929), II-13, p. 74, does not report any stories about King Shabur, but he does associate Mani's belief in two principles, one good and the other evil, with the belief of the ancients that a plurality including opposite effects could not come from one source. Like Duran and later Bibago, he says that Mani's followers are called minim, just as the followers of Epicurus, who denied the divine existence and providence, are called 'epiqursim.

Elijah Levita (1468-1549), in the entry under min in his Tishbi, says that the books of the Greeks speak of an irreligious man Mani and that his followers are called *minim*, just as *'epiqursim* are so called because of the man Epicurus. Levita's entry was reproduced by David de Pomis in his *Ṣemaḥ David*, and as late as the nineteenth century Moses Israel Landau, in his edition of the *ᶜArukh*, derived the word *min* from Mani.

Mani was born in Babylonia around 216 and was executed around 276. His syncretistic faith flourished under the tolerant reign of the Sassanid King Shapur I of Persia. On Mani and his doctrines, see Geo Widengren, *Mani and Manichaeism*, trans. C. Kessler (New York: 1965).

Many scholars agree that at least some of the numerous references to *minim* in the older rabbinic literature refer to dualistic and heretical Gnostics. See Gershom G. Scholem, *Major Trends in Jewish Mysticism* (New York, 1954), p. 359, n. 24; idem, *Jewish Gnosticism, Merkabah Mysticism and Talmudic Tradition* (New York, 1965), p. 84; George F. Moore, *Judaism in the First Centuries of the Christian Era: The Age of the Tannaim*, 3 vols. (Cambridge, Mass., 1927-30), 3:68; Saul Lieberman, "How Much Greek in Jewish Palestine?" in *Biblical and Other Studies*, ed. A. Altmann (Cambridge, Mass., 1963), p. 135.

The word *min* is used to refer to dualists or polytheists in Mishnah Sanhedrin 4:5, B.T. Hullin 87b, Genesis Rabba 8:8, and J.T. Berakhoth 9. According to Maimonides in his *Mishneh Torah*, "Hilkhoth Teshuvah," 3:7, one of the five types of *min* is he who believes that the world is governed by two or more rulers.

53. *DE* I-1, 4d: Sheshem 'epiqurus nigzar me'Epiqurus 'ish 'eḥad qadum.

54. *DE* I-1, 4b. Bibago refers here to Ps. 145:15. On the relationship between being changeable and inclining to either of two opposites, see Thomas Aquinas, *ST* I-xix-7, obj. 4.

55. *DE* I-1, 6b: zeh hahishtanuth hu' miṭevaᶜ haraṣon bemah shehu' raṣon she'im lo' yishtaneh lo' yihyeh raṣon. Also 7b. On the divine immutability, see *DE* I-3, 18c; III-3, 87b.

56. *DE* I-1, 4c. Bibago mentions Maimonides in this connection, perhaps referring to *MN* II-18, p. 37b (Arabic, p. 210). There Maimonides says that the will and essence of an immaterial being does not change even when it wishes one thing now and another tomorrow, for there is no likeness between our will and that of immaterial beings.

57. *Sefer ha-ᶜIqqarim*, II-2 and 3, especially pp. 13-17.

58. Ibid., pp. 19-25.

59. *DE* I-1, 6b, 7b. See n. 55. On change and the divine will, see also Crescas, *OH* III-i-4, p. 68b.

60. *DE* I-1, 4c. Also 7b.

61. *MN* II-18, second method, p. 37b. See n. 56. Also *MN* I-11 on the divine immutability. In describing the Aristotelian view that the world is eternal, Maimonides attributes to Aristotle the opinion that it is impossible that the divine will should change or that a new volition should arise in God. *MN* II-13, p. 31a (Arabic, p. 198).

62. Joseph ibn Ṣaddiq, *Sefer ha-ᶜOlam ha-Qatan*, ed. S. Horovitz (Breslau, 1903), pp. 44-45, 53-54. Ibn Ṣaddiq adds at the end that one should turn for a full discussion of the will to Empedocles, whom Bibago also mentions three times (*DE* I-2, 16a; I-3, 18d, 27b), although not in connection with the will.

63. *TAF* I.

64. See n. 5 above.

65. DE I-1, 3b. Also 4c and III-3, 87b. Cf. MN II-22, second proposition, and Abraham Shalom, Sefer Neweh Shalom (Venice, 1575), I-8, p. 9a.

66. Wolfson, Philo, 1:282-83; Salomon Munk, ed. and trans., Le guide des égarés (Paris, 1861), 2:172, n. 1; Herbert A. Davidson, The Philosophy of Abraham Shalom (Berkeley and Los Angeles, 1964), p. 47.

67. DE I-1, 3b-c; III-4, 89d.

68. DE I-1, 3b-c.

69. MN II-19, 22, and 24.

70. Sefer ha-Kuzari, II-6, IV-25, V-14.

71. Ibid., V-2. See also Harry A. Wolfson, "Hallevi and Maimonides on Design, Chance and Necessity," PAAJR 11 (1941): 109, 122, 125, and 162-63, reprinted in his Studies in the History of Philosophy and Religion, ed. I. Twersky and G. H. Williams (Cambridge, Mass., 1977), 2:5, 17, 20, and 58-59.

72. Another example: Joseph Albo, in his Sefer ha-^{c}Iqqarim, II-5, p. 20, says that agents by necessity are deficient and finite, whereas the divine agency, being of infinite power, is voluntary and perfect.

73. DE I-1, 3b-c. A page later, 4b-c, Bibago answers that if this limit were by necessity, it could not be by choice, which is of the essence of an infinite being.

74. DE III-4, 91c.

75. DE I-3, 18c. Cf. Die Epitome der Metaphysik des Averroes, trans. S. van den Bergh (Leiden, 1924), p. 142: "Denn ist es klar, dass, wenn die Sonne von grösserer Gestalt wäre und sich in geringerer Entfernung befände, alle Arten Pflanzen und Tiere durch die übermässige Hitze umkommen müssten. Gleichfalls, wenn sie kleiner wäre und ferner im Raume, würde alles durch die Kälte vernichtet werden. . . . Die Vorsehung zeigt sich auch in der Schiefe der Sonnensphäre."

76. Medieval arguments for the divine will and against necessity are, according to Wolfson, based on certain irregularities in the heavens that are inexplicable by the assumption of a law of necessary causality. This is the argument used by Maimonides. Arguments from the order evident in the universe establish that the world did not come about by chance, but these same arguments are traditionally used to prove that it came about instead by necessity, not by will. See MN II-20, p. 46. Arguments from the irregularities in the universe and from the principle of particularization (taḥṣiṣ) were used to establish the divine will by al-Ghazālī, Halevi, and Maimonides. Wolfson, "Hallevi and Maimonides," pp. 109, 128-29, 162-63, reprinted in his Studies, 2:4, 23-24, 57-58.

Because of the element of infinity in Bibago's arguments it is difficult to fit them into this framework. He is clearly arguing for the divine will and against the doctrine of the production of the world by necessity, so that, according to this framework, his arguments should be based either on certain irregularities in the universe or on examples of particularization. That Bibago's references to the universe in this regard are not citations of irregularities seems clear to me. His arguments may, however, be examples of particularization.

77. DE I-1, 4c.

78. Ibid.

79. See MN II-21, p. 47a (Arabic, p. 220). Also Alexander Altmann, "Essence and Existence in Maimonides," as reprinted in idem, Studies in Religious Philosophy and Mysticism (Ithaca, N.Y., 1969), pp. 126-27; and Emil L. Fackenheim, "The Possibility of the Universe

in al-Fārābī, ibn Sīnā and Maimonides," PAAJR 16 (1946-47): 68.

80. Heiko A. Oberman, Archbishop Thomas Bradwardine: A Fourteenth Century Augustinian (Utrecht, 1957), pp. 46, 52; Leff, Bradwardine, p. 12.

81. Wolfson, Philo, 1:282-83. Cf. Saadia Gaon, Sefer ha-'Emunoth, I-iii, seventh theory; also Judah Halevi, Sefer ha-Kuzari, ed. A. Ṣifroni, V-20, pp. 315-18. Gilson says that, whereas ibn Sīnā built a bridge of necessity between the necessary God and the possible world, Duns Scotus bridges the gap between the infinite God and finite beings by the divine will. Gilson, Christian Philosophy, p. 460.

82. See page 19 above.

83. DE III-1, 78a-c. Abraham Shalom defined a miracle as the instantaneous appearance of a form in a matter not prepared to receive it. Neweh Shalom, I-16, p. 26a; IX-1, p. 153a. Also H. A. Davidson, Abraham Shalom, p. 63.

84. DE III-5, 96a: pe^{c}uloth hashem be'emṣa^{c}im ^{c}al harov.

85. DE III-1, 78a-c.

86. DE I-3, 18c. See Maimonides' description of the origin of idolatry in his Mishneh Torah, "Hilkhoth Avodah Zarah," I-1, 2; II-1.

87. DE I-1, 3a-b. Also 4c-d. Retribution is not included in this list.

88. DE III-1, 78d: 'im naniaḥ ha^{c}olam qadmon, nimshakh 'aḥare haḥiyyuv. Also III-3, 87a.

89. DE I-1, 4c-d: 'aḥar shehassibbah hammeḥayyeveth qedumah, hineh hammehuyyav qadum.

90. DE III-1, 78d.

91. DE III-3, 86b: heyoth ha^{c}olam meḥudash . . . wiheyoth hashem yith' po^{c}el beraṣon. Also I-3, 20d.

92. DE III-3, 88c.

93. DE I-1, 3c.

94. Ibid.: habberiy'ah lo' teṣuyar bezulath happo^{c}el hareṣoni. Both Halevi and Maimonides agreed that we can learn from the scriptural story of creation that God acts by will. Harry A. Wolfson, "The Platonic, Aristotelian and Stoic Theories of Creation in Hallevi and Maimonides," in Essays in Honour of the Very Rev. Dr. J. H. Hertz, Chief Rabbi of Great Britain, ed. I. Epstein, E. Levine, and C. Roth (London, 1944), pp. 439-40, reprinted in Wolfson's Studies, 1:246-47.

95. MN II, 18-25. Abraham Shalom points out that Maimonides' goal in this discussion was not to prove that the world was created from nothing but only that it is the product of will and purpose and not the product of necessity, as those assert who believe in the eternity of the world. Having proved this, he could then accept the doctrine of creation on tradition. Neweh Shalom, I-8, p. 8a-b. See also Y. J. Guttmann, Ha-Pilosofiyah, pp. 153-54.

96. MN II-25, p. 51a (Arabic, p. 229). Cf. DE II-4, 49c.

97. MN II-21.

98. Sefer Shamayim Ḥadashim, printed as a commentary to MN II-19, p. 38a-b.

99. DE II-4, 49c. See n. 96 above.

100. See nn. 88 and 89 above.

101. DE II-4, 49c: hannifla'oth lo yihyu 'eṣel qadmuth ha^{c}olam . . . ^{c}im heyoth 'abuḥamid u-b's' ḥashvu meṣi'utham ^{c}im haqqadmuth. In DE III-1, 78d, Bibago mentions only the followers of ibn Sīnā as adherents of the consistency of miracles with the doctrine of the

eternity of the world. Al-Ghazālī's summary of the views of al-Fārābī and ibn Sīnā in his Maqāṣid al-Falāsifah (The Intentions of the Philosophers) (Egypt, 1936) was so impartial and effective that, upon its translation into Latin, Christian scholastics sometimes thought that al-Ghazālī agreed with the views of ibn Sīnā. Frederick Copleston, A History of Philosophy, vol. 2, pt. 1 (New York, 1962), pp. 220-21; also Arthur Hyman and James J. Walsh, eds., Philosophy in the Middle Ages: The Christian, Islamic and Jewish Traditions (New York, 1967), p. 263.

102. DE III-1, 78c. Also I-1, 6a.

103. DE I-1, 5b, 7b.

104. DE III-2, 85b-c.

105. Sefer ha-Kuzari, ed. A. Ṣifroni, I-83, pp. 38-39. Also V-6. Cf. Wolfson, "Hallevi and Maimonides," pp. 160-61, reprinted in his Studies, 2:56-57.

106. DE III-2, 84d.

107. DE I-1, 6b: haṣṣadiq hannosha[c] weharasha[c] hannishḥat hu' meharaṣon.

108. Ibid.: u-mizeh yeṣe' me[c]aṭ teshuvah lequshyath ṣadiq wera[c] lo. Also DE III-5, 98c.

109. DE III-5, 98c. Also DE I-1, 6b.

110. DE I-1, 6b.

111. DE I-3, 25c; DE III-5, 98c. Cf. MN III-51, 66b-67b (Arabic, pp. 460-61).

112. DE I-1, 3a-b, 4c-d. See n. 87 above.

113. DE II-6, 65d-66a; III-5, 100a. Also DE I-1, 6d, on Barukh ben Neriyyah; I-3, 20a and II-3, 44c.

114. DE III-5, 96d. To describe this necessary prophecy of Moses, Bibago uses the terms hekhraḥith and behekhraḥ, not beḥiyyuv, the term he uses to describe the agent that acts by necessity.

115. DE I-1, 6b; III-5, 98c. See n. 109 above.

116. DE III-2, 84d.

117. DE III-3, 86b.

118. DE I-1, 4c.

119. See page 19 above and nn. 47 and 48.

120. DE I-1, 5b. Also 4b, from Ps. 145:16.

121. DE I-1, 4c, 7b.

122. See page 20 above.

123. DE I-1, 6b, 7b.

124. For example, Clement of Alexandria says that will distinguishes God's action from that of fire. Stromata VII-vii-42. Al-Naẓẓam and his contemporary Mu[c]ammar b. [c]Abbād (ninth century) said that agents operate either naturally, as in the case of inanimate things like fire, or voluntarily, as in the case of animate beings like man. Al-Shahrastānī, Kitāb al-Milal wa'l-Niḥal (Book of Religious and Philosophical Sects), ed. W. Cureton (London, 1846), p. 46. Both al-Ghazālī and ibn Rushd attributed such a classification of agents to the philosophers (TAT III, p. 153) and Isaac Albalag also said that agents operate either by nature or by will. Vajda, Albalag, p. 68. Thomas Aquinas said that every mover is either natural or voluntary (ST I-xlvi-1, obj. 6) and Duns Scotus divides all active powers into either nature or will. Quaestiones subtilissimae in Metaphysicam Aristotelis, IX-xv-4, in Opera Omnia, ed. L. Wadding (Paris, 1891-95), 7:608b ff., referred to in Allan B. Wolter, Duns Scotus: Philosophical

Writings (Edinburgh, 1962), p. 184, n. 7. Cf. Albo, Sefer ha-cIqqarim, II-2, p. 12.

125. For example, Aristotle says that nature, necessity, and chance are thought to be causes, and also reason and everything that depends on man. Nicomachean Ethics III-3, 1112a31-32. Judah Halevi, in his Sefer ha-Kuzari, usually mentions the divine will, nature, and chance as causes (trans. J. ibn Tibbon, ed. A. Ṣifroni [Tel Aviv, 195?], II-50, p. 109), sometimes adding to this list human choice (V-20, p. 316), will (I-97, p. 51), or the stars (I-83, p. 39). See n. 105. Isaac ibn Pulgar (flourished in Spain in the fourteenth century) classifies the causes of actions as natural, voluntary, and accidental. Sefer cEzer ha-Dath, ed. G. Belasco (London, 1906), sec. 68, p. 60a.

126. DE I-1, 6d: hapeculoth . . . ṭivcith . . . macarakhith . . . beḥirith . . . miqrith. Also 7a.

127. DE I-1, 6d. It should be noted, however, that the four types of actions mentioned by Bibago, along with the divine will over them all, are exactly the five types of actions mentioned by Judah Halevi in his various lists in his Sefer ha-Kuzari. See n. 125.

128. In MN II-48, Maimonides has four lists of intermediate causes. I specify these four lists in their order of occurrence. The first list (p. 96b, Arabic, p. 292) enumerates the three basic types of causes: essential-natural (caṣmiyoth-ṭivciyoth), choice (babeḥirah), and chance (bamiqreh). Maimonides immediately explains that "choice" includes the choice of man as well as the will (raṣon) of other animals, thus adopting Aristotle's extension of voluntary action to animals and his limitation of rational choice to man. See Nicomachean Ethics III-2, 1111b7-9, 1112a16-17.

The second list will be described in n. 130.

Maimonides' third list of causes emerges from his analysis of some biblical verses in terms of these intermediate causes. This third list of causes (p. 97a-b; Arabic, pp. 293-94) has four members: nature, human choice, will, and chance. The "essential-natural" cause of the first list is here called simply "natural," and the "choice" of the first list is here broken up into human choice and animal will, as Maimonides had specified immediately following the first list.

Maimonides' fourth and last list of causes (p. 97b; Arabic, p. 294) also has four members and is almost exactly like the third list. The exception is that the "essential-natural" cause of the first list, which had become the "natural" cause of the third list, is here simply the "essential" cause.

Although the third and fourth lists each have four members, we can follow in these two lists the procedure that Maimonides followed in the first list. We can collapse human choice and animal will into one voluntary cause. We can then say that Maimonides basically divides these intermediate causes into natural, voluntary, and accidental ones. "Natural" and "essential" seem to be used interchangeably in these lists.

Bibago's addition of the constellations of stars as a fourth cause to the three mentioned by Maimonides (see n. 126) does not indicate any inclination toward astrology on Bibago's part. Bibago in fact devotes a long section of I-3 (pp. 18c-21b) to refuting the claims of astrology. He remarks at the end of that discussion (21b) that he elaborated so much on astrology because so many in his day believed in its claims.

129. See Aristotle's *Physics* II-5 and 6, especially 198a2-10.

130. In his second list of intermediate causes in *MN* II-48, pp. 96b-97a (Arabic, p. 293), Maimonides mentions animal will, human choice, and nature, three of the four members of the third and fourth lists. He then adds that chance is what is left after things are accounted for by nature, and most things are accounted for by either nature or will or choice. Since therefore chance can be eliminated, and human choice and animal will can be combined into one voluntary cause, as in Maimonides' first list in this chapter, we are left with most causes being either natural or voluntary.

131. *DE* I-2, 8b. See also Saadia Gaon, *Sefer ha-'Emunoth*, I-3, the first and second objections to the ninth theory about the beginning of the world, the theory of chance.

132. *DE* I-1, 6d.

133. See p. 18 above.

134. Plato, *Republic* VII, 535E; Aristotle, *Nicomachean Ethics* III-1, 1109b35-36, 1111a23. Also Wolfson, *Philo*, 1:434-35.

135. *TAT* III, p. 156.

136. *MN* II-7, p. 24b.

137. Vajda, *Albalag*, p. 68.

138. *DE* I-1, 2d: hapo^{c}el beṭeva^{c} yipared mehayedi^{c}ah.

139. Flourished in southern France at the end of the fourteenth and the beginning of the fifteenth century. *Encyclopaedia Judaica* (English, Jerusalem, 1971), 4:1198, s.v. "Bonafos, Menaḥem ben Abraham."

140. *Sefer ha-Gedarim* (Salonica, 1567), pt. 2, s.v. *po^{c}el beṭeva^{c}*, *po^{c}el beraṣon*.

141. His "Commentary" on *MN* II-22, p. 48a and on III-13, pp. 16b-17a.

142. Ibn Sīnā, *Kitāb al-Shifā'*, VIII-7, pp. 366-67; IX-4, pp. 402-03. A view similar to that of ibn Sīnā appears in al-Fārābī's *^{c}Uyūn al-Masā'il* (*The Main Questions*). See *Alfārābī's Philosophische Abhandlungen*, ed. F. Dieterici (Leiden, 1890), p. 96. The authorship of this essay has been questioned, however, and it is not certain whether the generation of the world, according to al-Fārābī, is necessary and eternal or voluntaristic and in time. Hyman and Walsh, eds., *Philosophy in the Middle Ages*, pp. 212, 214.

143. *TAF* V, pp. 155-56; XI, pp. 214-15.

144. *Sefer ha-Kuzari*, V-18, ninth axiom.

145. *MN* II-20, 46a (Arabic, p. 219).

146. *DE* I-1, 3a. Also 3b.

147. For example, *Enneads*, V-iii-12.

148. Ibid., V-vi-1, VI-ix-3, 6.

149. On necessity in Plotinus, see nn. 12-14 above. On the divine thought in Aristotle, see *Metaphysics* XII-7, 9, and *MN* I-68.

150. *TAF* XI.

151. *Kitāb al-Shifā'*, VIII-7, p. 367.

152. Ibid., p. 366.

153. *DE* I-1, 3a.

154. *Kitāb al-Shifā'*, VIII-7, p. 366.

155. Deut. 11:26-29.

156. See n. 134.

157. Harry A. Wolfson, "St. Augustine and the Pelagian Controversy," in idem, *Religious Philosophy*, pp. 158-59.

158. Wolfson, Philo, 1:436-37, 456-57; or idem, "Philo on Free Will," pp. 150, 163-64.

159. Sefer ha-Kuzari, V-18, ninth axiom.

160. Al-Ghazālī, Al-Risālah al-Qudsiyyah (English title: Tract on Dogmatic Theology), ed. and trans. A. L. Tibawi (London, 1965), p. 21 (p. 41 in the English translation). On al-Ghazālī's defense of the Kalām concept of the will and its influence on Maimonides, see Shlomo Pines's introduction to his translation of Maimonides' Guide of the Perplexed (Chicago, 1964), pp. cxxvii-cxxviii.

161. MN II-18, p. 37a (Arabic, p. 210).

162. MN II-22, third proposition, p. 48a (Arabic, p. 221).

163. MN I-73, p. 124a (Arabic, pp. 147-48).

164. John Duns Scotus, Opus Oxoniense, ed. L. Wadding (Paris, 1893), vol. 9, bk. 1, distinction 39; bk. 2, distinction 25, translated in Hyman and Walsh, eds., Philosophy in the Middle Ages, pp. 593, 598. Also William of Ockham, Super 4 Libros Sententiarum (London, 1962), I-38b, and Quodlibeta Septam IV-1, the latter also translated in Hyman and Walsh, Philosophy in the Middle Ages, p. 644.

In regard to what God does not will necessarily, Thomas Aquinas says that God can choose one of two opposites because He can will a thing to be or not to be. ST I-xix-10. The general thrust of Aquinas's discussion of the divine will, however, reflects Aristotle's analysis of the will as a combination of appetency and reason. ST I-xix-1; Aristotle, De Anima III-10, 433a23-25.

165. Hyman and Walsh, eds., Philosophy in the Middle Ages, p. 556.

166. Yiṣḥaq F. Baer, "Sefer Minḥath Qena'oth shel 'Avner me-Burgos we-hashpa[c]atho [c]al Ḥasdai Crescas," Tarbiṣ 11 (1940): 191-92. After his conversion Abner was known as Alphonso of Valladolid.

167. Sefer ha-[c]Iqqarim, II-2, pp. 12, 16.

168. The philosopher referred to in this first section may be al-Fārābī, who does not mention the divine knowledge in his description of the necessary generation of the world from God in his Kitāb al-Siyāsat al-Madaniyyah.

169. The philosopher intended here is ibn Sīnā. Since the sun had been used as an example of an agent operating by natural necessity (see above, p. 24), al-Ghazālī here notes that the knowledge the sun has is not the cause of its light and that the divine knowledge may similarly not be causal. Shem Ṭov ben Joseph ibn Shem Ṭov and Efodi (Profiat Duran), in their commentaries on MN II-20 (p. 46a), reproduce this opinion that the sun has knowledge that is not causal.

170. TAF XI, pp. 214-15.

171. Aristotle, Metaphysics IX-2, 1046b4-24.

172. Ibid., IX-5, 1048a8-11.

173. TAT XI, pp. 438-39; XII, p. 450. Cf. Moses Narboni, Be'ur la-"Sefer Moreh Nevukhim," ed. J. Goldenthal (Vienna, 1852), on MN III-25, p. 61a. Also the "Commentary" of Shem Ṭov ben Joseph ibn Shem Ṭov on MN III-25, p. 39a, and on II-22, p. 48a.

174. TAT I, p. 54; IV, p. 276.

175. TAT III, p. 148; XI, pp. 426, 438, 444; XII, p. 450. Isaac ibn Pulgar describes the deficiency of the human will, in contrast to the divine will, in [c]Ezer ha-Dath, secs. 47-48, p. 43a.

176. TAT III, pp. 148-49. This interpretation of the passage is based on a somewhat similar passage dealing with natural and voluntary agents in the church father Athanasius, referred to by Harry A. Wolfson

in his Philosophy of the Church Fathers (Cambridge, Mass., 1970), 1:228-29.

177. TAT I, p. 6; III, p. 148; XI, p. 439; XII, pp. 449-50.

178. TAT III, p. 160; XI, p. 427.

179. Sefer Tiqqun ha-De[c]oth, ed. G. Vajda (Jerusalem, 1973), pp. 47 and 78-79. Also in Y. H. Schorr, "R. Yiṣḥaq Albalag," He-Ḥaluṣ, 7 (1865): 158, 167.

180. Vajda, Isaac Albalag, pp. 108-09.

181. Ibid., p. 68.

182. Ibid., pp. 269-74.

183. See pages 19 and 25.

184. Aristotle, Nicomachean Ethics III-2, 1111b6-10. See also n. 128.

185. Aristotle, De Anima III-10, 433a9-13, b28-31.

186. Donald James Allan, The Philosophy of Aristotle, The Home University Library of Modern Knowledge, no. 222 (London, 1952), pp. 75, 95, 181.

187. Aristotle, Nicomachean Ethics III-2, 1111b6-15, 1112a13-18.

188. Wolfson, "St. Augustine," in idem, Religious Philosophy, pp. 159-60.

189. Quaestiones subtilissimae, IX-xv-4, in Opera Omnia, 7:608b ff., referred to in Wolter, Duns Scotus, p. 184, n. 7.

190. MN II-48. See n. 128.

191. DE II-6, fifth premise, 65a.

192. Ibid.; also I-4, 33b.

193. DE III-5, 98b.

194. DE II-6, fifth premise, 65b. Bibago here seems to disagree with Maimonides, who in MN II-7, 24b, says that the celestial intellects or angels apprehend their acts and have will and free choice.

195. DE I-3, 19b.

196. The critical reference occurs in a letter by Maimonides to Samuel ibn Tibbon, the translator of the Guide of the Perplexed into Hebrew. See Alexander Marx, "Texts By and About Maimonides," JQR, n.s. 25 (1935): 379.

197. See Shlomo Pines's "Introduction" to his English translation of Maimonides' Guide of the Perplexed, pp. xciii-xciv. On ibn Rushd's charge that ibn Sīnā introduced Kalām notions into philosophy, see TAT I, p. 54; IV, p. 276. On ibn Sīnā's attempt to harmonize philosophy and Kalām on the issue of the possibility or necessity of the universe, see Fackenheim, "The Possibility of the Universe," pp. 42-43, 51-52.

198. MN I-73, p. 124a (Arabic, pp. 147-48).

199. See pp. 25-26 above.

200. DE I-1, 4c.

201. See p. 26 above.

202. MN II-21.

203. In his Shamayim Ḥadashim, printed as a commentary to MN II-19, p. 38b.

204. OH III-i-5, p. 69a. On the opposition of Crescas's concept of the divine will to that of Maimonides, see Y. J. Guttmann, Ha-Pilosofiyah, p. 211. Also Isidore Epstein, "Das Problem des göttlichen Willens in der Schöpfung nach Maimonides, Gersonides und Crescas," MGWJ 75 (1931): 335-47.

In his arguments against the theory of chance in the beginning of the next chapter, Bibago says that the essential agency of the divine will has a greater duration than chance occurrences do. DE I-2, 8b-c. This great duration of the agency of the divine will may seem to imply that it is eternal and therefore necessary and that Bibago may here agree with Crescas on the consistency of will and necessity! As we shall see, however, this duration argument against chance does not refer to a voluntary and eternal divine agency but to the completion and perfection of the action.

205. See pp. 17 and 25 above.

206. Contra Duas Epistolas Pelagianorum, I-ii-5. See Wolfson, "St. Augustine," in idem, Religious Philosophy, pp. 170-74.

207. DE I-1, 2d, 3a.

208. DE I-3, 18c.

209. MN II-20, 46a (Arabic, p. 218).

210. DE I-2, 8b-c: haddavar hammathmid 'i 'efshar heyotho bemiqrah 'aval be^{c}eṣem. Cf. Aristotle, Physics II-8, 199b15-18: "For those things are natural which, by a continuous movement originated from an internal principle, arrive at some completion: the same completion is not reached from every principle, nor any chance completion, . . . " (Trans. R. P. Hardie and R. K. Gaye, in The Works of Aristotle, ed. W. D. Ross, vol. 2 [Oxford: Clarendon Press, 1930].)

211. DE I-2, 9d.

212. "Commentary" on MN III-13, p. 17a. Shem Ṭov uses the phrase po^{c}el be^{c}aṣmuth, not be^{c}eṣem, the phrase used by Bibago.

213. MN II-48. See n. 128 above.

214. Metaphysics V-4, 1015a13-15.

1014b18-20: ("Nature" means) the source from which the primary movement in each natural object is present in it in virtue of its own essense.

1014b36: "Nature" means the essence (ousia) of natural objects.

1015a12-13: Every essence (ousia) in general has come to be called a "nature," because the nature of a thing is one kind of essence. (Trans. W. D. Ross, second edition, in The Works of Aristotle, ed. W. D. Ross, vol. 8 [Oxford: Clarendon Press, 1928].)

215. Sefer ha-Kuzari, I, 70-75. Cf. Aristotle, Physics II-1, 192b22-23: "Nature is a source or cause of being moved and of being at rest in that to which it belongs primarily, in virtue of itself and not in virtue of a concomitant attribute."

216. Orationes Contra Arian, III-62, referred to in Wolfson, Church Fathers, 1:228-29.

217. Wolfson, Church Fathers, 1:128-29, 132.

218. Sefer Tiqqun ha-De^{c}oth, pp. 55-56. First published in Schorr, "R. Yiṣhaq Albalag," p. 161. As has already been noted, Abner of Burgos said that a voluntary agent could perform either of two opposite actions in accordance with its nature. See n. 166 above. In view of the preceding discussion, it is likely that Abner's phrase "in accordance with its nature" (miṭiv^{c}o) is equivalent to Bibago's "essentially" (be^{c}eṣem). Since Baer's text is his Hebrew translation of a Spanish translation from the original Hebrew, one wonders if the original text may have spoken of essential actions.

Although Joseph Albo describes a voluntary agent as Bibago does, as one that can perform opposite actions, Albo does not specify, as Bibago does, that these actions are performed essentially. He does say that a natural agent can perform only one action essentially, as the heat of fire only heats. Sefer ha-ᶜIqqarim, II-2, p. 12.

219. DE I-1, 5b-6b, 6d-7b.

220. DE I-1, 5d; III-4, 91b-c.

221. DE I-1, 7b; also 6a-b and I-2, 8b.

222. DE I-1, 5d. On the philosopher's view that nature lacks intelligence and is guided by a higher intellectual principle, see Judah Halevi, Sefer ha-Kuzari, I-76, 77; MN III-13, p. 17b (Arabic, p. 324); Wolfson, "Hallevi and Maimonides," pp. 135, 141-42, 148-49, 154-58, reprinted in his Studies, 2:30, 36-37, 44-45, 49-54.

223. Deut. 8:3.

224. DE I-1, 6a.

225. DE I-3, 23c.

226. DE I-1, 5b.

227. DE I-1, 5d-6a. Bibago's example, which he says he took from the sage (ḥakham), is somewhat reminiscent of the stories in MN II-17, p. 35a (Arabic, pp. 205-06), and in ibn Sīnā's and ibn Ṭufayl's Ḥayy ibn Yaqẓān. In these latter instances, boys growing up on deserted islands acquire philosophy naturally on their own. In Maimonides' example, the boy's restricted experience leads him to make a gross error that helps Maimonides illustrate his point. Bibago's example differs in that a man is born with fully developed physical and mental powers, but as in Maimonides' example, his restricted experience leads him to make an error that illustrates Bibago's point.

228. DE III-5, 96a. See n. 84 above.

229. DE I-1, 7b. Abraham Shalom feels that the inability to perpetuate themselves would indicate an imperfection in the things divinely created. He concludes, in agreement with Gersonides (MH VI-i-7), that it is not necessary for God to constantly emanate the world anew and that God's maintenance of the world in existence (evidently such as Bibago is defending) should therefore be distinguished from His constant re-emanation of the world. Neweh Shalom, I-9, 10, pp. 11a-12b. See also H. A. Davidson, Abraham Shalom, p. 46. Shalom's remarks against the theory of the constant emanation of the world are directed, it should be noted, against Ḥasdai Crescas.

230. DE I-7a, 7b.

231. It has in fact been called Neophilonism. Harry A. Wolfson, "Causality and Freedom in Descartes, Leibniz and Hume," in idem, Religious Philosophy, pp. 196-98.

232. MN I-73, sixth premise.

233. Oberman, Archbishop Bradwardine, pp. 57, 78-79; Leff, Bradwardine, p. 50. In this discussion I have borrowed the term "divine coefficiency" from Oberman. Leff uses the term "divine participation" to describe this concept.

234. Sefer ha-Kuzari, IV-26, V-20. Most medieval Jewish philosophers maintained man's freedom of the will, but Ḥasdai Crescas, while admitting that the essence of the human will is its ability to do either of two opposites, followed ibn Sīnā in regarding the human will as determined by external causes. OH II-v-3. Isaac Abravanel and Abraham Shalom, Bibago's contemporaries, had already noted Crescas's dependence upon the Islamic philosophers in this regard. Yiṣḥaq J. Guttman, "Baᶜayath ha-Beḥirah ha-Ḥafshith be-Mishnatham shel Ḥasdai Crescas weha-'Arisṭoṭel'ayim ha-Muslamim," in idem, Dath U-Madaᶜ, ed. S. Bergman and N. Rotenstreich; trans. S. Esh (Jerusalem, 1956), pp. 149-50, 157-61.

Crescas has often been classed with al-Ghazālī and Judah Halevi because of his critique of Aristotelian philosophy. On the differences between them, however, see Y. J. Guttmann, Ha-Pilosofiyah, p. 207. See also Harry A. Wolfson, Crescas' Critique of Aristotle (Cambridge, Mass., 1929), pp. 11-18, on the question of whether Crescas was acquainted with al-Ghazālī's Tahāfut al-Falāsifah. Further, in regard to the divine will, as we have already seen, and now in regard to the human will, it seems that Crescas has certain affinities with ibn Sīnā.

235. See p. 20 above.

236. TAT I, p. 36.

237. MN II 18-25.

238. "Qol Yehudah" on Sefer ha-Kuzari (Israel: Hadaran, 1958-59), II-6, p. 20.

239. DE III-1, 78d; III-3, 86d. Bibago's discussion of creation is in III-3, pp. 86b-89c.

240. See n. 5 above.

241. DE I-1, 7d.

242. Ibid. In the course of this second explanation, Bibago offers an interpretation of Isa. 45:7, "Who forms light and creates darkness, Who makes peace and creates evil." This interpretation is repeated in I-2, 15b and I-4, 31d.

243. DE I-1, 7d, 8a.

244. DE I-1, 7b: takhlith hapo^cel wetakhlith hapa^cul.

245. DE I-1, 7b-c.

246. Physics II-8.

247. Wolfson, "Hallevi and Maimonides," p. 141, reprinted in his Studies, 2:36. For a forceful statement of the view that Aristotle's teleology is purely natural and immanent and divorced from the conscious purpose of a divine artisan, see John Herman Randall, Jr., Aristotle (New York, 1960), pp. 228-29.

248. Randall, Aristotle, pp. 228-29. Maimonides says that final ends in nature are proof of a purposive being. MN III-13, p. 17b (Arabic, p. 324). For an interesting interpretation of the passage, cf. Wolfson, "Hallevi and Maimonides," p. 154, reprinted in his Studies, 2:49. Abraham Shalom had interpreted this passage in Maimonides to mean that final ends indicate an agent that acts by will, not necessity. Neweh Shalom, I-9, p. 9b.

249. DE I-1, 7c.

250. See pp. 16-17.

251. MN III-13, p. 18b (Arabic, pp. 326-27).

252. ST I-xix-1, obj. 1 and reply; OH II-vi-5, p. 60b, III, introduction, p. 61b. Spinoza, in the appendix to pt. 1 of his Ethics, rejects this solution of the problem.

Chapter
The Divine Knowledge

1. DE I-1, 2d: 'Az hu' yith' 'im hayah yode^ca hannimṣa'oth u-peraṭehem ḥaser lefi shehu' yishalem behaskalatham. . . . On knowledge implying a deficiency, see TAF XI. Also DE I-3, 17c.

2. DE I-2, 8a.

3. Ibid. Maimonides attributes the first opinion he records concerning providence in MN III-17, the theory of chance, to Epicurus. Alexander of Aphrodisias, in his treatise On Providence, says that this is also the opinion of Democritus. See Shlomo Pines's

"Introduction" to his translation of The Guide of the Perplexed (Chicago, 1964), p. lxv, n. 13.

4. DE I-2, 8b: Hahizdammen hi' sibbah bemiqreh u-mith'aḥereth mimmah shebe^{c}eṣem . . . ki hi' baddevarim 'asher ^{c}al hamme^{c}aṭ. . . . See Aristotle's Physics II, 4-6, especially 5:196b10-12: "First then we observe that some things always come to pass in the same way, and others for the most part. It is clearly of neither of these that chance is said to be the cause."

Also 6:198a5-10: "Spontaneity and chance are causes of effects which, though they might result from intelligence or nature, have in fact been caused by something incidentally. Now since nothing which is incidental is prior to what is per se, it is clear that no incidental cause can be prior to a cause per se. Spontaneity and chance, therefore, are posterior to intelligence and nature." (Trans. R. P. Hardie and R. K. Gaye, in The Works of Aristotle, ed. W. D. Ross, vol. 2 [Oxford: Clarendon Press, 1930].)

Three explanations of chance--Democritus's theory of spontaneity, Aristotle's theory of incidental causes, and Epicurus's theory of causelessness--were indiscriminately lumped together in medieval philosophy. Harry A. Wolfson, "Hallevi and Maimonides on Design, Chance and Necessity," PAAJR 11 (1941): 105, 132-33, reprinted in his Studies in the History of Philosophy and Religion, ed. I. Twersky and G. H. Williams (Cambridge, Mass., 1973-77), 2:1, 28-29. See nn. 129-32 in ch. 4.

5. DE I-2, 8b. See n. 210 in ch. 4. It is a sign of divine punishment when God abandons the people of Israel to chance. In this regard Bibago, following ibn Ezra, Kimḥi, and Maimonides (MN III-36), derives the word qeri in Lev. 26:21, 24, and 28 from the Hebrew word often used for chance, miqreh.

Three of the characteristics of chance mentioned by Bibago--namely, its inconsistency because of its relative character, its occurrence in a minority of cases, and its inconstancy--occur also in the description of chance by Saadia Gaon in his Sefer ha-'Emunoth weha-De^{c}oth, I-3, the ninth theory.

6. DE I-2, 8b. The theory of chance seems to have been the theory against which a number of the religious philosophers were arguing, especially in their defense of the divine will. Plotinus, for example, contends that chance (túke) cannot be the basic principle of the world and that the One is self-caused by His will and does not just happen to be (sunébe). Enneads VI-viii-8 (end), 10, 13-14, 16 (ed. F. Creuzer, 2:1358, 1361, 1369, and 1375). Judah Halevi seems to direct his defense of the divine will, especially in the last part of his book, against the theory of chance. Sefer ha-Kuzari, V, 3, 5-8. Also Harry A. Wolfson, "Hallevi and Maimonides on Design, Chance and Necessity," PAAJR 11 (1941): 121-22, 131-34, 162-63, reprinted in his Studies, 2:16-17, 26-29, 58-59.

In his defense of the divine will, Bibago, like Maimonides (MN II, 18-25 , also Wolfson, "Hallevi and Maimonides," pp. 162-63), directs his arguments against the theory of necessity, as we have seen. Also like Maimonides (MN II-13, III-17), however, he occasionally mentions the theory of chance in his lists of alternative theories, as he does here.

Judah Moscato notes two different concepts of the will. In the philosophical theory, will is the opposite of chance. In the second theory, will involves purpose and a deficiency in the agent and allows the possibility of opposite actions. "Qol Yehudah" on Sefer ha-Kuzari (Israel: Hadaran, 1958-59), II-6, p. 19. The philosophical theory of the will is like the theory of Plotinus and, as Moscato himself says, is described by Maimonides in MN II-20. The problem in the Sefer ha-Kuzari is that Halevi seems to be arguing against the theory of chance in defense of the second theory of the will, not in defense of the philosophical theory of the will that often opposes chance. Halevi does not seem to defend the philosophical theory of the will because he says at the beginning of the book that the philosopher totally rejects the notion of a divine will.

7. DE I-2, 8c.

8. MN III-17, first and second opinions, p. 23. IN DE I-3, 16c, Bibago says that the various opinions concerning the divine providence are parallel to those concerning the divine knowledge. Concerning this second opinion on providence, Bibago says that it is not the view of Aristotle, although both ibn Sīnā and Maimonides attributed it to him. It is rather the interpretation of Alexander. DE I-3, 17b.

9. DE I-2, 8c-d.

10. DE I-2, 9a.

11. DE I-2, 8d. Bibago refers again to the science of talismans in I-3, 22c and II-3, 47b. In the latter instance Bibago says that this is how ibn Ezra interpreted the Arabic fable-book Kelilah we-Dimnah.

Maimonides says that the use of talismans in order to cause spirits to descend, a description also used here by Bibago, is one of the idolatrous practices that he found in the Sabian book The Nabatean Agriculture. Maimonides also mentions several books on talismans, one of them attributed to Aristotle. MN III-29, p. 43. See Abraham Shalom, Sefer Neweh Shalom (Venice, 1575), V-4, p. 66a. In MN I-63, p. 94b, Maimonides says that the use of talismans to call down spirits is a type of idolatrous prophecy. In his Hebrew translation, Samuel ibn Tibbon adds, after the word "talismans," "perush ṣuroth hammedabberoth." See Le guide des égarés, ed. and trans. with commentary by S. Munk (Paris, 1856), 1:281, n. 1.

12. These imaginary forms, it should be noted, are worshiped not as intermediaries between man and God but as beings divine in themselves. DE I-2, 9a. Bibago discusses shedim at some length in II-2, 39b-40a. In preference to Naḥmanides' theory, he adopts there the explanation of ibn Rushd that shedim are spiritual beings related to the imagination as angels are related to reason. In 38d-39b, Bibago associates the imagination with matter, privation, and the evil impulse. On shedim, see also II-5, 54d. Bibago's tolerance of partisans of both sides of the issue of shedim is characteristic of his generally moderate attitude. DE I-2, 9b. Unlike Bibago's attempt to explain shedim away, Abraham Shalom affirms the existence of shedim because they are attested to by rabbinic texts, although the philosophers denied them. Neweh Shalom, II-1, p. 29a. Shalom's explanation of shedim as imperfect combinations of the lighter elements of fire and air is similar to that of Naḥmanides in his commentary on Lev. 17:7. On ᶜaza'el see B. T. Yoma 67b.

13. DE I-2, 9a; I-3, 18a.

14. DE I-2, 9b. Bibago mentions Themistius again in II-3, 44b and III-4, 92c. Themistius, a fourth-century Neoplatonic philosopher prized by the church fathers, is known mainly for his paraphrases of

Aristotle's works. Maimonides, who was evidently decisively influenced by Alexander of Aphrodisias, quotes Themistius only once in the Guide (MN I-71, pp. 108b-109a), but ibn Rushd refers to Themistius frequently. See Eduard Zeller, Die Philosophie der Griechen in ihrer Geschichtlichen Entwicklung (Leipzig, 1881), 3:739-42; Valentin Rose, "Über eine angebliche Paraphrase des Themistius," Hermes 2 (1867): 191-213, and Pines's "Introduction" to his translation of The Guide of the Perplexed, p. lxiv.

15. DE I-2, 9b, 14c.

16. DE I-2, 15c: 'Aḥar shehapperaṭiyuth 'amnam yavo' miṣṣad haḥomer . . . gam haḥomer . . . yada[c] 'otho yith'. Also 16a: Zeh takhlith happele' 'eykh yada[c] habilti hiyyula'ni haddevarim hahiyyula'nim . . . mikal sheken shehu' yode[c]a [c]aṣmutho.

17. DE I-2, 9b. See ch. 3, nn. 51-54.

18. DE I-2, 9c.

19. Ibid. On the divine immateriality, see DE I-1, 4c.

20. DE I-2, 9c-d. See ibn Rushd, Die Epitome der Metaphysik des Averroes, trans. S. van den Bergh (Leiden, 1924), p. 129.

21. DE I-3, 17b-c. See Aristotle, Categories, ch. 5, 2a11-16: "Substance, in the truest and primary and most definite sense of the word, is that which is neither predicable of a subject nor present in a subject; for instance, the individual man or horse. But in a secondary sense those things are called substances within which, as species, the primary substances are included, also those which, as genera, include the species."

Also 3b10-12, 15-16: "All substance appears to signify that which is individual. In the case of primary substance this is indisputably true, for the thing is a unit. In the case of secondary substances, . . . the impression is not strictly true, for a secondary substance is not an individual, but a class with a certain qualification." (Trans. E. M. Edghill in The Works of Aristotle, ed. W. D. Ross, vol. 1 [Oxford: At the University Press, 1928].)

Also Spinoza's Short Treatise on God, Man and His Well-Being, I-6: "Although those who follow Aristotle say, indeed, that these things (i.e., general Ideas) are not real things, only things of Reason, they nevertheless . . . have clearly said that his providence does not extend to particular things but only to kinds; . . . They say also that God has no knowledge of particular and transient things, but only of the general, which, in their opinion, are imperishable. We have, however, rightly considered this to be due to their ignorance. For it is precisely the particular things, and they alone, that have a cause, and not the general, because they are nothing." (Ed. and trans. Abraham Wolf [1910; reissued, New York: Russell & Russell, 1963], p. 50.)

22. Ibn Sīnā, Kitāb al-Shifā': al-Ilāhiyyāt, ed. G. Anawati et al. (Cairo, 1960), VIII-6, pp. 307-08; cf. ibn Rushd, TAT XIII. See also Narboni on MN III-20, p. 57a: Ramaz bazzeh [c]al 'ibn Sini shehari'shon yaskil hannimṣa'oth kulam beminehem.

23. ST I-xiv-6.

24. ST I-xiv-11.

25. MN III-16.

26. MH III-4, 23b-24a. Gersonides' assertion that God knows particulars insofar as they are derived from the general order of forms is interpreted by Guttmann to mean that the divine knowledge is limited to this general order of forms. Yiṣḥaq J. Guttmann,

Ha-Pilosofiyah shel ha-Yahaduth, ed. Ṣ. Wislavski; trans. Y. Barukh (Jerusalem, 1963), pp. 196-97. Wolfson, on the other hand, interprets this to mean that God does indeed know the particulars and that Gersonides rejects the limitation of divine knowledge to the general order of forms. Harry A. Wolfson, The Philosophy of Spinoza (Cambridge, Mass., 1934), 2:31.

27. OH II-i-1, 3, 5. Abraham Shalom also criticizes Gersonides' position. In regard to Crescas, although Shalom agrees with Crescas that God knows particulars as particulars, he criticizes the arguments that Crescas uses to establish this position. Neweh Shalom, III-2, 3, and 5.

28. DE I-2, 10a. See also ibn Rushd, TAT XI, p. 444.

29. DE I-2, 9d. See also Spinoza, Ethics, I-16, corol. 2.

30. DE I-2, 9d: ᶜAṣmo hu' haththalah lenimṣa'o' ki hu' yith' poᶜel 'otham 'im ken hekhraḥ sheyadaᶜ 'eth ᶜaṣmo bihyotho teḥillah lenimṣa'o' we'im ken yadaᶜ hannimṣa'o'. See also Moses Narboni's Be'ur la-"Sefer Moreh Nevukhim," ed. J. Goldenthal (Vienna, 1852), on MN III-20, p. 57b.

31. DE I-2, 9d; MN I-16.

32. MN III-21. See also ibn Rushd, TAT XI, pp. 435-36, 442, and 451; Gersonides, MH III-4, p. 23b; and Wolfson, Spinoza, 2:13-15.

33. DE I-2, 13d: U-vehasagtho 'eth 'aṣmo yasig 'eth hannimṣa'oth ki hem hem ᶜaṣmo bimeṣi'utho hammeshubaḥ. Also 14a: Hashem yith' hu' hannimṣa'oth kullam bimeṣi'uth hammeᶜulah wehammeshubaḥ.

34. TAT III, p. 217; XIII, pp. 462-63.

35. Be'ur on MN III-20, p. 57b; also his "Epistle on 'Shiᶜur Qomā'," ed. A. Altmann, in idem, Jewish Medieval and Renaissance Studies (Cambridge, Mass., 1967), pp. 259-60 (English, p. 279). See also Y. J. Guttmann, Ha-Pilosofiyah, p. 190.

36. "Commentary" on MN III-21, p. 31b.

37. DE I-2, 11c.

38. MN III-21; OH II-i-4, pp. 32b-33a.

39. 'Ohev Mishpaṭ (Vienna, 1589), II-6, p. 11a.

40. DE I-1, 3b: . . . sheyediᶜatho 'asher hu' ᶜaṣmo. See MN I-53, p. 77; III-20, p. 30. Also Duran, 'Ohev Mishpaṭ, II-6, p. 12a.

41. Immediately after these four arguments, Bibago inserts a digression consisting of a lengthy interpretation of the midrash at the end of Seder ᶜOlam Rabba, ch. 30. DE I-2, 10a-11c.

42. DE I-2, 11c. See the end of chapter 3.

43. DE I-2, 11c.

44. DE I-2, 11d-12a; MN III-20, p. 30 (Arabic, p. 349).

45. DE I-2, 11d.

46. MN III-20, p. 30a.

47. MH III-2, p. 21d; III-5, 25a.

48. See also Crescas, OH II-i-2, p. 29a; Spinoza's Ethics, II-4.

49. MN III-20, p. 30a-b.

50. Ibid., p. 29b (Arabic, p. 348). See MN III-16, p. 22b (Arabic, p. 334).

51. MH III-5, p. 25a: Hasheni mehem wehu' sheyediᶜatho nithleth beheᶜder hu' davar mibilti meḥuyav. Also MH III-2, pp. 21d-22a. See Spinoza's Ethics, II-8, and Wolfson, Spinoza, 2:27-31.

52. DE I-2, 11d: Hasheni sheyediᶜatho yith' tithleh beheᶜder wezeh meḥuyyav. Shem Ṭov ben Joseph ibn Shem Ṭov, in his "Commentary" on MN III-20, p. 30b, interprets Maimonides in a similar way but objects that we do in fact know nonexistents that cannot possibly

exist, as in mathematics. Gersonides says that the objects of mathematics do exist in a general way. *MH* III-2, p. 22a.

53. *MN* III-20, p. 30b.

54. *Ibid.*, p. 29b.

55. *MH* III-5, p. 25a-b. Also III-2, p. 22a-b.

56. *DE* I-2, 11d: Shelishith ki yedi^{c}atho yith' maqqefeth bemah she'eyn takhlith lo wezeh nimna^c liyedi^{c}ah ha'enoshith ki hayyedi^{c}ah taqqif wetagbil. See *MH* III-2, p. 22a: Wehashelishi . . . sheyedi^{c}atho yith' maqqefeth bemah she'eyn lo takhlith . . . wezah ^{c}inyan bilti 'efshar . . . biyedi^{c}atenu . . . yedi^{c}ah teḥuyav sheyihyeh hayyidu^{c}a ^{c}inyan mugbal u-muqaf. Shem Ṭov ben Joseph ibn Shem Ṭov may have had Gersonides in mind in his comment on *MN* III-20, p. 30b.

57. *MH* III-5, 25b.

58. *MN* III-20, p. 30a.

59. *MH* III-5, p. 25b.

60. *DE* I-2, 11d-12a.

61. *Ibid.*, 12a. See *MH* III-2, p. 22b. Also Shalom, *Neweh Shalom*, XII-ii-1, p. 208b.

62. *DE* I-2, 12a.

63. *Neweh Shalom*, XII-ii-2, p. 211. Shalom also offers a second explanation that was well known in Jewish philosophy and according to which God had certain knowledge of the future, not just probable knowledge. The explanation is that God's knowledge is no more the determining cause of the future events that He knows than is our knowledge such a cause of the events that we know at present. For the eternity of the divine knowledge, all events are present events. Ibid., p. 211b. See Herbert A. Davidson, *The Philosophy of Abraham Shalom* (Berkeley and Los Angeles, 1964), pp. 72-73.

This argument evidently could not be used by Maimonides and the other philosophers for whom the divine knowledge was indeed causal. See for example *MN* III-21. William of Ockham rejects the notion that all future contingencies are present to God and so he also could not use the explanation. Ockham said that the statement, "God knows that this side of the contradiction will be true," is a contingent, not a necessary statement. *Ordinatio*, XXXVIII-1, in P. Boehner, ed., *Ockham: Philosophical Writings* (Edinburgh, 1957), p. 134. Bibago also does not use or mention this explanation of the divine foreknowledge.

64. *DE* I-2, 12a.

65. *MN* III-20, p. 30b. Also p. 10 and III-16, p. 22b.

66. *MH* III-2, p. 22c.

67. *MH* III-5, p. 25b.

68. *DE* I-2, 12a.

69. *DE* I-2, 12b.

70. *MH* III-2, p. 21a-c.

71. *DE* I-2, 12b-c.

72. *Ibid.*, 12c.

73. *MH* III-3, p. 22d. Gersonides uses *shittuf* as a general term of comparison, of which priority and posteriority are a subclass. He uses the phrase *shittuf gamur* for the equivocal relationship that the ibn Tibbon Hebrew translation of Maimonides calls simply *shittuf*.

In Arabic philosophy the term "equivocal," unless modified by the term "pure" or "absolute" or contrasted with the term "ambiguous," does not necessarily mean the equivocal relationship in its strictest sense but may also include an ambiguous relationship such as that of priority and posteriority. Harry A. Wolfson, "St. Thomas on Divine

Attributes," Mélanges offerts a Etienne Gilson (Paris, 1959), pp. 689-90, reprinted in Wolfson's Studies, 2:513-14.

On the ambiguous or amphibolous character of the relationship of priority and posteriority in Gersonides, see Harry A. Wolfson, "Maimonides and Gersonides on Divine Attributes as Ambiguous Terms," Mordecai M. Kaplan Jubilee Volume (New York, 1953), English Section, pp. 515-16, 520, reprinted in Wolfson's Studies, 2:231-32, 236.

74. Wolfson, "Maimonides and Gersonides," pp. 517-19, reprinted in Wolfson's Studies, 2:233-35. In "Crescas on the Problem of Divine Attributes," JQR, n.s. 7 (1916-17): 34-40, reprinted in his Studies, 2:280-84, Wolfson derives Gersonides' theory of priority and posteriority from the influence of ibn Rushd.

A medieval Christian critic of Maimonides raised an objection to the theory of equivocality that is similar to this first criticism by Gersonides. The anonymous critic said that, since our perfections are derived from the perfections of God and the agent or cause always makes the effect similar to itself, pure equivocality between divine and human attributes of the same name is impossible. Isaac Husik, "An Anonymous Medieval Christian Critic of Maimonides," JQR, n.s. 2 (1911): 175.

Although many Arabic philosophers and later Christian and Jewish philosophers before the fifteenth century did not agree with Maimonides' purely equivocal and negative interpretation of the divine attributes, Simon ben Ṣemaḥ Duran (1361-1444), somewhat like Bibago, rejected Gersonides' prior and posterior interpretation of the divine knowledge and said Maimonides was right. 'Ohev Mishpaṭ, p. 12a.

75. DE I-2, 12d. Plotinus had said that, although God causes intellect, sense, and inspiration, He is none of these Himself. Enneads, V-iii-14. See Harry A. Wolfson, "Albinus and Plotinus on Divine Attributes," HTR 45 (1952): 123, reprinted in Wolfson's Studies, 1:123.

76. DE I-2, 12c. See MH III-3, pp. 22d-23a.

77. Wolfson, "Maimonides and Gersonides," pp. 520-22, reprinted in Wolfson's Studies, 2:236-38.

78. Opus Oxoniense, I-iii-2, no. 6, referred to by Frederick Copleston in A History of Philosophy (New York, 1962), vol. 2, pt. 2, pp. 227-28.

79. DE I-2, 13a. See Aristotle, Physics VII-4.

80. OH I-iii-3, p. 25a.

81. DE I-2, 13a, 14a.

82. Be'ur on MN I-68. Narboni, however, distinguishes human knowledge from the divine because human knowledge is not actual all the time. See also the "Commentary" of Shem Ṭov ben Joseph ibn Shem Ṭov on MN I-68 and the references there to Narboni.

According to Guttmann, who associates Gersonides' opinion on the divine knowledge with the view of ibn Sīnā (see n. 26 above), Narboni in this respect is closer to the view of ibn Rushd. Y. J. Guttmann, Ha-Pilosofiyah, pp. 189-90. If this is so, then Bibago here is again defending Maimonides by interpreting him according to ibn Rushd. At the end of his response to Gersonides' second objection, Bibago admits that he is reading his interpretation into Maimonides. DE I-2, 14a: 'Im neḥabber zeh lema'ama' harav hayah haddibur torani weshalem . . . 14b: We'im lo' yekhawweyn 'el zeh kevod ma^calatho yekhapper.

83. MN I-56.

84. MN I-68. At the end of MN I-1, p. 13b, Maimonides says that

the divine and human intellects are only apparently alike but are not really the same. In DE I-3, 21d, Bibago notes that in MN I-1 Maimonides says that the divine and human intellects are only apparently similar but are not really the same.

The "Ma'amar beyiḥud ha-Bore'" (Treatise on the Unity of the Creator) attacks descriptions of the unity of the divine intellect because they are inconsistent with the doctrine of the equivocality of the divine attributes. Alexander Altmann, "Ma'amar beyiḥud ha-Bore'," Tarbiṣ 27 (1957): 302-03.

85. Albalag says at one point that divine and human knowledge are related as the prior and posterior. Sefer Tiqqun ha-De^coth, ed. G. Vajda (Jerusalem, 1973), pp. 66-68. Also in Y. H. Schorr, "R. Yiṣḥaq Albalag," He-Ḥaluṣ 7 (1865): 164-66. The similarity, however, is in name only, so that his theology is essentially negative. Georges Vajda, Isaac Albalag (Paris, 1960), pp. 126-28.

86. DE I-4, 29a.

87. MN I-26, 46, and 47.

88. MH III-3, 23a.

89. ST I-xiii-2; Opus Oxoniense, I-iii-1 and 2. Shlomo Pines noted similarities in this passage of Gersonides to the work of Thomas Aquinas and Duns Scotus. Pines, "Scholasticism," pp. 34-36.

90. DE I-2, 12c.

91. DE I-2, 14b.

92. According to Harry A. Wolfson, Gersonides' fourth objection is that, if the divine attributes were all equivocal, none would be more worthy of being ascribed to God than any other. "Maimonides and Gersonides," pp. 523-24, reprinted in Wolfson's Studies, 2:239-40. Bibago evidently considers this passage in Gersonides to be part of his third objection. In his response to the fourth objection, Bibago admits that it is not counted among the other objections. DE I-2, 14b: Zeh hassafeq 'eyno nimneh bakkelal hassefeqoth. . . .

93. MH III-3, p. 23a-b.

94. DE I-2, 12d.

95. DE I-2, 14b-c.

96. DE I-2, 16b.

Chapter Six
The Divine Providence

1. DE I-3, 16b: Hassafeq hayyadu[c]a beṣaddiq wera[c] lo. . . . 'asher ba[c]avuro salqu hahashgaḥah wehayyedi[c]ah. . . .

2. MN III-16, pp. 22a, 23a; III-51, p. 67a (Arabic, pp. 333-34, 460-61).

3. MH IV-2, p. 26b-c; IV-3, p. 27b-c; IV-6, pp. 28c-d, 29a-b. Joseph Albo says that even those who admit the divine knowledge deny divine providence because of the disorder of worldly goods and evils, the righteous faring as the wicked should and vice versa. Sefer ha-[c]Iqqarim, ed. and trans. I. Husik (Philadelphia, 1929), IV-7, pp. 50-51. Crescas had also said that the apparent disorder of the suffering of the righteous poses a great problem for the belief in divine providence. OH II-ii-2, p. 35b.

4. MH IV-2, p. 26c; IV-3, p. 27c; IV-6, p. 29c-d.

5. DE I-3, 16d: Wehaḥush lif[c]amim yekazzev u-lezeh 'eyn lahem levaqqesh hammishpaṭ mehaḥush ki 'im mehassekhel.

6. DE I-3, 17a: Hannissim wehannifla'oth. . . . zeh kullo moreh

^{c}al hahashgaḥah . . . wehammakhḥish 'othah makhḥish haddevarim hammuḥashim. See also 17d.

7. DE III-2, 83b: Geder hannes . . . haṭṭov hammequbbal behashgaḥah. Also 84b. Bibago distinguishes a miracle (nes) from a wonder (pele') on the one hand and from signs and portents ('othoth u-mofthim) on the other in regard to intermediaries. A wonder (pele') occurs without any intermediary, a miracle (nes) occurs through the intermediacy of an angel or separate intellect, and signs and portents ('othoth u-mofthim) are conveyed first to prophets. DE III-2, 84b-c. In DE I-4, 31b, Bibago associates the miracle (nes) with providence and with the use of the Tetragrammaton.

8. MN III-17, p. 25b (Arabic, p. 340).

9. MN III-17, p. 26a-b (Arabic, p. 342); III-18, p. 26b (Arabic, p. 343); III-51, pp. 66b-67a (Arabic, p. 460).

10. MN III-17, p. 25b (Arabic, p. 340).

11. MN III-51, p. 67a-b (Arabic, pp. 460-41).

12. MH IV-6, p. 29c.

13. MH IV-4, pp. 27d-28a.

14. MN III-17, p. 23b (Arabic, p. 335). This is Aristotle's opinion, as reported by Maimonides, namely, that providence overflows from the celestial spheres to the sublunar species but not to their individuals. In MN III-17, pp. 25b-26a (Arabic, pp. 340-42), Maimonides says that he agrees with Aristotle's view of providence in regard to animal species other than man and that biblical verses referring to divine providence for animals refer only to the species. See also MN III-23, p. 36a (Arabic, p. 360). For Gersonides' view concerning providence in regard to animals, see MH IV-5, p. 28a.

15. DE I-3, 18a: Hahashgaḥah kefi hassekhel. Also 21c, 22c, and II-1, 37c.

16. DE I-3, 21c. In regard to the actions of animals, the theory of Aristotle, which was adopted by Maimonides (see n. 128 in ch. 4), was that animals as well as men act voluntarily and that man is distinguished by his rational choice. Bibago also seems to adopt this Aristotelian theory in DE II-6, Fourth Premise, 65b: Habba^{c}aley ḥayyim habbilti medabberim hem ba^{c}aley raṣon 'akh lo' ba^{c}aley beḥirah weraṣon. In the passage under consideration here, however, in I-3, 21c, Bibago says that animals do not act completely voluntarily.

17. DE I-3, 21a: Hahashgaḥah . . . hu' be'ishey hammin ha'enoshi levado. In 21c: 'ishey ha'adam hem qayyamim be'ish behash'aruth nafsham.

18. DE I-3, 21c-d; DE III-2, 82a, 84d.

19. DE I-3, 21d. Joseph Albo, citing Maimonides, also says that the degree of divine providence one enjoys is dependent upon the degree to which he has perfected his intellect. Sefer ha-^{c}Iqqarim, IV-10, p. 78. According to Gersonides, providence according to intellect for the prophets means that they are informed of the evil and good in store for them so that they can avoid the evil and prepare for the good. MH IV-5, p. 28b.

20. DE I-3, 21d, 22b. Maimonides and Gersonides agree that an ignorant human being has no individual providence and in this regard is like an animal, coming only under general providence. MN III-18, p. 27a (Arabic, p. 343); MH IV-4, p. 28a. Thomas Aquinas criticized Maimonides for limiting individual providence in this corruptible world to human beings. He said that the divine providence, like the divine knowledge, extends to all particulars, whether or not they

possess intellect. ST I-xxii-2.

21. DE I-3, 22b, 22c.

22. DE I-3, 22b-c. Saadia Gaon had said that man is the purpose of creation. See n. 11 in ch. 4. Maimonides said that man is the most noble and perfect thing in the sublunar world and that all other things in the sublunar world exist for his sake. MN III-12, p. 15a (Arabic, p. 319); III-13, pp. 18a, 19b (Arabic, pp. 325, 328). In comparison to the spheres, stars, and separate intellects, however, man is contemptible and cannot possibly be the purpose of these vast and superior beings. MN III-12, p. 15a; III-13, p. 19b (Arabic, pp. 319, 328); and III-14.

Bibago's reference to man's being the purpose of the universe could well refer to Saadia, since, like Saadia, Bibago also calls man the purpose of creation. Bibago's reference to those who think man is the purpose of the sublunar world but not the celestial world is probably a reference to Maimonides. By saying that the rational part of the universe, including both men and angels, is the purpose of creation, Bibago is defending Saadia's view against Maimonides.

23. DE I-3, 21d, 22b.

24. OH II-ii-4, p. 38a-b.

25. OH II-ii-3, p. 36b. Crescas does speak of a natural and for the most part general providence that attaches to the human species as a whole because of its intellect. This is somewhat more specialized than the natural and absolutely general providence that attaches to all animal species. This natural providence, however, that attaches to the human species because of its intellect is not individual and varies from individual to individual not according to their excellence but according to the celestial influences present at their birth. Individual providence for Crescas is based on reward and punishment. OH II-ii-1, p. 35a.

26. DE I-3, 18a. See also III-5, 98b.

27. MN III-16, p. 23a (Arabic, p. 335). Also Simon ben Ṣemaḥ Duran, 'Ohev Mishpaṭ (Vienna, 1589), p. 10a.

28. DE III-5, 102d: 'Eyn hayyedi^c^ah wehahashgaḥah sheney ^c^iqqarim mithḥalfim le'emunah ki hahashgaḥah hen hi' hayyedi^c^ah.

29. DE I-3, 16c. See n. 8 in ch. 5.

30. See p. 34 above.

31. DE III-5, 98b.

32. See pp. 33-34 above.

33. The realm of chance is opposed to that of providence in DE II-5, 58b. Also III-4, 95a. The rule of the stars is opposed to divine providence in DE I-3, 16c and 16d.

34. MN III-17, p. 25b (Arabic, p. 340); III-51, p. 67b (Arabic, p. 461).

35. MN III-51, p. 67a-b (Arabic, pp. 460-61).

36. See p. 23 above.

37. MH IV-6, p. 29a.

38. For example, OH II-ii-4, pp. 37b-38a.

39. As we shall see, Bibago, like Maimonides, distinguished this suffering of the righteous as a result of chance from the just punishment visited upon them by providence.

40. See p. 28 above.

41. See pp. 28 and 35 above.

42. DE I-2, 8c.

43. DE I-3, 19c-20a.

44. DE I-3, 19d-20a.

45. DE I-3, 18d.

46. DE I-3, 19d. This conjectural heat is instrumental in the acquisition of forms according to both ibn Sīnā, for whom the forms come from above, and ibn Rushd, for whom the forms develop out of matter. Ibid. In 20c, Bibago uses the term "natural heat" (haḥom haṭṭivᶜi). In II-6, 63a, Bibago distinguishes this peculiar and divine heat from the elemental (yesodi) heat that is negative and destructive. On the conjectural heat (ḥom meshuᶜar), see, for example, Gersonides, MH V-4, pp. 41d, 42d, and on the heat from the spheres, see Isaac Albalag, Sefer Tiqqun ha-Deᶜoth, ed. G. Vajda (Jerusalem, 1973), pp. 48-49, also in Y. H. Schorr, He-Ḥaluṣ 7 (1865): 158-59. On the elemental heat (ḥom yesodi), see MH V-4, p. 42a-c.

47. Meteorologica I-2, 339a20-33; DE I-3, 19c.

48. DE I-3, 19d.

49. MN II-12, p. 29a (Arabic, p. 195). Bibago quotes this passage in DE I-3, 19b.

50. DE I-3, 19b.

51. The foolish people who understand only material matters limit providence to this physical influence. DE I-3, 16d. Joseph Albo, in his Sefer ha-ᶜIqqarim, IV-4, distinguishes two theories about the influence of the celestial spheres upon the earth. One is the opinion of the philosophers that the motions of the heavenly bodies move the elements here in this world and prepare them to receive various forms. The philosophers deny, however, that the stars determine human circumstances such as wealth and poverty. The other theory is the belief of the astrologers that the stars decree everything that happens to human beings. Albo raises objections against the theories of both the philosophers and the astrologers. Judah Halevi, like Maimonides and Bibago, also admits that terrestial generation/decay and heat/cold are a result of the influence of the spheres. Sefer ha-Kuzari, IV-9 and I-77. Crescas similarly says that there is no doubt that the heavenly causes move and combine the elements through the four qualities and prepare them to receive their natural forms. The question is whether or not these celestial causes also determine our human circumstances and events. OH IV-4, p. 98a.

52. DE I-3, 19d-20a. Bibago seems to be saying that the human mind, even in prophecy, does not encompass all the celestial causes. It is knowledge of the essential cause, the divine will, that enables the prophet to predict. Judah Halevi similarly says that the material influence of the spheres on this earth does not permit the astrologer to predict the future and that such predictions can only come through prophecy. Sefer ha-Kuzari, IV-9. Zarkali was an eleventh-century Spanish astronomer and instrument designer. See n. 95 in ch. 1.

53. DE I-3, 21b: He'erakhti bazeh leṣorekh hashaᶜah ki ra'ithi pirsum zoth he'emunah biggedole bene ᶜamenu.

54. Yiṣḥaq F. Baer, A History of the Jews in Christian Spain (Philadelphia, 1966), 2:256.

55. DE II-7, 70c-d.

56. Heiko A. Oberman, Archbishop Thomas Bradwardine: A Fourteenth Century Augustinian (Utrecht, 1957), pp. 29-30; Gordon Leff, Bradwardine and the Pelagians (Cambridge, 1957), p. 28.

57. Alexander Marx, ed., "The Correspondence Between the Rabbis of Southern France and Maimonides About Astrology," HUCA 3 (1926):

311-58 (the Hebrew text of Maimonides' letter is on pp. 349-58); MT, "Hilkhoth 'Avodath Kokhavim" XI, 8-9, "Hilkhoth Teshuvah" V-4, and 'Iggereth Teman, ch. 3.

58. DE I-3, 18d-19a.

59. DE I-3, 19a. Also 19b: Sof davar hamma'amin bememsheleth hammazzaloth makhḥish hattorah kullah. Bibago explains that man, having been created by God in the divine image because of his reason, is higher than the stars and that God would not therefore subjugate man to the rule of these same stars.

60. DE I-3, 20b.

61. DE I-3, 20b, 21b. Gersonides and Crescas had both said that the stars control human events but that man can rise above this through his rational choice. MH II-2; OH IV-4.

62. DE I-3, 20d: Shem mazzal meshuttaf wekolel pa^{c}am yirṣu bo kokhav wepa^{c}am koaḥ shemaymiyi wepa^{c}am 'ey zeh mashpiya^{c} sheyihyeh. Also 21a.

63. DE I-3, 20c.

64. DE I-2, 12b.

65. DE I-3, 19b.

66. On Maimonides, see p. 41 above.

67. DE I-2, 12b: Safeq he^{c}eder hasseder wehayyosher hishtadel lehattiram beve'aro hara^{c}oth. In MN III-17, p. 26a, Maimonides says that the prophet Habakkuk explains (Hab. 1:12-14) that the evils perpetrated by Nebuchadnezzar are not the result of the people being left to chance like animals. According to Maimonides, the prophet denies that the evils are due to the withdrawal of providence and asserts instead that they are just punishments deserved by the people.

68. OH II-ii-3, p. 37a.

69. See p. 27 above.

70. MN III-51, p. 67b (Arabic, p. 461).

71. DE II-5, 58b-c.

72. DE I-3, 27c.

73. DE I-3, 16d-17a. See also I-1, 4c.

74. DE I-3, 17a.

75. The three parts of the existent universe are the separate intellects or angels, the celestial spheres, and this lowly world of generation and corruption. See DE I-2, 10d; I-3, 30c-d, 31d; II-1, 36d; II-2, 40c, 43a; III-1, 73b; III-2, 80a-b; III-4, 90b. Also MN II-10, p. 27a (Arabic, p. 190); II-11, p. 27b (Arabic, p. 191); and Herbert A. Davidson, The Philosophy of Abraham Shalom (Berkeley and Los Angeles, 1964), p. 43.

76. DE I-1, 4c; I-3, 25a; and III-1, 75a.

77. DE III-1, 75a: 'im nivdal miṣṣad she'eyn lo ^{c}eruv wehith'aḥduth ^{c}im ḥeleq meḥelqe ha^{c}olam we'im shehu' nimṣa' ^{c}imo lefi sheyesh lo ^{c}imo heqsher meṣi'uth.

78. DE III-1, 74d. Bibago here also says that the human mind and body are like the burning bush that Moses saw. The bush was not consumed because it was related to the fire by a connection of existence in the same way that the body is related to the mind. This analogy of the burning bush is also used in II-3, 45c and III-5, 97a. Bibago reiterates on numerous occasions that the human mind, although it is in the body, is not mixed or blended with the body. DE I-3, 23d; II-1, 36d; II-2, 40a, 41b; II-5, 55d. Aristotle had insisted that the human mind is not blended with the body. De Anima III-4, 429a19-24, 430a18. For a derivation of the terms heqsher meṣi'uth

and heqsher ^{c}eruv from Greek terms used by Aristotle in De Anima II-2 and I-4, see Harry A. Wolfson, Crescas' Critique of Aristotle (Cambridge, Mass., 1929), p. 560.

79. DE III-2, 81c, and III-3, 89a.

80. DE III-1, 75a. Bibago here quotes MN I-72, p. 115a. Maimonides in that passage is discussing the last of three differences between the world as a whole and a human individual. The difference is that the rational faculty of the human individual, according to Maimonides, subsists in his body and is not separate from it. God, however, is separate from all parts of the world, although His providence accompanies the world in a way that is hidden from us. Bibago, as we have just seen, seems to differ from Maimonides in this regard as well. Bibago says that the human intellect is separate from the body as God is separate from the world.

Maimonides had previously explained, however, that by the term "rational faculty" (hakkoaḥ hammedabber) he meant the hylic intellect (p. 114a). In the passage immediately following the one under discussion (p. 115a-b), Maimonides compares the relationship between God and the world to the relationship between the acquired intellect (hassekhel hanniqneh) and the body. The acquired intellect, unlike the hylic intellect, is separate from the body.

81. DE III-1, 75a. On ibn Sīnā's "oriental" or "illuminative" philosophy, of which only the part on logic is extant, see A. Nallino, "Filosofia 'orientale' od 'illuminativa' d'Avicenna," Rivista degli studi orientali 10 (1925): 367-433, and S. Pines, "La 'Philosophie orientale' d'Avicenne et sa polémique contre les Bagdadiens," Archives d'histoire doctrinale et littéraire du moyen âge, année 27, tome 19 (1952): 5-37.

According to Pines, the term translated by "oriental" refers to ibn Sīnā's own city of Bukhāra, which is east of Baghdad. The issue separating the schools of the two cities was the immortality of the soul. The Christian peripatetics of Baghdad rejected the possibility of the existence of the soul without the body.

Maimonides says that, according to ibn Bājja's commentary on Aristotle's Physics, the Sabeans believed that God was the spirit of the sphere and that the sphere and stars were His body. This belief that the heaven was the deity led them to uphold the eternity of the world. MN III-29, p. 42 (Arabic, p. 375).

82. DE III-1, 75a. In Physics VIII-5, 256b25-27, Aristotle says that mind has supreme control because it is unmixed.

83. Harry A. Wolfson, "Notes on Proofs of the Existence of God in Jewish Philosophy," HUCA 1 (1924): 589, reprinted in his Studies in the History of Philosophy and Religion, ed. I. Twersky and G. H. Williams (Cambridge, Mass., 1973-77), 1:575; Étienne H. Gilson, The Spirit of Medieval Philosophy, trans. A. Downes (New York, 1940), p. 80; A. Goichon, "The Philosopher of Being," in the Avicenna Commemoration Volume, ed. V, Courtois (Calcutta, 1956), pp. 113-14.

84. DE I-3, 25d, 27b. In MN I-72, Maimonides compares the world as a whole to a human individual and more specifically the heavens as the source of motion in the world to the heart as the source of motion in the body. See especially pp. 110b, 112a, 113b-114b (Arabic, pp. 127, 129, and 132).

85. DE I-3, 27a.

86. DE I-3, 25d and 27b. Joseph Albo says that the heretical Epicureans believed that God is the soul of the celestial sphere

(nefesh haggalgal). Sefer ha-[c]Iqqarim, III-18, pp. 159, 165. From the other phrase, however, that Albo uses on p. 159 to describe the Epicurean belief about God, namely, the phrase koaḥ be-guf, it is apparent that the heretical aspect of this Epicurean belief that God is the soul of the world is the belief that He is a corporeal, immanent power. As Bibago phrases it in describing the Sabean belief attributed by ibn Sīnā to Aristotle (see n. 81 above), it is the belief that God is not separate from the world or the sphere. Bibago, however, as we have seen, carefully specifies that both God and the soul are separate from the world and the body respectively because the relation in both cases is a connection of existence. See especially DE I-3, 27b, the fifth of five similarities between God and the soul, and III-1, 75a.

According to Maimonides, the soul and the hylic intellect are in the body and are not separate from it. MN I-72, p. 115a (see n. 80 above); II-introduction, eleventh premise; II-1, first proof, p. 13a (Arabic, pp. 133, 166, 170). Since God is of course separate from matter (MN I-70 , p. 104b [Arabic, p. 119] and MN II-1), He can be compared to the acquired intellect, which, as we have seen, is separate from matter. When, Maimonides says, the term "soul" (nefesh) is used of God, it refers to the divine will. MN I-41.

In regard to the relationship between the rational faculty and the body, Moses Narboni (in Be'ur la-"Sefer Moreh Nevukhim," ed. J. Goldenthal [Vienna, 1852], on MN II, introduction, premise eleven, p. 22b) criticizes Maimonides for believing that the soul and intellect are corporeal powers and says that Maimonides was misled in this matter by ibn Sīnā. According to Aristotle, says Narboni, the intellect and soul are not corporeal powers intermixed in the sphere. They are rather separate from it and related to it by a connection of existence. Following Narboni, Ḥasdai Crescas also criticizes Maimonides here for asserting that the intellect and soul are corporeal powers. Aristotle's doctrine, says Crescas, is the opposite of this. He believes that the acquired intellect is related to the body by a connection of existence, not a connection of mixture. OH I-i-11, p. 10a. Both Narboni and Crescas, evidently following ibn Rushd, also mention that the separate intellect is the soul of the sphere because it is its mover. See Wolfson, Crescas' Critique, pp. 264-67 and 605-11, especially p. 607.

Abraham Shalom tries to defend Maimonides against these charges of Narboni and Crescas. When Maimonides says that the rational faculty or the hylic intellect is a power in a body, says Shalom, Maimonides does not mean that it is intermixed in the body but that it is in the body by a connection of existence. Sefer Neweh Shalom (Venice, 1575), VIII-3, p. 125b; 4, p. 126a. Bibago, however, compares the connection of existence to wearing clothes or shoes and implies that the phrase involves a sense of being separate as well as connected. DE III-1, 74d-75b. If this is so, then Shalom's defense would not hold, since Maimonides says that the rational faculty is not only a faculty in the body but is also not separable from it, whereas God is separate from all parts of the world. MN I-72, p. 115a (Arabic, p. 133).

On the soul being in matter but separate from it, see Thomas Aquinas, ST I-lxxvi-1, reply to obj. 1. On the separability of the intellect from the body, see Harry A. Wolfson, The Philosophy of Spinoza (Cambridge, Mass., 1934), 2:53-56, and H. A. Davidson, Abraham Shalom, pp. 79-82.

Finally, it should be noted that Judah Halevi refers to God as the soul and intellect of the world. Sefer ha-Kuzari (trans. J. ibn Tibbon, ed. A. Ṣifroni [Tel Aviv, 195?], IV-3, p. 230).

87. DE III-4, 95b.

88. DE II-2, 38a. Abravanel, and Shem Ṭov and Efodi as well, in their commentaries on MN I-25, note that Maimonides invokes two meanings of "indwelling" (shekhinah) in regard to God. One, the created light ('or nivra'), refers to a physical apparition in some place. The other, providence, refers to the divine attachment to something other than place, such as the people Israel. Maimonides also mentions the created light and providence in connection with the shekhinah in MN I-27, p. 43a (Arabic, p. 38).

89. See Moses Naḥmanides' Perush ha-Torah on Gen. 46:1. Naḥmanides speaks there of the shekhinah in terms of the created glory (kavod nivra'), not the created light that Maimonides mentions in MN I-25 and I-27 as one meaning of shekhinah. In MN I-64, p. 96a (Arabic, p. 107), however, Maimonides says that the phrase "the glory of God" sometimes refers to the created light that God causes to indwell (hishkhin in the Hebrew ibn Tibbon translation) in a place.

Saadia Gaon also interprets "the glory of God" in terms of a created light. Sefer ha-'Emunoth weha-Deᶜoth II-12. On the concept of the created glory in the thought of Saadia, on its sensual character and its connection with light and the shekhinah, see A. Altmann, "Saadya's Theory of Revelation: Its Origin and Background," in idem, Studies in Religious Philosophy and Mysticism (Ithaca, N.Y., 1969), pp. 145, 153, and 157.

Underlying Naḥmanides' criticism of Maimonides could be the contention of the mystics that the sefiroth, of which the shekhinah is one, are emanations within God, not outside Him like the Neoplatonic hypostases that are intermediaries between God and the world. See Gershom G. Scholem, Major Trends in Jewish Mysticism (New York, 1954), pp. 208-09.

90. DE II-2, 38a. As we saw in the previous note, our text of Naḥmanides' Perush ha-Torah mentions the created glory, not the created light, as Bibago has it here. Bibago also mentions here his essay, not otherwise known, in which he defends Maimonides against the criticisms found in Naḥmanides' Perush ha-Torah.

91. DE I-2, 10d: Hashekhinah shokheneth ᶜimo shehu' hassekhel happoᶜel. On Abraham Abulafia's identification of the shekhinah with the Active Intellect, see Scholem, Jewish Mysticism, p. 143. According to Bibago, the shekhinah is also the vehicle of prophecy that miraculously comes to whomever God so wills to receive it. DE II-3, 44c.

92. In MN III-17, in the second and fifth opinions and in Maimonides' own opinion, providence is said to apply to the species of the sublunar world and to individuals only within the human species. Maimonides does not use the term "general providence," although this is what he describes as applying beyond the individual providence that extends to human beings. He says that he agrees with Aristotle in regard to providence for animals (p. 26a, Arabic, p. 341). Crescas speaks of both general and individual providence in the beginning of his discussion of providence. OH II-ii-1. See H. A. Davidson, Abraham Shalom, pp. 73-74.

93. DE I-3, 18a, and III-5, 99d.

94. DE III-5, 99d.

95. Crescas says that the providence that extends to the people of Israel is a result of the divine will and grace and has nothing to

do with intellect. *OH* II-ii-1, p. 35a.

96. *DE* I-3, 22c: Hahashgaḥah . . . be'umathenu lema^{c}alah mikkal 'uma . . . ki ha'umah hayyisra'elith hen hi' sikhlith bepo^{c}el miṣṣad hattorah hashelemah. . . . 'im ken hahashgaḥah . . . be'umathenu.

97. *DE* II-6, 61d.

98. *DE* I-3, 18c, 22d-23a; III-4, 93d-94a.

99. *DE* III-4, 94c-d.

100. *DE* I-3, 24b-d; II-2, 39d.

101. *DE* I-3, 23a.

102. *DE* I-3, 23b-c.

103. *DE* I-3, 23d.

104. Edom was a medieval Jewish epithet for Christianity. See, for example, J. Albo, *Sefer ha-^{c}Iqqarim*, IV-42, pp. 428-29. For the historical development of this epithet, see Gerson D. Cohen, "Esau as Symbol in Early Medieval Thought," in *Jewish Medieval and Renaissance Studies*, ed. A. Altmann (Cambridge, Mass., 1967), especially pp. 27-29.

105. *DE* I-3, 23d-24a. On 23d Bibago lists about six similarities between the people of Israel and the human intellect.

106. *DE* I-3, 23d: Ha'umah hayyisra'elith hi' levadah nimshekheth 'aḥare hassekhel hannaqi. . . . 'asher lazeh hi' 'adam be'emeth. . . . See also 24a. The distinction that Bibago attributes here to the land and people of Israel is reminiscent of the distinction attributed to them by Judah Halevi, especially the identification of the people of Israel with the quintessence of mankind. See Ḥaim Hillel Ben-Sasson, ed., *A History of the Jewish People* (Cambridge, Mass.: Harvard University Press, 1976), p. 612. Halevi, however, does not base the superiority of the land of Israel on its moderate qualities. He also compares Israel among the nations to the heart within the body, not to the intellect. On the superiority of the people of Israel, see *Sefer ha-Kuzari*, I, 26-43 and 95-97. On the superiority of the land of Israel, see II, 9-18, 22-24. For the parable of the heart, see II, 35-44.

107. See pp. 41 and 44.

108. *DE* I-3, 24a.

109. *DE* II-7, 72c: Gidrah . . . qinyan sikhli meṣuyyar mehaqdamoth mequbbaloth.

110. *DE* II-5, 53b: Hadderekh hammevi' 'el hahaṣlaḥah hu' derekh ha'emunah levadah asher bah yeṣe' hassekhel min haḥesron 'el hashelemuth u-min hakkoḥiyyuth 'el happe^{c}ulah.

111. Ibid., 50c.

Bibliography

BIBAGO'S WORKS

Published

Derekh 'Emunah. Constantinople, 1521. Reprint. Farnborough, England: Gregg, 1969. Jerusalem: Meqoroth, 1970 (pp. 98-101 missing). Abridged edition with introduction and notes by Ḥava Fraenkel-Goldschmidt. Jerusalem: Mosad Bialik, Sifriyyath 'Doroth', 1978.
Zeh Yenaḥamenu. [Salonica] 1522.

Manuscripts

("H.U." precedes the number of the manuscript in the Institute of Microfilmed Hebrew Manuscripts at the National and Hebrew University Library in Jerusalem.)

"Derekh 'Emunah." Moscow-Ginzberg 1754, indexes of verses, sayings, and topics. Paris 747 (H.U. 12053). Paris 995.2 (H.U. 14680). Munich 43.17 (H.U. 1150). Cambridge-Trinity College 121 (H.U. 12215). Montefiore 289 (H.U. 5247), summary of second and third parts.
"Commentary on Aristotle's Posterior Analytics." Vatican 350 (H.U. 381), autograph. Paris 959.2
"Essays in Philosophy." Paris 1004.3 (H.U. 14689).
"Ma'amar be-Ribuy ha-Ṣuroth." Paris 1004.1 (H.U. 14689).
"Sefer ᶜEṣ Ḥayyim." Paris 995.1 (H.U. 14680).
"Supercommentary to ibn Rushd's 'Middle Commentary on Aristotle's Metaphysics.'" Munich 357.6 (H.U. 1679). Munich 57.2 (H.U. 1153).
Two Letters to Moses Arondi. Parma 457.4 (H.U. 13547).
"Zeh Yenaḥamenu." New York, Jewish Theological Seminary-Rab. 80 (originally Adler 28). Paris 995.3 (H.U. 14680).

PRIMARY SOURCES

Aaron ben Elijah. ᶜEṣ Ḥayyim; System des Religionsphilosophie. . . . Edited by Franz Delitzsch. Leipzig, 1841.
Abraham bar Ḥiyya. Sefer Hegyon ha-Nefesh or Sefer ha-Musar. Edited

by Eisik Freimann. Leipzig, 1860. Reprint. Jerusalem: Sifriyah lemaḥsheveth Yisra'el, 1966-67.
___. Sefer Megillath ha-Megalleh. Edited by A. S. Poznanski. Berlin: Mekiṣe Nirdamim, 1924. Reprint. Jerusalem, 1967-68.
Abraham ben David ha-Levi (ibn Daud, RaBaD). Sefer ha-'Emunah ha-Ramah. Translated and edited by Simson Weil. Frankfurt a. M., 1852. Reprint without the German translation. Jerusalem: Sifriyah lemaḥsheveth Yisra'el, 1966-67.
Abravanel, Isaac ben Judah. ᶜAtereth Zeqenim. Warsaw, 1894. Reprint, Jerusalem, 1967-68.
___. Mifᶜaloth 'Elokim. 1592. Lvov, 1863.
___. Rosh 'Amanah. 1505. Tel Aviv: Sifriyati, 1958.
___. Shamayim Ḥadashim. Rödelheim, 1828. Reprint. Jerusalem, 1966. Also included in Abravanel's "Commentary" on the Moreh Nevukhim.
Abravanel, Isaac ben Judah, and Ashkenazi, Saul ben Moses ha-Kohen. She'eloth leha-Ḥakham . . . Shaul ha-Kohen . . . : Shesha'al me'eth ha-Ḥakham . . . Yiṣḥaq Abravanel. . . . Venice, 1574. Reprinted as Teshuvoth R. Yiṣḥaq Abravanel ᶜal She'eloth Shesha'alu R. Shaul ha-Kohen. Jerusalem, 1966-67.
Albalag, Isaac. Sefer Tiqqun ha-Deᶜoth. Edited by Georges Vajda. Jerusalem: Publications de l'académie nationale des sciences et des lettres d'Israel, 1973. First published in Yehoshua Heschel Schorr, "R. Yiṣḥaq Albalag," He-Ḥaluṣ 4 (1859): 83-94, 6 (1861): 86-94, 7 (1865): 157-69.
Albo, Joseph. Sefer ha-ᶜIqqarim. Edited and translated by Isaac Husik. 4 vols. in 5. The Schiff Library of Jewish Classics. Philadelphia: Jewish Publication Society of America, 1929.
Alkabeṣ, Solomon ben Moses ha-Levi. 'Ayeleth 'Ahavim: Perush ᶜal "Shir ha-Shirim." Lemberg, 1888. Reprint. [Jerusalem, 1973?] First edition. Venice, 1552.
___. Manoth ha-Levi: Perush ᶜal "Megillath Esther." Lemberg, 1911. Reprint. [Tel Aviv, 1973] First edition. Venice, 1585.
Aquinas, Thomas, Saint. See Thomas Aquinas, Saint.
Arama, Isaac ben Moses. ᶜAqedath Yiṣḥaq. 5 vols. Bialystok, 1911.
Aristotle. Works. Translated into English under the editorship of William David Ross. 12 vols. Oxford: Clarendon Press, 1910-52.
Ashkenazi, Saul ben Moses ha-Kohen. See Abravanel, Isaac ben Judah.
Averroes. See ibn Rushd, Abū l-Walīd Muḥammad ibn Aḥmad.
Avicenna. See ibn Sīnā, Abū ᶜAlī al-Ḥusain.
Bonafos, Menaḥem ben Abraham. Sefer ha-Gedarim: Mikhlal Yofi. Commentary by Isaac Satanov. Berlin, 1798. First edition. Salonica, 1567.
Bradwardine, Thomas. De causa Dei contra Pelagium. . . . Edited by Henry Savile. London, 1618.
Crescas, Ḥasdai. Sefer 'Or ha-Shem. Vienna, 1859. Reprint. [Tel Aviv, 1962] First edition. Ferrara, 1556. Reprint, with introduction by Eliezer Shweid. Jerusalem: Maqor, 1970.
Delmedigo, Joseph Solomon. "'Iggereth 'Aḥuz." In Melo' Ḥofnayim, edited by Abraham Geiger, pp. 1-28. Berlin, 1840.
___. Maṣref le-Ḥokhmah. Warsaw, 1890. First edition. Basel, 1629.
Duns, John, Scotus. Opera Omnia. Edited by Luke Wadding. 26 vols. Paris: L. Vives, 1891-95.
___. Philosophical Writings. Edited and translated by Allan B. Wolter. Edinburgh: Thomas Nelson and Sons, 1962.
___. A Treatise on God as First Principle. Translated by Allan B.

Wolter. Chicago: Franciscan Herald Press, 1966.
Duran, Simon ben Ṣemaḥ. Sefer Magen 'Avoth: Ha-Ḥeleq ha-Pilosofi. Livorno, 1785. Reprint. Jerusalem: Meqor [1969].
___. 'Ohev Mishpaṭ: Sefer ha-Hashgaḥah. Vienna, 1589.
Eusebius Pamphili. Praeparatio Evangelica, Introduction and Books 1-10. Edited by Karl Mras. Die Griechischen Christlichen Schriftsteller der Ersten Jahrhunderte, vol. 8. Berlin: Akademie-Verlag, 1954.
Falaquera, Shem Ṭov ben Joseph. Moreh ha-Moreh: . . . Be'ur ledivre . . . RaMBaM . . . besifro . . . "Moreh Nevukhim." Pressburg, 1837. Reprint in Sheloshah Qadmone Mefarshe ha-Moreh. Jerusalem: n.p., 1960-61.
al-Fārābī, Abū Naṣr Muḥammad. Kitāb Ārā' Ahl al-Madīnah al-Fāḍilah. Cairo, 1959.
___. Der Musterstaat, aus Londoner und Oxforder Handschriften hrsg. Arabic text edited by Friedrich Dieterici. Leiden, 1895. Translation by idem. 1900. Die Philosophie der Araber im 10 Jahrhundert, vol. 16.
___. Kitāb al-Siyāsat al-Madaniyyah. Hyderabad Arabic Series, no. 64. 1927.
___. "Sefer ha-Hatḥaloth." In Sefer ha-'Asif, edited by Herschell E. Filipowski. Leipzig, 1849.
___. Alfarabi's Philosophische Abhandlungen, aus Londoner, Leidener und Berliner Handschriften hrsg. Edited by Friedrich Dieterici. Leiden, 1890. Translation by idem. 1892. Die Philosophie der Araber im 9 und 10 Jahrhundert, vols. 14 and 15.
___. Alfarabi's Philosophy of Plato and Aristotle. Translated by Muhsin Mahdi. Revised edition. Ithaca, N.Y.: Cornell University Press, Agora Paperbacks, 1969.
___. Die Staatsleitung von Al-Fārābī. Translated by Friedrich Dieterici. Edited by Paul Brönnle. Leiden, 1904.
Gersonides. See Levi ben Gershon.
al-Ghazālī, Abū Ḥamid Muḥammad al-Ṭūsī. Algazel's Metaphysics: A Medieval Translation. Edited by Joseph Thomas Muckle. Toronto: St. Michael's College, 1933.
___. Maqāṣid al-Falāsifah. Egypt, 1936.
___. Tahāfut al-Falāsifah. Edited by Maurice Bouyges. Bibliotheca Arabica Scolasticorum, Série arabe, vol. 2. Beirut: Imprimerie catholique, 1927.
___. Al-Risālah al-Qudsiyyah (English title: Tract on Dogmatic Theology). Edited and translated by Abdul L. Tibawi. London: Luzac, 1965. Also in Islamic Quarterly, vol. 9, nos. 3-4.
Ibn Bājja, Abū Bakr al-Ṣa'igh. Risālat al-Widā^c. In Miguel Asín Palacios, "La 'Carta de Adiós' de Avempace," Al-Andalus 8 (1943): 1-87.
___. Kalām fī Ittiṣāl al-^{c}Aql bi'l-'Insān. In Miguel Asín Palacios, "Tratado de Avempace sobre la union del intellecto con el hombre," Al-Andalus 7 (1942): 1-47.
Ibn Gabbai, Meir ben Ezekiel. Sefer Derekh 'Emunah. Padua, 1562.
___. Sefer ^{c}Avodath ha-Qodesh. Warsaw, 1883. First edition. Venice, 1566-68.
Ibn Ḥabib, Jacob ben Solomon. ^{c}En Ya^{c}aqov. 5 vols. in 3. Vilna, 1894. First edition. Venice, 1546.
Ibn Kaspi, Joseph ben Abba Mari. ^{c}Amude Kesef u-Maskiyoth Kesef: Shene Perushim ^{c}al sefer ha-"Moreh" leha-RaMBaM. Edited by

Solomon Werbluner. Frankfurt a. M., 1848. Reprint in Sheloshah Qadmone Mefarshe ha-Moreh. Jerusalem: n.p., 1960-61.

___. Mishneh Kesef: Shene Be'urim ^{c}al ha-Torah. Edited by Isaac Last. Vol. 1. Tirath Kesef. Pressburg, 1904. Vol. 2. Maṣref le-Kesef. Cracow, 1905-06. Reprint. Jerusalem: Meqoroth, 1969-70.

Ibn Khaldūn, ^{c}Abd al-Raḥmān Abu Zayd. The Muqaddimah: An Introduction to History. Translated by Franz Rosenthal. Second edition. 3 vols. Bollingen Series, no. 43. New York: Pantheon, 1967.

Ibn Pulgar, Isaac ben Joseph. Sefer ^{c}Ezer ha-Dath. Edited by George S. Belasco. London: J. Jacobs, 1906.

Ibn Rushd, Abū l-Walīd Muḥammad ibn Aḥmad (Averroes). Des Averroës Abhandlungen: "Über die Möglichkeit der Conjunction," oder "Über den Materiellen Intelleckt." Translated and edited by Ludwig Hannes. Halle, 1892.

___. Die Epitome der Metaphysik des Averroes. Translated by Simon van den Bergh. Leiden: E. J. Brill, 1924.

___. Drei Abhandlungen über die Conjunction des Separaten Intellekts mit dem Menschen von Averroës (Vater und Sohn). Translated by Samuel ibn Tibbon. Edited by J. Hercz. Berlin, 1869.

___. Kitāb Faṣl al-Maqāl. Leiden, 1959.

___. On the Harmony of Religion and Philosophy. Translated by George F. Hourani. E. J. W. Gibb Memorial Series, n.s. 21. London: Luzac, 1961.

___. Die Metaphysik des Averroës. Translated by Max Horten. Halle: M. Niemeyer, 1912. Reprint. Frankfurt a. M., 1960.

___. Tahāfut al-Tahāfut. Edited by Maurice Bouyges. Bibliotheca Arabica Scholasticorum, Série arabe, vol. 3. Beirut: Imprimerie catholique, 1930.

___. Tahāfut al-Tahāfut: The Incoherence of the Incoherence. Translated with notes by Simon van den Bergh. 2 vols. London: Luzac, 1954.

Ibn Ṣaddiq, Joseph ben Jacob. Sefer ha-^{c}Olam ha-Qatan. Edited by Saul Horovitz. Jahres-Bericht des jüdisches-theologischen Seminars. Breslau, 1903. Reprint. [Jerusalem:] Sifriyah lemaḥsheveth Yisra'el [1967?].

Ibn Shem Ṭov, Joseph ben Shem Ṭov. Kevod 'Elokim. Ferrara, 1556-57. Reprint. [Jerusalem? 1966?].

Ibn Shem Ṭov, Shem Ṭov. Sefer ha-'Emunoth. Ferrara, 1556-57. Reprint. Jerusalem: n.p., 1968-69.

Ibn Sīnā, Abū ^{c}Alī al-Ḥusain (Avicenna). Das Buch der Genesung der Seele: Eine Philosophische Enzyklopädie Avicennas. Series 2. Die Philosophie. Section 3 and part 13. Die Metaphysik, Theologie, Kosmologie und Ethik. Translated by Max Horten. Halle and Leipzig, 1907-09. Reprint. Frankfurt a. M.: Minerva, 1960.

___. Kitāb al-Shifā': al-Ilāhiyyāt. Edited by G. C. Anawati et al. Cairo: Organisation générale des imprimeries governementales, 1960.

___. The "Metaphysica" of Avicenna (ibn Sīnā): A Critical Translation-Commentary and Analysis of the Fundamental Arguments in Avicenna's "Metaphysica" in the "Dānish Nāma-i ^{c}alā'ī" (The Book of Scientific Knowledge). By Parviz Morewedge. Persian Heritage Series, no. 13. London: Routledge and Kegan Paul, 1973.

Ibn Tibbon, Samuel ben Judah. Ma'amar Yeqqavu ha-Mayim. Edited by Mordecai L. Bisliches. Pressburg, 1837. Reprint. [Jerusalem:] Sifriyah lemahsheveth Yisra'el, n.d.

Ibn Verga, Solomon. Sefer Shevet Yehudah. Edited with introduction by Yiṣḥaq F. Baer. Notes by Azriel Shoḥeṭ. Jerusalem: Mosad Bialik, 1947.

Ibn Yaḥya, Gedalya ben Joseph. Shalsheleth ha-Kabbalah. Warsaw, 1881. Reprint. Jerusalem: n.p., 1962. First edition. Venice, 1586.

Isaac ben Shesheth. She'eloth u-Teshuvoth. Edited by Israel H. Daiches. Vilna, 1878. Reprint. Jerusalem, 1967-68.

Josel of Rosheim. Sefer ha-Miqnah. Edited by Ḥava Fraenkel-Goldschmidt. Jerusalem: Meqiṣe Nirdamim, 1970.

Judah Halevi. Sefer ha-Kuzari. Arabic text, with the Hebrew translation of Judah ben Saul ibn Tibbon. Edited by Hartwig Hirshfeld. Leipzig, 1887.

___. Sefer ha-Kuzari. Translated by Judah ben Saul ibn Tibbon. Commentaries: "Qol Yehudah," by Judah Aryeh Moscato, and "'Oṣar Neḥmad," by Israel Zamosc. Warsaw, 1880. Reprint. Israel: Hadaran, 1958-59.

___. Sefer ha-Kuzari. Translated by Judah ben Saul ibn Tibbon. Edited by Abraham Ṣifroni. [Tel Aviv:] Maḥberoth lesifruth and Mosad ha-Rav Kuk [195?].

Levi ben Gershon (Gersonides, RaLBaG). Sefer Milḥamoth ha-Shem. Riva di Trento, 1560. Reprint. [Jerusalem? 1966?].

Maimonides, Moses. See Moses ben Maimon.

Moscato, Judah Aryeh. See Judah Halevi.

Moses ben Joshua of Narbonne (Narboni). "Babeḥirah." In Divre Ḥakhamim, edited by Eliezer Ashkenazi. Metz, 1849.

___. Be'ur la-"Sefer Moreh Nevukhim." Edited by Jacob Goldenthal. Vienna, 1852. Reprint in Sheloshah Qadmone Mefarshe ha-Moreh. Jerusalem: n.p., 1960-61.

___. Ma'amar bishelemuth ha-Nefesh. Edited by Alfred L. Ivry. Jerusalem: Ha-'akademyah ha-Le'umith ha-Yisra'elith lemadaᶜim, 1977.

Moses ben Maimon (Maimonides, RaMBaM). Dalālat al-ḥā'irīn. Edited by Salomon Munk and Issachar Joel. Jerusalem: Judah Junovitch, 1930.

___. Le guide des égarés. Edited and translated with commentary by Salomon Munk. 3 vols. Paris, 1856-66. Reprint. Paris, 1960.

___. The Guide of the Perplexed. Translated by Shlomo Pines. Chicago: University of Chicago Press, 1964.

___. 'Iggereth Teman (Epistle to Yemen). Arabic original and 3 Hebrew translations edited by Abraham S. Halkin. English translation by Boaz Cohen. New York: American Academy for Jewish Research, 1952.

___. Ma'amar Teḥiyyath ha-Metim. Translated by Samuel ben Judah ibn Tibbon. Edited by Joshua Finkel. PAAJR 9 (1939).

___. Milloth ha-Higgayon (Treatise on Logic). Original Arabic and 3 Hebrew translations edited and translated into English by Israel Efros. PAAJR 8 (1938).

___. Mishneh Torah: Ha-Yad ha-Ḥazaqah. Warsaw-Vilna edition with commentaries, including the "Kesef Mishneh" by Joseph Karo. 6 vols. New York: S. Goldman, 1955-56.

___. Sefer Moreh Nevukhim. Translated by Samuel ben Judah ibn Tibbon. Commentaries by Isaac Abravanel, Asher Crescas, Profiat Duran (Efodi), and Shem Ṭov ben Joseph ibn Shem Ṭov. Jerusalem: n.p., 1959-60.

___. Perush la-Mishnayoth. In standard editions of the Babylonian

Talmud.

Moses ben Naḥman (Naḥmanides, RaMBaN). Kitve Rabbenu Mosheh ben Naḥman. Edited by Charles B. Chavel. 2 vols. Jerusalem: Mosad ha-Rav Kuk, 1963-64.

___. Perush ha-Torah lerabbenu Mosheh ben Naḥman. Edited by Charles B. Chavel. 2 vols. Jerusalem: Mosad ha-Rav Kuk, 1959-60. Also in standard editions of Miqroth Gedoloth.

Naḥmanides. See Moses ben Naḥman.

Narboni. See Moses ben Joshua.

Ockham, William of. Philosophical Writings: A Selection. Edited and translated by Philotheus Boehner. Edinburgh: Thomas Nelson and Sons, 1957.

___. Predestination, God's Foreknowledge, and Future Contingents. Translated by Marilyn M. Adams and Norman Kertzmann. New York: Appleton-Century-Crofts, 1969.

Plotinus. Plotini Opera: Enneads 1-5. Edited by Paul Henry and Hans-Rudolf Schwyzer. 2 vols. Paris: Desclée, de Brouwer, 1951-59.

___. Plotinou Apanta: Plotini Opera Omnia (Enneads). Edited by Fr. Creuzer. 2 vols. Oxford, 1835.

___. The Enneads. Translated by Stephen MacKenna. Third edition revised by B. S. Page. London: Faber [1962].

Rossi, Azariah ben Moses, de. Sefer Me'or [c]Enayim. Edited by David Cassel. Vilna, 1866. Reprint. Jerusalem: Meqor, 1969-70. First edition. Mantua, 1573-75.

Saadia ben Joseph, Gaon. Sefer ha-'Emunoth weha-De[c]oth. Translated by Judah ben Saul ibn Tibbon. Yosefow, 1885.

Saul ben Moses ha-Kohen Ashkenazi. See Abravanel, Isaac ben Judah.

al-Shahrastānī, Muḥammad ibn [c]Abd al-Karīm. Kitāb al-Milal wa'l-Niḥal (Book of Religious and Philosophical Sects). Edited by William Cureton. London, 1846.

___. Kitāb Nihāyat al-Iqdām fī [c]Ilm al-Kalām. Edited and translated by Alfred Guillaume. London: Oxford University Press, 1934.

Shalom, Abraham ben Isaac. Sefer Neweh Shalom. Venice, 1575. Reprint. 2 vols. [Jerusalem:] Sifriyah lemaḥsheveth Yisra'el [1966-67].

Spinoza, Benedict (Barukh). Opera, ed. Carl Gebhardt. 4 vols. Heidelberg: C. Winter, [1925]. Reprint. [c. 1972].

___. Ethic. Translated by William Hale White and Amelie H. Stirling. Fourth edition revised. London: Oxford University Press, H. Milford [1923].

Thomas Aquinas, Saint. Summa Theologica. Latin text and English translation. 60 vols. New York: McGraw-Hill, 1964-76.

Zacuto, Abraham ben Samuel. Sefer Yuḥasin ha-Shalem. London, 1857. Reprint. Jerusalem, 1962-63. First edition. Constantinople, 1566.

SECONDARY SOURCES

Altmann, Alexander. "The Divine Attributes: An Historical Survey of the Jewish Discussion." Judaism 15 (1966): 40-60.

___. "Moses Narboni's 'Epistle on Shi[c]ur Qomā': A Critical Edition of the Hebrew Text with an Introduction and an Annotated English Translation." In his Jewish Medieval and Renaissance Studies, Philip W. Lown Institute of Advanced Judaic Studies, Brandeis

University, Studies and Texts, vol. 4, pp. 225-88. Cambridge, Mass.: Harvard University Press, 1967.

___. "Ma'amar beyiḥud ha-Bore'." Tarbiṣ 27 (1957): 301-09.

___. Studies in Religious Philosophy and Mysticism. Ithaca, N.Y.: Cornell University Press, 1969.

Altmann, Alexander, and Stern, Samuel M. Isaac Israeli, A Neoplatonic Philosopher of the Early Tenth Century: His Works Translated with Comments and an Outline of his Philosophy. Scripta Judaica, vol. 1. Oxford: Clarendon Press, 1958.

Assemani, Stefano Evodio, and Assemani, Giuseppe Simone, eds. Bibliothecae Apostolicae Vaticanae Codicum Manuscriptorum Catalogus. Vol 1. Codices Ebraicos et Samaritanos. Rome, 1756. Reprint. Paris: Maisonneuve frères, Libraire orientale et americaine, 1926.

Azulai, Hayyim Joseph David. Shem ha-Gedolim. Vilna, 1852. Reprint. New York, n.d.

Baer, Yiṣḥaq Fritz. A History of the Jews in Christian Spain. Vol. 2. Philadelphia: Jewish Publication Society of America, 1966.

___. Die Juden im Christlichen Spanien. Vol. 2. Berlin: Akademie Verlag, 1936.

___. "Sefer Minḥath Qena'oth shel Avner me-Burgos we-hashpa[c]atho [c]al Ḥasdai Crescas." Tarbiṣ 11 (1940): 188-206.

Baron, Salo Wittmayer. A Social and Religious History of the Jews. Second edition, revised and enlarged. Vols. 11, 13. New York: Columbia University Press, 1967, 1969.

Bartolocci, Giulio. Bibliotheca Magna Rabbinica. . . . Vol. 1. Rome, 1675. Reprint. Farnborough, England: Gregg, 1965.

Bass, Shabbethai ben Joseph. Sifte Yeshenim. Amsterdam, 1680.

Ben-Sasson, Ḥaim Hillel. "Dor Goley Sefarad [c]al [c]Asmo." Zion 26 (1961): 23-64.

___. "Jewish-Christian Disputation in the Setting of Humanism and Reformation in the German Empire." HTR 59 (1966): 369-90.

Ben-Sasson, Ḥaim Hillel, ed. A History of the Jewish People. Cambridge, Mass.: Harvard University Press, 1976.

Blumberg, Harry. "Ha-Rambam [c]al Musag al-Tajwiz beshetatam shel ha-Mutakallimūn." Tarbiṣ 39 (1970): 268-76.

Carmoly, Eliakim. "Analecten: 8. Plagiate." Israelitische Annalen, 29 March 1839, p. 101.

___. "Toldoth Don Yiṣḥaq Abravanel." In 'Oṣar Neḥmad, edited by Ignaz Blumenfeld, 2:47-65. Vienna, 1857.

Castro, Americo. The Structure of Spanish History. Translated by Edmund L. King. Princeton: Princeton University Press, 1954.

Chaytor, Henry John. A History of Aragon and Catalonia. London: Methuen and Co., 1933.

Copleston, Frederick Charles. A History of Philosophy. New revised edition. Vols. 1-3. Garden City, N.Y.: Doubleday, Image Books, 1962-63.

Courtois, V., ed. Avicenna Commemoration Volume. Calcutta: Iran Society, 1956.

Davidson, Herbert Alan. "John Philoponus as a Source of Medieval Islamic and Jewish Proofs of Creation." JAOS 89 (1969): 357-91.

___. The Philosophy of Abraham Shalom: A Fifteenth-Century Exposition and Defense of Maimonides. University of California Near Eastern Studies, no. 5. Berkeley and Los Angeles, 1964.

Diesendruck, Zevi. "Die Teleologie bei Maimonides." HUCA 5 (1928): 415-534.
___. "Samuel and Moses ibn Tibbon on Maimonides' Theory of Providence." HUCA 11 (1936): 341-66.
Dreyer, John Louis Emil. A History of Astronomy from Thales to Kepler (formerly History of the Planetary Systems from Thales to Kepler, Cambridge 1905). Second edition, revised. New York: Dover Publications, 1953.
___. "Medieval Astronomy." In Studies in the History and Method of Science, edited by Charles Singer, vol. 2, pp. 102-20. Oxford: Clarendon Press, 1921.
Duhem, Pierre Maurice Marie. Le Système du monde: Histoire des doctrines cosmologiques de Platon à Copernic. 10 vols. Paris: A. Hermann et fils, 1954-59.
Encyclopedia ᶜIvrith. 30 vols. to date. Jerusalem, 1949--.
The Encyclopaedia of Islam: A Dictionary of the Geography, Ethnography and Biography of the Muhammadan Peoples. Edited by M. Th. Houtsma, Arent J. Wensinck, et al. 4 vols. Leiden: E. J. Brill, 1924.
The Encyclopaedia of Islam, New Edition. 4 vols. Leiden: E. J. Brill; London: Luzac, 1960--.
Encyclopaedia Judaica. 10 vols. Berlin: Verlag Eschkol, 1929-34.
Encyclopaedia Judaica (English). 16 vols. Jerusalem, 1971.
The Encyclopedia of Philosophy. 8 vols. New York: Macmillan, 1967.
Epstein, Isidore. "Das Problem des göttlichen Willens in der Schöpfung nach Maimonides, Gersonides und Crescas." MGWJ 75 (1931): 335-47.
Fackenheim, Emil Ludwig. "The Possibility of the Universe in al-Fārābī, ibn Sīnā and Maimonides." PAAJR 16 (1946-47): 39-70.
Fakhry, Majid. A History of Islamic Philosophy. Studies in Oriental Culture, no. 5. New York: Columbia University Press, 1970.
___. Islamic Occasionalism and its Critique by Averroes and Aquinas. London: George Allen and Unwin, 1958.
Feldman, Seymour. "Gersonides' Proofs for the Creation of the Universe." PAAJR 35 (1967): 113-37.
Fünn, Samuel Joseph. Keneset Yisra'el. Warsaw, 1886.
Gandz, Solomon. "Studies in Hebrew Mathematics and Astronomy." PAAJR 9 (1939): 5-50.
Gans, David. Ṣemah David. Warsaw, 1859. Reprint. Jerusalem: Huminer, 1966. First edition. Prague, 1591.
Gardet, Louis. La Pensée religieuse d'Avicenne (ibn Sīnā). Études de philosophie médiévale, 41. Paris: J. Vrin, 1951.
Gauthier, Léon. Ibn Rochd (Averroès). Paris: Presses universitaires de France, 1948.
Gilson, Étienne Henry. The Christian Philosophy of St. Thomas Aquinas. Translated by L. K. Shook. New York: Random House, 1956.
___. History of Christian Philosophy in the Middle Ages. New York: Random House, 1955.
___. The Spirit of Medieval Philosophy. Translated by Alfred H. C. Downes. New York: C. Scribner's Sons, 1940.
Goldstein, Bernard Raphael. The Arabic Version of Ptolemy's Planetary Hypotheses. Transactions of the American Philosophical Society, New Series, vol. 57, pt. 4. Philadelphia, 1967.
Graetz, Heinrich. Geschichte der Juden. Vol. 8. Leipzig, 1890.
Guttmann, Jakob. "Die Familie Schemtob in ihren Beziehungen zur

Philosophie." MGWJ 57 (1913): 177-95, 326-40, 419-51.
___. Die Religionsphilosophischen Lehren des Isaak Abravanel. Breslau: Marcus, 1916.
Guttmann, Yiṣḥaq Julius. Dath U-Mada^c. Translated by Saul Esh. Edited by Samuel H. Bergman and Nathan Rotenstreich. Jerusalem: Hebrew University, Magnes Press, 1956.
___. "Elia del Medigos Verhaltnis zu Averroes in seinen Bechinat ha-dat." In Jewish Studies in Memory of Israel Abrahams, edited by George A. Kohut, pp. 192-208. New York: Press of the Jewish Institute of Religion, 1927.
___. Ha-Pilosofiyah shel ha-Yahaduth. Translated by Y. L. Barukh. Edited by Ṣevi Wislavski. Jerusalem: Mosad Bialik, 1963. Translated into English as Philosophies of Judaism: The History of Jewish Philosophy from Biblical Times to Franz Rosenzweig by David W. Silverman. New York: Holt, Rinehart and Winston, 1964.
Hakker, Yosef. "Meqomo shel R. Avraham Bivag' be-Maḥloqeth ^cal Limud ha-Pilosofiyah u-Ma^camadah be-Sefarad be-Me'ah ha-15." In Proceedings of the Fifth World Congress of Jewish Studies, 3:151-58. English Abstract: "The Role of Rabbi Abraham Bibago in the Polemic on the Place of Philosophy in Jewish Life in Spain in the 15th Century," 3:94-95. Jerusalem: World Union of Jewish Studies, 1972.
Hammond, Robert. The Philosophy of Alfarabi and its Influence on Medieval Thought. New York: Hobson Book Press, 1947.
Highfield, John Roger Loxdale, ed. Spain in the Fifteenth Century 1369-1516. Translated by Francis M. Lopez-Morillas. London: Macmillan, 1972.
Hirschfeld, Hartwig. Descriptive Catalogue of the Hebrew MSS. of the Montefiore Library. London: Macmillan, 1904.
Husik, Isaac. "An Anonymous Medieval Christian Critic of Maimonides." JQR, n.s. 2 (1911): 159-90.
___. A History of Medieval Jewish Philosophy. Second edition. Philadelphia: Jewish Publication Society of America, 1941.
___. Philosophical Essays: Ancient, Medieval and Modern. Edited by Milton C. Nahm and Leo Strauss. Oxford: Basil Blackwell, 1952.
Hyman, Arthur, and Walsh, James Jerome, eds. Philosophy in the Middle Ages: The Christian, Islamic and Jewish Traditions. New York: Harper and Row, 1967.
Ivry, Alfred Lyon. "Moses of Narbonne's 'Treatise on the Perfection of the Soul,' A Methodological and Conceptual Analysis." JQR, n.s. 57 (1967): 271-97.
The Jewish Encyclopedia. 12 vols. New York: Funk and Wagnalls, 1901-06.
Jüdisches Lexikon: Ein enzyklopädisches Handbuch des jüdischen Wissens. . . . Edited by Georg Herlitz and Bruno Kirschner. 4 vols. in 5. Berlin: Jüdischer Verlag, 1927-30.
Kaufmann, David. Geschichte der Attributenlehre in der jüdischen Religionsphilosophie des Mittelalters von Saadja bis Maimuni. Gotha, 1877.
___. Studien über Salomon ibn Gabirol. Jahresbericht der Landes-Rabbinerschule in Budapest für das Schuljahr 1898-99.
Klatzkin, Jacob. 'Oṣar he-Munaḥim ha-Pilosofiyim we-Antologiyah Pilosofith. 5 vols. Berlin: Eschkol, 1926-33.
Krauss, Samuel. "The Jews in the Works of the Church Fathers: IV Eusebius." JQR 6 (1894): 82-88.

Leff, Gordon. Bradwardine and the Pelagians: A Study of his "De Causa Dei" and its Opponents. Cambridge Studies in Medieval Life and Thought, New Series, vol. 5. Cambridge: At the University Press, 1957.

———. The Dissolution of the Medieval Outlook: An Essay on Intellectual and Spiritual Change in the Fourteenth Century. New York: Harper and Row, 1976.

———. Gregory of Rimini: Tradition and Innovation in Fourteenth Century Thought. Manchester: Manchester University Press, 1961.

———. Richard FitzRalph, Commentator of the 'Sentences': A Study in Theological Orthodoxy. Manchester: Manchester University Press, 1963.

Levinger, Yaᶜaqov. "Nevu'ath Moshe Rabenu be-Mishnath ha-RaMBaM." In Divre ha-Congress ha-ᶜOlami ha-Reviᶜi le-Madaᶜe ha-Yahaduth, 2:339-355. Jerusalem, 1969.

Lewy, Hans. "Aristotle and the Jewish Sage According to Clearchus of Soli." HTR 31 (1938): 205-35.

Llubera, I. Gonzalez. "Spain in the Age of Abravanel." In Isaac Abravanel: Six Lectures, edited by John B. Trend and Herbert Loewe, pp. 17-37. Cambridge: At the University Press, 1937.

Loewe, Herbert. Catalogue of the Manuscripts in the Hebrew Character Collected and Bequeathed to the Trinity College Library by the late William Aldis Wright. Cambridge: At the University Press, 1926.

Luzzatto, Samuel David. "Über die angeblichen Plagiate Abrabanel's und Muscato's." Israelitische Annalen, 10 and 17 January 1840, pp. 17, 24-25.

Maier, Anneliese. Ausgehendes Mittelalter: Gesammelte Aufsätze zur Geistegeschichte des 14. Jahrhunderts. Storia e letteratura, vols. 97, 105, 138. Rome: Edizioni di storia e letteratura, 1964, 1967, 1977.

Marx, Alexander, ed. "The Correspondence Between the Rabbis of Southern France and Maimonides About Astrology." HUCA 3 (1926): 311-58.

———. "Texts By and About Maimonides." JQR, n.s. 25 (1935): 371-428.

Merton, Robert King. On the Shoulders of Giants: A Shandean Postscript. New York: Free Press, 1965.

Michal, Ḥayyim. 'Or ha-Ḥayyim. Frankfurt a. M., 1891. Reprint. Jerusalem: Mosad ha-Rav Kuk, 1965.

Michalski, Konstanty. Le Problème de la volonté à Oxford et à Paris au XIVe siècle. Studia Philosophica, vol. 2. Lvov, 1937. Reprinted in his La Philosophie au XIVe siècle: six études. Opuscula Philosophica, vol. 1. Edited by Kurt Flasch. Frankfurt: Minerva, 1969.

Mihaly, Eugene. "Isaac Abravanel on the Principles of Faith." HUCA 26 (1955): 481-502.

Munk, Salomon. Mélanges de philosophie juive et arabe. Paris, 1859. Reprint. Paris: J. Vrin, 1955.

Nallino, Carlo Alfonso. "Filosofia 'orientale' od 'illuminativa' d'Avicenna." Rivista degli studi orientali 10 (1925): 367-433.

Nasr, Seyyed Hossein. An Introduction to Islamic Cosmological Doctrines: Conceptions of Nature and Methods Used for its Study by the Ikhwān al-Safā', al-Bīrūnī and ibn Sīnā. Cambridge, Mass.: Harvard University Press, 1964.

Netanyahu, Ben Zion. Don Isaac Abravanel: Statesman and Philosopher.

Second edition. Philadelphia: Jewish Publication Society of America, 1968.

___. The Marranos of Spain from the Late XIVth to the Early XVIth Century According to Contemporary Hebrew Sources. New York: American Academy for Jewish Research, 1966.

Neumark, David. Geschichte der jüdischen Philosophie des Mittelalters nach Problemem dargestellt. Vol. 1. Berlin: Georg Reimer, 1907.

Nicholson, Reynold Alleyn. A Literary History of the Arabs. Cambridge: At the University Press, 1930.

Nuriel, Avraham. "'Emunah we-Sekhel be-Mishnath R. Abraham Bibago." In Hithgaluth 'Emunah Tevunah, pp. 35-43. Ramath Gan, Israel: Bar-Ilan University, 1976.

___. "Ḥidush ha-ᶜOlam 'o Qadmutho ᶜal pi ha-RaMBaM." Tarbiṣ 33 (1964): 372-87.

___. "Mishnatho ha-Pilosofith shel R. Avraham ben Shem Ṭov Bibago." Ph.D. dissertation, Hebrew University, 1975.

___. "Ha-Raṣon ha-'Elohi beMoreh Nevukhim." Tarbiṣ 39 (1969): 39-61.

Oberman, Heiko Augustinus. Archbishop Thomas Bradwardine: A Fourteenth Century Augustinian. Utrecht: Kemink and Zoon, 1957.

___. Forerunners of the Reformation: The Shape of Late Medieval Thought Illustrated by Key Documents. Translations by Paul L. Nyhus. New York: Holt, Rinehart and Winston, 1966.

___. The Harvest of Medieval Theology: Gabriel Biel and Late Medieval Nominalism. Cambridge, Mass.: Harvard University Press, 1963.

Peters, Francis Edwards. Aristoteles Arabus: The Oriental Translations and Commentaries on the Aristotelian Corpus. New York University Department of Classics: Monographs on Mediterranean Antiquity, vol. 2. Leiden: E. J. Brill, 1968.

___. Aristotle and the Arabs: The Aristotelian Tradition in Islam. New York University Studies in Near Eastern Civilization, no. 1. New York, 1968.

Pines, Shlomo. "A Tenth Century Philosophical Correspondence." PAAJR 24 (1955): 103-36.

___. "Ha-Ṣuroth ha-'Ishiyoth be-Mishnatho shel Yedaᶜyah Bedershi." Harry Austryn Wolfson Jubilee Volume, vol. 3, Hebrew Section, pp. 187-201. Jerusalem: American Academy for Jewish Research, 1965.

___. "La 'Philosophie orientale' d'Avicenne et sa polémique contre les Bagdadiens." Archives d'histoire doctrinale et littéraire du moyen âge, année 27, tome 19 (1952): 5-37.

___. "Scholasticism after Thomas Aquinas and the Teachings of Ḥasdai Crescas and his Predecessors." Proceedings of the Israel Academy of Sciences and Humanities, vol. 1, no. 10, pp. 1-101. Jerusalem, 1967.

___. "Studies in Abu'l-Barakāt al-Baghdadi's Poetics and Metaphysics." Scripta Hierosolymitana [Jerusalem] 6 (1960): 120-98.

Rahman, Fazlur. Prophecy in Islam: Philosophy and Orthodoxy. London: George Allen and Unwin, 1958.

Reines, Alvin Jay. Maimonides and Abravanel on Prophecy. Cincinnati: Hebrew Union College Press, 1970.

Renan, Ernest. Averroes et l'averroisme: essai historique. Paris: Calmann-Lévy [1859].

Rosin, David. "Die Religionsphilosophie Abraham ibn Esra's." MGWJ 42 (1898): 17+; 43 (1899): 22+.

Rossi, Giovanni Bernardo, de. Historisches Wörterbuch der jüdischen Schriftsteller und ihrer Werke. Translated by C. H. Hamberger.

Leipzig, 1839. Reprint. Amsterdam: Philo Press, 1967.
___. MSS. Codices Hebraici Biblioth. 3 vols. Parma, 1803.
Sarachek, Joseph. Don Isaac Abravanel. New York: Bloch, 1938.
___. Faith and Reason: The Conflict over the Rationalism of Maimonides. Williamsport, Pa.: Bayard Press, 1935.
Sassoon, David Solomon, ed. 'Ohel Dawid: Descriptive Catalogue of the Hebrew and Samaritan Manuscripts in the Sassoon Library. Vol. 2. London: Oxford University Press, 1932.
Schechter, Solomon. "The Dogmas of Judaism." In his Studies in Judaism: First Series, pp. 147-81. Philadelphia: Jewish Publication Society of America, 1911. Reprinted in his Studies in Judaism: Selections, pp. 73-104. Philadelphia: Jewish Publication Society of America, 1958.
Scholem, Gershom Gerhard. Das Buch Bahir. Leipzig: W. Drugulin, 1923.
___. Jewish Gnosticism, Merkabah Mysticism, and Talmudic Tradition. New York: Jewish Theological Seminary of America, 1965.
___. Major Trends in Jewish Mysticism. Third revised edition. New York: Schocken Books, 1954.
___. Ursprung und Anfänge der Kabbala. Berlin: Walter de Gruyter, 1962.
Sharif, Mian Mohammad, ed. A History of Muslim Philosophy. 2 vols. Wiesbaden: Otto Harrassowitz, 1963-66.
Shorter Encyclopedia of Islam. Edited by Hamilton A. R. Gibb and Johannes H. Kramers. Leiden: E. J. Brill, 1953.
Sirat, Colette. "Moses Narboni's Pirqei Moshe." Tarbiṣ 39 (1970): 287-306.
___. Haguth-pilosofith bime ha-Benayim. Jerusalem: Keter Publishing House, 1975.
Steenberghen, Fernand van. Aristotle in the West: The Origins of Latin Aristotelianism. Translated by Leonard Johnston. Second edition. Louvain: E. Nauwelaerts, 1970.
___. La Philosophie au XIIIe siècle. Philosophes médiévaux, vol. 9. Louvain: Publications universitaires, 1966.
___. The Philosophical Movement in the Thirteenth Century. Edinburgh: Thomas Nelson and Son, 1955.
Steinschneider, Moritz. "Abraham Bibago's Schriften." MGWJ 32 (1883): 79-96, 125-44, 239-40.
___. Catalogus Liborum Hebraeorum in Bibliotheca Bodleiana. . . . Berlin, 1852-60. Reprint. Berlin: Welt-verlag, 1931.
___. "Études sur Zarkali, astronome arabe du XIe siècle et ses ouvrages." 6 parts. Bulletino della bibliografia e della storia delle scienze mathematiche e fisiche [Rome] 14 (1881): 171-82; 16 (1883): 493-527; 17 (1884): 765-94; 18 (1885): 343-60; 20 (1887): 1-36, 575-604.
___. Al-Fārābī: Des Arabischen Philosophen Leben und Schriften. . . . Buchdruckerei der Kaiserlichen Akademie der Wissenschaften, series 7, vol. 13, no. 4. St. Petersburg, 1869. Reprint. Amsterdam: Philo Press, 1966.
___. Hebräische Bibliographie 15 (1875): 44-45; 20 (1880): 134; 21 (1881-82): 82-83.
___. Die Hebräischen Handschriften der K. Hof- und Staatsbibliothek in München. Munich, 1875. Second edition. Munich, 1895.
___. Die Hebräischen Übersetzungen des Mittelalters und die Juden als Dolmetscher. Berlin, 1893. Reprint. Graz: Akademische Druck- u. Verlagsanstalt, 1956.

___. "Josef b. Schemtob's Commentar zu Averroes' grosserer Abhandlung über die Möglichkeit der Conjunction." MGWJ 32 (1883): 459-77, 514-21.

Stern, Selma. Josel of Rosheim. Translated by Gertrude Hirschler. Philadelphia: Jewish Publication Society of America, 1965.

Strauss, Leo. "On Abravanel's Philosophical Tendency and Political Teaching." In Isaac Abravanel: Six Lectures, edited by John B. Trend and Herbert Loewe, pp. 93-129. Cambridge: At the University Press, 1937.

___. "Der Ort der Vorsehungslehre nach der Ansicht Maimunis." MGWJ 81 (1937): 93-105.

___. Persecution and the Art of Writing. Glencoe, Ill.: Free Press, 1952. Reprint. Westport, Conn.: Greenwood Press, 1973.

Touati, Charles. "Dieu et le monde selon Moïse Narboni." Archives d'histoire littéraire du moyen-age, 1956, pp. 80-102.

___. La Pensée philosophique et theologique de Gersonide. [Paris] Les Editions de minuit [1973].

Twersky, Isadore. Rabad of Posquières: A Twelfth-Century Talmudist. Cambridge, Mass.: Harvard University Press, 1962.

Vajda, Georges. Introduction à la pensée juive du moyen âge. Paris: J. Vrin, 1947.

___. Isaac Albalag: Averroiste juif, traducteur et annotateur d'al-Ghazālī. Paris: J. Vrin, Librairie philosophique, 1960.

___. Juda ben Nissim ibn Malka: Philosophe juif Marocain. Paris: Larose, 1954.

Vicens Vives, Jaime. Juan II de Aragon: Monariquia y revolucion en la España del siglo XV. Barcelona: Teide, 1953.

Walzer, Richard. Greek into Arabic: Essays on Islamic Philosophy. Oriental Studies, vol. 1. Oxford: Bruno Cassirer, 1962.

Watt, William Montgomery. Free Will and Predestination in Early Islam. London: Luzac, 1948.

Waxman, Meyer. A History of Jewish Literature. Second edition, revised. Vol. 2. New York: Thomas Yoseloff, 1960.

Wensinck, Arent Jan. The Muslim Creed: Its Genesis and Historical Development. Cambridge: At the University Press, 1932.

Werner, Karl. Die Scholastik des späteren Mittelalters. 4 vols. Vienna, 1881-87.

Wickens, G. M., ed. Avicenna, Scientist and Philosopher: A Millenary Symposium. London: Luzac, 1952.

Wilensky, Sarah Heller. R. Yiṣḥaq Arama u-Mishnatho. Jerusalem: Mosad Bialik, 1956.

Wirszubski, Chaim, ed. Flavius Mithridates Sermo de Passione Domini. Jerusalem: Israel Academy of Sciences and Humanities, 1963.

Wolf, Johann Christoph. Bibliotheca Hebraea. 4 vols. Hamburg, 1715-36.

Wolfson, Harry Austryn. Crescas' Critique of Aristotle: Problems of Aristotle's Physics in Jewish and Arabic Philosophy. Harvard Semitic Series, vol. 6. Cambridge, Mass.: Harvard University Press, 1929. Reprint. 1971.

___. "Joseph ibn Ṣaddik on Divine Attributes." JQR, n.s. 55 (1965): 277-98.

___. "The Kalām Arguments for Creation in Saadia, Averroes, Maimonides, and St. Thomas." In Saadia Anniversary Volume, edited by Boaz Cohen, pp. 197-245. American Academy for Jewish Research Texts and Studies, vol. 2. New York and Philadelphia: Press of the

Jewish Publication Society, 1943.
___. Philo: Foundations of Religious Philosophy in Judaism, Christianity and Islam. Revised edition. 2 vols. Structure and Growth of Philosophic Systems from Plato to Spinoza, no. 2. Cambridge, Mass.: Harvard University Press, 1962.
___. "Philo on Free Will and the Historical Influence of his View." HTR 35 (1942): 131-69.
___. "Philosophical Implications of the Problem of Divine Attributes in the Kalām." JAOS 79 (1959): 73-80.
___. The Philosophy of the Church Fathers. Vol. 1: Faith, Trinity, Incarnation. Structure and Growth of Philosophic Systems from Plato to Spinoza, no. 3. Third revised edition. Cambridge, Mass.: Harvard University Press, 1970.
___. The Philosophy of the Kalam. Structure and Growth of Philosophic Systems from Plato to Spinoza, no. 4. Cambridge, Mass.: Harvard University Press, 1976.
___. The Philosophy of Spinoza. 2 vols. Cambridge, Mass.: Harvard University Press, 1934. Reprint. 2 vols. in 1. New York: Schocken Books, 1969.
___. Religious Philosophy: A Group of Essays. Cambridge, Mass.: Harvard University Press, 1961. Reprint. New York: Atheneum, 1965.
___. Studies in the History of Philosophy and Religion. 2 vols. Edited by Isadore Twersky and George H. Williams. Cambridge, Mass.: Harvard University Press, 1973-77.
Zedner, Joseph, ed. Catalogue of the Hebrew Books in the Library of the British Museum. London, 1867.
Zeller, Eduard. Die Philosophie der Griechen in ihrer Geschichtlichen Entwicklung. Third edition. 3 vols. Leipzig, 1881.
Zinberg, Israel. A History of Jewish Literature. Translated and edited by Bernard Martin. Vol. 3. The Struggle of Mysticism and Tradition Against Philosophic Rationalism. Cleveland and London: Press of the Case Western Reserve University, 1973.
Zotenberg, Hermann. Catalogues des Manuscrits Hébreux et Samaritains de la Bibliothèque Impériale. Paris, 1866.
Zumkeller, A. "Die Augustinerschule des Mittelalters: Vertreter und Philosophisch-theologische Lehre." Analecta Augustiniana 27 (1964): 167-262.

Allan Lazaroff is a visiting associate professor of religion, Boston University, Boston, Massachusetts.

Index of Hebrew, Greek, and Arabic Terms

General Index

a priori and a posteriori demonstration, 8-9, 10, 11, 67-68 (nn. 7-8)
Abner of Burgos (Alphonso of Valladolid): on voluntary and natural agents, 25, 90 (n. 218)
Abraham: taught through speculation, 67 (n. 2)
Abravanel, Isaac: letter from Saul ha-Kohen, 5; borrowed from Bibago in his Rosh 'Amanah, 6, 64 (n. 168), 65 (n. 171), 72 (n. 10); on creation and necessity, 22; on will and necessity, 28; defended Jewish theology, 58 (n. 89); does not mention Bibago by name, 65 (n. 169); existence and truth, 73 (n. 15); on Crescas on essential attributes, 77 (n. 55)
Abu'l-Barakāt al-Baghdadī, 72 (n. 6)
Accident(s), 15, 28-29, 43; existence as, 13; and substance, 73 (n. 16); of body, 76 (n. 40). See also Agents; Causes; Forms
Actions, 44; essential, 28-29, 90 (n. 218); accidental, 28-29; purposive, 10, 15, 16; of God, 12, 15, 16, 17, 18, 31, 71 (n. 3), 77 (n. 58); their perfection, 10, 90 (n. 204); opposite, performed by will, 18, 19, 20, 24, 25, 27, 28, 29, 81 (n. 51), 90 (n. 218); voluntary, 24, 41, 86 (nn. 125, 128); types of, 23, 86 (nn. 125, 127); by knowledge, 28. See also Agents; Causes
Active Intellect: conjunction with, 57 (n. 77). See also Intellect
Agency: essential, 29, 43, 90 (n. 204)
Agent(s), 17, 18; natural, 18-19, 23, 24, 25, 26, 28-29, 81 (n. 48), 85 (n. 124), 88 (n. 176), 90 (n. 218); voluntary, 18-19, 22-24, 25, 26, 28-29, 80 (n. 51), 85 (n. 124), 88 (n. 176), 90 (n. 218); first, 80 (n. 13); by necessity, 19-23, 24, 25, 26, 29, 83 (n. 72), 85 (n. 114); his perfection, 16; essential, 25, 28-29, 35; accidental, 29, 35; deficient, 19, 31, 83 (n. 72); classification of, 25, 26
Albalag, Isaac: divine will as delight, 18, 26; on voluntary agents, 24; on intermediate agent by necessity, 26, 32; on essential agents, 29; on negative attributes, 39; on two senses of "existence," 73 (n. 16); agents by nature or will, 85 (n. 124); influenced Bibago, 26
Albinus: first classification of negative attributes, 72 (n. 4)
Albo, Joseph: praises Maimonides' third proof, 10; on divine attributes, 14, 74 (n. 20); on divine goodness, 15; on change in the divine will, 20; not cited by name by Bibago, 56 (n. 60); on Rabad's criticism of Maimonides, 57 (n. 65), 64 (n. 168); defended Jewish theology, 58 (n. 89); on being as actuality, 73 (n. 16);